DECISIONS AT FORTS
HENRY AND DONELSON

OTHER BOOKS IN THE COMMAND DECISIONS IN AMERICA'S CIVIL WAR SERIES

Decisions at Stones River
Matt Spruill and Lee Spruill

Decisions at Second Manassas
Matt Spruill III and Matt Spruill IV

Decisions at Chickamauga
Dave Powell

Decisions at Chattanooga
Larry Peterson

Decisions of the Atlanta Campaign
Larry Peterson

Decisions of the 1862 Kentucky Campaign
Larry Peterson

Decisions at The Wilderness and Spotsylvania Court House
Dave Townsend

Decisions at Gettysburg, Second Edition
Matt Spruill

Decisions of the Tullahoma Campaign
Michael R. Bradley

Decisions at Antietam
Michael S. Lang

Decisions of the Seven Days
Matt Spruill

Decisions at Fredericksburg
Chris Mackowski

Decisions at Perryville
Larry Peterson

Decisions of the Maryland Campaign
Michael S. Lang

Decisions at Shiloh
Dave Powell

Decisions at Franklin
Andrew S. Bledsoe

Decisions of the 1862 Shenandoah Valley Campaign
Robert Tanner

Decisions at Kennesaw Mountain
Larry Peterson

Decisions of the Vicksburg Campaign
Larry Peterson

Decisions of the Galveston Campaigns
Edward T. Cotham Jr.

Decisions of the Red River Campaign
Michael S. Lang

DECISIONS
AT FORTS HENRY AND DONELSON

The Twenty-One Critical Decisions
That Defined the Battles

Hank Koopman

Maps by Alex Mendoza

Command Decisions
in America's Civil War
Matt Spruill and Larry Peterson,
Series Editors

The University of Tennessee Press / Knoxville

Copyright © 2025 by The University of Tennessee Press / Knoxville.
All Rights Reserved.
First Edition.

All images are from the Library of Congress unless otherwise noted.

Library of Congress Cataloging-in-Publication Data

Names: Koopman, Hank (Historian), author. |
Mendoza, Alexander, 1970–, cartographer.
Title: Decisions at Forts Henry and Donelson : the twenty-one critical decisions
that defined the battles / Hank Koopman ; maps by Alex Mendoza.
Other titles: Command decisions in America's Civil War.
Description: First edition. | Knoxville : The University of Tennessee Press, [2024] |
Series: Command decisions in America's Civil War | Includes bibliographical references and index. | Summary: "The Battles of Forts Henry and Donelson took place in
February of 1862 and were early indicators of the success the US would have in the
Civil War's Western Theater. Due to Kentucky's neutrality at the time, Adna Anderson
of Tennessee was instructed to find suitable sites for fortifications along the
Tennessee and Cumberland Rivers but just inside the state boundaries of Tennessee.
Forts Henry and Donelson were constructed in the summer and fall of 1861 and were
quickly identified by Gen. Ulysses S. Grant as strategic fortifications that, if conquered,
would open the Federal Army's path to Alabama and Mississippi. Fort Henry fell to
Federal control on February 6, 1862, and Fort Donelson fell ten days later. With the
Tennessee and Mississippi Rivers now open to Federal gunboats, Grant and his army
would head southwest to Memphis and on to Vicksburg"—Provided by publisher.
Identifiers: LCCN 2024024775 (print) | LCCN 2024024776 (ebook) | ISBN
9781621908470 (paperback) | ISBN 9781621908494 (adobe pdf)
Subjects: LCSH: Fort Henry, Battle of, Tenn., 1862. | Fort Donelson,
Battle of, Tenn., 1862. | Command of troops—Case studies.
Classification: LCC E472.9 .K66 2024 (print) | LCC E472.9 (ebook) |
DDC 973.7/31—dc23/eng/20240808
LC record available at https://lccn.loc.gov/2024024775
LC ebook record available at https://lccn.loc.gov/2024024776

CONTENTS

Preface	ix
Introduction	1
Chapter 1. Before the Battles	9
Chapter 2. Battle for Fort Henry: Thursday, February 6, 1862	21
Chapter 3. Between the Battles	35
Chapter 4. Day of Decisions: Friday, February 14, 1862	67
Chapter 5. Day of Battle: Saturday, February 15, 1862	101
Chapter 6. Day of Shame: Sunday, February 16, 1862	145
Chapter 7. Aftermath and Conclusions	163
Appendix I. Battlefield Guide to the Critical Decisions at Forts Henry and Donelson	181
Appendix II. Union Order of Battle	207
Appendix III. Confederate Order of Battle	213
Notes	217
Bibliography	249
Index	259

ILLUSTRATIONS

Photographs

Snow-covered Cannon	xiii
Maj. Gen. Henry Halleck	10
Brig. Gen. Ulysses S. Grant	22
Fort Henry	24
Flag Officer Andrew Foote	26
USS *Essex*	27
USS *Tyler*	28
Brig. Gen. Lloyd Tilghman	29
Brig. Gen. Don Carlos Buell	40
Gen. Albert Sidney Johnston	44
Brig. Gen. Bushrod Johnson	45
Brig. Gen. Gideon Pillow	49
Brig. Gen. Simon Bolivar Buckner	51
Commander Henry Walke	57
USS *Carondelet*	58
Brig. Gen. John Floyd	62
Widow Crisp farm	71
Brig. Gen. Lew Wallace	73
Fort Donelson Upper Battery	79
Fort Donelson from downriver	80
Fort Donelson Lower Battery	81

Brig. Gen. John McClernand	92
Col. John McArthur	94
Col. William Baldwin	96
Col. Nathan Bedford Forrest	98
Col. Charles Cruft	108
View from Buckner's trenches	114
Col. John Thayer	121
Wynn's Ferry Road	122
Brig. Gen. Charles Ferguson Smith	134
Col. James Tuttle	139
Forge Road	143
Dover Hotel	155

Maps

Western Theater	8
January Demonstrations	15
Attack on Fort Henry, February 6	25
Escape from Fort Henry	33
Union Movement to Fort Donelson	56
End of February 13	68
Valentine's Day	95
Morning of February 15	102
Afternoon, February 15	124
Grant Arrives	136
Lew Wallace's Counterattack	138
Smith's Attack	140
End of Day, February 15	146
Lick Creek Crossings of Charlotte and Forge Roads	152
Tour Stops of Critical Decisions	182

PREFACE

My compelling interest in the battles for Forts Henry and Donelson is rooted in the fact that my great-great-grandfather fought at Fort Donelson with the Fifty-Eighth Illinois Volunteer Infantry Regiment. With the intent of recording the history of the Fifty-Eighth Illinois, I walked the battlefields of Forts Henry and Donelson and spent many hours in archives and libraries across the United States. This effort resulted in an understanding of what happened at those strongholds in the first half of February 1862. The quest to determine those events led me to study why things happened as they did.

Discovering why things occurred adds depth to knowledge about the fighting at Forts Henry and Donelson. I applied critical-decision methodology to analyze the events leading up to the battles, the battles themselves, and the end of the engagements. A person with an understanding of what happened during the battles can use critical decisions to understand why events happened that way and what the circumstances that caused them were. Those who comprehend how the critical-decision concept is derived can apply it to battles and campaigns of any war.

It was not just random occurrences that led the campaign and battles for Forts Henry and Donelson to be waged as they were. Events occurred as recorded due to decisions made by men at differing levels of command on each side of the conflict. They made these choices during the weeks preceding the Union invasion into Tennessee, and then during the battles. Many normal decisions were reached as both sides recognized that the Union forces would, at some point, move to strike at Forts Henry and Donelson. A smaller number of decisions were more important, but a select number of decisions affected the way the Union forces invaded Tennessee and how the battles for Forts Henry and Donelson were fought. These are identified as the critical decisions.

Critical decisions are found throughout the entire spectrum of war. This includes organization, strategy, operations, tactics, personnel, and logistics. Only three of these classifications of critical decisions were made during the battles for Forts Henry and Donelson. There were two personnel decisions, six tactical decisions, and a preponderance of thirteen operations decisions. During the fighting some choices appeared minor in the beginning, but because they ended up having a major impact on how events unfolded, they were elevated to the status of a critical decision.

It is imperative that readers understand the concept of a critical decision. If not, this work will present as just an unseemly short and selective description of the history of the Union campaign for possession of Forts Henry and Donelson. The book goes beyond being just a limited narrative. Its pages contain a new concept explaining why battles and campaigns developed as they did—*the why instead of the what.*

This chart shows the decisions hierarchy. At the bottom are the many and various decisions, above those are a smaller number of important decisions, and at the top are even fewer critical decisions.

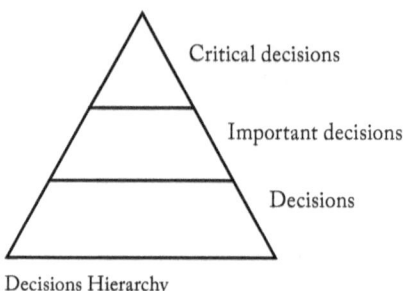

Decisions Hierarchy

The criterion for a critical decision is that it is of such magnitude that it shaped not only the events immediately following, but also the campaign or battle from that point on. If these choices had not been made, or if different ones had been made, the sequence of events for the battles by the North to take Forts Henry and Donelson would have been significantly different.

Twenty-one critical decisions for the Battles of Forts Henry and Donelson are grouped into six specific time periods:

Chapter 1, "Before the Battles"
- (1) Halleck Orders Demonstrations into Kentucky, January 10–22, 1862
- (2) Halleck Orders Grant to Take Fort Henry, January 30, 1862

Chapter 2, "Battle for Fort Henry, Thursday, February 6, 1862"
- (3) Grant Attacks Fort Henry
- (4) Tilghman Defends Fort Henry

Chapter 3, "Between the Battles"
- (5) Halleck Supports Grant's Attack on Fort Donelson
- (6) Buell Sends Reinforcements to Halleck
- (7) Johnston Orders Pillow to Fort Donelson, February 9, 1862
- (8) Grant Orders an Immediate Attack on Fort Donelson, February 12, 1862
- (9) Johnston Orders Floyd to Fort Donelson, February 13, 1862

Chapter 4, "Day of Decisions, Friday, February 14, 1862"
- (10) Grant Orders Lew Wallace to Fort Donelson
- (11) Foote Attacks Fort Donelson
- (12) Floyd Orders Breakout Attack against the Union Right Flank
- (13) McClernand Sends McArthur's Brigade to the Far-Right Flank

Chapter 5, "Day of Battle, Saturday, February 15, 1862"
- (14) Grant Leaves the Battlefield to Visit Foote
- (15) Lew Wallace Orders Cruft's Brigade to Aid McClernand
- (16) Buckner Breaks His Promise
- (17) Lew Wallace Orders Thayer's Brigade to Stem the Rebel Tide
- (18) Pillow Orders the Rebels to Return to the Entrenchments
- (19) Floyd Sustains Pillow's Order to Buckner
- (20) Grant Orders Counterattacks

Chapter 6, "Day of Shame, Sunday, February 16, 1862"
- (21) Floyd Surrenders Fort Donelson

Chapter 7, "Aftermath and Conclusions"

The critical decisions discussed in the book were chosen based on a study of the terrain surrounding Forts Henry and Donelson, along with an analysis of the ground between the forts and the roads that existed at the time of the battles. I studied the weather during the campaign because it played an important part in decision-making and troop performance. At the start of the campaign heavy rains resulted in rising water levels in the rivers, a development to the Union's advantage. But the February weather in Tennessee turned nasty, and Union and Confederate troops fighting for Fort Donelson were unprepared for snow and plunging nighttime temperatures. In addition, I reviewed available primary and secondary material. Choosing the critical decisions for the campaign against the forts is subjective, and other historians could arrive at different decisions. But the critical decisions featured in this book affected the way the battles evolved. If these decisions had not been made as they were, the fighting would have been altered, and subsequent choices would have changed the sequence of events as we now know them to have occurred.

This is not to imply that the South could have held on to Forts Henry and Donelson and sent Grant packing back to Cairo had different critical decisions been made. The North had a brand-new fleet of ironclad gunboats and numerical superiority. Different determinations could have resulted in a land attack on Fort Henry and a siege at Fort Donelson. The South might have sent more forces to oppose Grant in a timely fashion. Had Fort Donelson's generals shown more gumption on the morning of February 16, 1862, and allowed the stronghold's defenders to attempt to fight their way out, a larger portion of the army might have escaped.

This is not a full, comprehensive history of the Battles of Forts Henry and Donelson. The fighting in these engagements is not complex when compared with other battles later in the war. Fort Henry fell to the gunboat attack, and fewer troops were involved at Fort Donelson than in other battles. Moreover, the area of the land battle was confined to just outside the hastily dug trenches around the fort and the town of Dover. This book does not intend to provide a new interpretive history of the action. The critical decisions chosen depict how the campaign evolved over the months prior to February 1862, and how those choices affected the actual fighting that occurred. This study includes important details, and it is designed to help readers understand why the campaign and battles developed as they did.

The critical decisions are grouped into six different time periods. The number of such choices discussed in each time period varies extensively from seven to one. Each critical decision is presented with a description of the situation and options available to the decision-makers. The final determination

Preface

is identified and analyzed as to its results and impact. In some cases I discuss what might have happened if a different option had been chosen.

When a critical decision is made, there is always the possibility of unforeseen circumstances or just plain luck affecting the outcome. Misfortune can make an otherwise good critical decision look like a bad one. Conversely, a bad choice can look good if good luck is encountered. Generally, a critical decision is not identified as a good one or a bad one, as the emphasis is on informing the reader as to why events happened as they did. However, some critical decisions made during the campaign for Forts Henry and Donelson have resounded through history as being pretty poor. These bad decisions are noted, as is any good decision that had particularly positive results. However, the main emphasis of the study is to highlight the consequences of the critical decisions and how they affected the battles for the forts.

No matter how hard an author, or battle participant, might try to describe the terrain of a battlefield, there is no better way to gain an understanding of that ground than by walking it. There is value in seeing what the participants saw during the fight. Standing near the location where a critical decision was made or carried out provides valuable insights as to the landscape and tactical situation facing the decision-maker. The early critical decisions affecting the

Present day photograph of a snow-covered cannon that illustrates the extreme winter conditions the soldiers faced during the battle for Fort Donelson. Photograph by the author.

campaign for Forts Henry and Donelson were made away from the battlefields. However, once the attacks on the forts commenced, most of the critical decisions were reached or implemented on or near the battlefields, and it is possible to stand on the very spots in question, or at least close to them. To aid the reader, this work includes an appendix with a tour of the sites associated with critical decisions. At these locations the terrain can be studied to enhance understanding of what happened during the fighting and why, and to develop additional insight into how critical decisions shaped the results.

I trust this book and the battlefield guide appendix will provide a firm foundation for further reading, analysis, and reflection on and appreciation for the North's successful campaign against Confederate Forts Henry and Donelson.

This book relied heavily on research and publications from earlier authors who wrote about the campaign for Forts Henry and Donelson. I was fortunate to have spent time discussing the battles on site at Fort Donelson with Ed Bearss, Benjamin Franklin Cooling, Kendall Gott, Tim Smith, and Jim Jobe. All are authors of works about Fort Donelson.

Dr. Cooling graciously reviewed the manuscript, and his suggestions improved the final work.

Retired Lieutenant Colonel James Vaughan was generous with his time and voluminous research on Fort Donelson. We spent a day on the battlefield and Colonel Vaughan shared with me the complete list he has accumulated of the Confederate soldiers who were captured at Fort Donelson and died in Northern prisons.

Thanks to Series Editors Larry Peterson and Matt Spruill for the opportunity to work with them and contribute to the Command Decisions in America's Civil War Series.

INTRODUCTION

When Gen. Pierre Gustave Toutant Beauregard ordered Confederate batteries to open fire on Fort Sumter on April 12, 1861, the Confederacy consisted of seven states: South Carolina, Mississippi, Florida, Alabama, Georgia, Louisiana, and Texas. Upon Lincoln's call for volunteers to save the Union, Virginia joined the Confederacy.[1]

Army general-in-chief Winfield Scott devised a plan that he believed would bring the seceding states back into the Union with a minimum of bloodshed. In early May 1861 Scott put forth what became known as his Anaconda Plan, which called for a blockade of the southern coastline from Virginia to Texas. The strategy also involved a combined army and navy expedition to establish Union control of the Mississippi River from Illinois to New Orleans. Scott wanted to suffocate the South from the outside to avoid the bloody consequences of invading rebel territory. By the end of May, North Carolina and Arkansas joined the Confederacy. Tennessee passed a declaration of independence requiring the people to vote in a June referendum on secession.[2]

George B. McClellan was commissioned major general of the Ohio militia on April 23, 1861, and he promptly let Lieut. Gen. Scott know his plans for bringing the Southern states back into the Union. McClellan advocated a drive toward Richmond in the East and an advance on Nashville in the West. Despite major differences with Scott on how to conduct the war, McClellan was given a major generalship in the Union army (he ranked second only to Scott), and he was given command of the new Department of the Ohio, which covered Ohio, Indiana, and Illinois, on May 13, 1862. The new commander showed an early interest in taking Nashville and prioritized that goal.³

President Lincoln declared a blockade of Southern ports on April 19, and the navy initiated efforts to increase the number of oceangoing vessels to enforce it. But inland waterways were under the control of the United States Army, and no suitable vessels were available for combat on the brown-water rivers. The navy commenced the Western Flotilla program to help the army develop a fleet of gunboats for use on the western waterways.⁴

Because designing and constructing ironclad gunboats would take time, the Union immediately addressed the necessity for river gunboats capable of attacking enemy batteries and forts. James Buchanan Eads of St. Louis had amassed a fortune salvaging shipwrecks on the Mississippi River. Eads and Attorney General Edward Bates were friends, and Bates invited Eads to Washington, DC, to present his ideas about what was needed to establish Union control of the western rivers. In late April 1861 Eads wrote a letter to Secretary of the Navy Gideon Welles proposing a blockade of river traffic at Cairo, Illinois. Welles forwarded Eads's proposition to Secretary of War Simon Cameron, who passed it along to McClellan in Cincinnati. Lieut. Gen. Scott weighed in after reviewing a memorandum about the design of river gunboats prepared by John Lenthall, chief of the Navy Bureau of Construction, Equipment, and Repair. Scott concluded the army required a total of sixteen gunboats.⁵

Cairo, became the operational base for the Western Flotilla. On May 16 Welles ordered Commander John Rodgers to help McClellan acquire the necessary vessels for river service. Naval constructor Samuel M. Pook traveled to Cairo and aided Rodgers by developing design criteria for constructing a fleet of gunboats.⁶

The priority was to quickly obtain three gunboats to defend Cairo and stop the movement of contraband between the North and the South. Rodgers found three steamboats in Cincinnati that the Union purchased and then modified with timber planking to protect sailors from small-arms fire. The boats were armed with an assortment of cannon. On August 12 the timberclads *A. O. Tyler*, *Lexington*, and *Conestoga* arrived at Cairo and commenced patrolling the Mississippi, Ohio, Tennessee, and Cumberland Rivers.⁷

On July 18, 1861, the War Department solicited bids for seven ironclad gunboats that became known as the City-Class gunboats. Eads won the contract with a bid of $89,600 per vessel. The contract was awarded on August 6, with delivery required in just sixty-five days on October 10. Eads used shipbuilding facilities at Carondelet, Missouri, and Mound City, Illinois. The *St. Louis*, *Carondelet*, *Pittsburg*, and *Louisville* were constructed at Carondelet, located approximately eleven miles south of St. Louis. The *Cairo, Cincinnati,* and *Mound City* were built at Mound City. Construction delays and design changes delayed delivery of the gunboats.[8]

Friction developed between Rodgers and Maj. Gen. John C. Frémont, and on September 6 Rodgers was replaced by Capt. Andrew Foote, who oversaw the completion of the gunboats. While Foote struggled to find crews, the vessels arrived for duty at Cairo. January 1862 witnessed intense interest in when the gunboats would be ready for action.[9]

In addition to the seven City-Class gunboats, Eads built the ironclad *Essex* by modifying an existing steamboat, and he transformed his own snag boat into the powerful *Benton*. The *Essex* was commissioned on October 15, 1861, while the *Benton* was commissioned on February 24, 1862. On January 16, 1862, Foote commissioned all seven City-Class gunboats at Cairo but lacked the crews to man them all. However, the flag officer was anxious to advance against the enemy, and he had enough men to put at least four of the gunboats into service.[10]

On June 8, 1861, Tennessee became the last state to join the Confederacy when its voters approved secession. Union success depended on invasion of the South, but the neutral position of Kentucky blocked the most advantageous routes into Tennessee.[11] Governor Isham Harris bore the responsibility to defend Tennessee. He entered into a military league with the Confederate States of America and started to recruit men for the Provisional Army of Tennessee in early May. In addition, Harris commissioned Gideon Pillow a major general and Bushrod Johnson a colonel. Johnson served as chief engineer in the army and played a key role in the siting of Forts Henry and Donelson.[12]

In June 1861 the Confederate government's priority was defense of Richmond and Virginia. Harris received minimal assistance from the Confederacy as storm clouds formed along the Ohio River. The North built up forces in key locations such as Cairo, Illinois; Jeffersonville, Indiana; and Cincinnati, Ohio. Tennessee regiments spread across the state from Memphis to Knoxville. In Eastern Tennessee state troops dealt with Union loyalists who wanted no part of secession.[13]

Southerners recognized the necessity to block invasions via the Mississippi, Tennessee, and Cumberland Rivers. With the dawn of the age of the ironclad ship the advantage of fixed fortresses diminished. However, in the summer of 1861 the South possessed few gunboats and stuck with the strategy of constructing fixed forts to stop invaders.

In May 1861 Governor Harris instructed Adna Anderson to survey the Cumberland and Tennessee Rivers in Tennessee to locate sites for construction of the two forts. The locations chosen were near the Kentucky-Tennessee border, where the two rivers are approximately twelve miles apart. Fort

Donelson was situated on the west bank of the Cumberland River and occupied a bluff about ninety feet above it. Unfortunately, there were no suitable bluffs on the east side of the Tennessee River, so Fort Henry was located as near as possible to Fort Donelson at the cost of being in the floodplain. Bushrod Johnson approved the sites, and work commenced immediately on Fort Henry. However, progress on Fort Donelson lagged far behind.[14]

The Lincoln administration suffered over six months of bad news, commencing with the collapse of Union troops at the First Battle of Bull Run on July 21, 1861. Three weeks later on August 10, 1861, a secessionist army of Missouri State Guard forces and Confederate troops defeated Federals at Wilson's Creek in Missouri.[15]

Maj. Gen. George McClellan's success at Philippi on June 3 and Rich Mountain on July 11 pried away the northwest counties of Virginia and kept them under Union control. After the debacle of Bull Run, McClellan arrived in Washington, DC, in late July to take charge of the Military Division of the Potomac. At the end of August Union spirits were buoyed by the capture of Forts Clark and Hatteras that established Federal control of the North Carolina sounds. Moreover, there was strong Unionist sentiment in northwest Virginia, and strong actions kept Maryland in the Union. McClellan organized the Army of the Potomac and increased its numbers, but the months passed with no signs of a move against the rebels.[16]

The neutrality dam burst on September 3, 1861, when Maj. Gen. Leonidas Polk sent Brig. Gen. Gideon Pillow into Kentucky to occupy the Mississippi River bluffs at Columbus. From Cairo, Brig. Gen. Ulysses S. Grant countered the move by seizing Paducah, Kentucky, on September 6, thus setting the stage for the struggle to control the state.[17]

Polk defended the rebel advance to Kentucky's legislature by claiming Kentucky permitted the North to operate recruitment camps, allowed the seizure of the property of Confederate States citizens in Paducah, let the North cut Kentucky timber to build gunboats, and provided men and supplies to the United States to pursue the war against the Confederacy. Observing a Union troop buildup in Missouri in preparation for advancing into Kentucky to seize Columbus, Confederates considered it urgent to prevent the North from occupying the Kentucky town. Polk offered to withdraw the rebels from Kentucky if the Union troops were also withdrawn.[18]

Kentucky Governor Beriah Magoffin believed in states' rights and sided with the South. But in early August Kentuckians elected a strong pro-Union legislature with veto-proof majorities in the Kentucky House and Senate. In response to Polk's proclamation, the legislature passed a resolution ordering the South out of the state. Magoffin wanted to include the same requirement of the North, but the legislators passed their resolution over his veto. On September 13 Governor Magoffin ordered the Confederates out of Kentucky.[19]

On September 10, 1861, Gen. Albert Sidney Johnston received command of the western Department No. 2, replacing Polk. Johnston was tasked with defending claimed Confederate territory stretching approximately one thousand miles from the Appalachian Mountains through the Indian Territory west of Arkansas. The general had to protect the northern portions of Louisiana, Mississippi, and Alabama, and the department included Missouri and Kentucky, even though those states had not seceded. The Confederacy focused on the defense of Richmond, New Orleans, and the southern coastline between them. Johnston was undermanned to defend the long northern boundary of the Confederacy. It was up to him to raise men and arms to bolster his meager forces. Johnston therefore admonished the governors of Tennessee, Mississippi, and Arkansas to send fifty thousand troops to bolster the defense of Tennessee. Requests to the government for soldiers from areas not threatened bore no fruit. Governor Harris responded aggressively, but Tennessee alone could not furnish enough men.[20]

On September 14 Johnston arrived in Nashville and immediately decided to ignore Kentucky's resolution and advance more troops into the state to hold it. He formed a four-hundred-mile defensive line starting at Columbus, where Polk, with eleven thousand men, had shattered Kentucky's neutrality, driving that state toward the Union camp. The line dipped southward into Tennessee at Forts Henry and Donelson, which were barely under construction at this time. Brig. Gen. Simon Bolivar Buckner, with four thousand men, was ordered from Nashville to occupy Bowling Green, sending the defensive line northward into Kentucky from the river forts. On his way from Richmond to Nashville, Johnston had stopped at Knoxville and approved Brig. Gen. Felix Zollicoffer's plan to immediately occupy the Cumberland Gap, where the defensive line ended with four thousand men.[21]

Johnston had approximately twenty-seven thousand men to hold this line. The general let Confederate president Jefferson Davis know he had not half enough armed men to protect the line, but he adhered to the Confederate strategy of trying to hold all important positions. The lack of men meant Johnston could not go on the offensive; he could only try to hold his positions until he had more men. Few troops arrived from other states, and volunteers from Kentucky were much fewer than Johnston had expected. Maj. Gen. William Hardee's small army of four thousand men traveled from Arkansas to Bowling Green. A regiment from Texas joined Johnston's Command and became Terry's Texas Rangers, with Johnston providing the horses. With Kentucky neutrality a thing of the past, Johnston's defensive positions to hold Nashville and Tennessee stretched through a state that had declared for the Union.[22]

Paducah and Smithland became Union strongpoints in Kentucky, located in the Western Department of the United States. The North operated Camp Dick Robinson southwest of Lexington, Kentucky, to muster in recruits, organize regiments, and provide arms to volunteers.[23]

Rebel forces moved on to Lexington, Missouri, and from September 12 through September 20, 1861, laid siege to Union forces defending the town. This action resulted in the surrender of approximately three thousand Federal troops. Missouri suffered from secessionists battling Union loyalists throughout the state.[24]

Johnston adopted a defensive strategy of deception by feigning aggressiveness to keep Union troops at bay while he built up his deficient army. The ploy worked and flummoxed Gens. Robert Anderson, William Sherman, and Don Carlos Buell. Both sides in Kentucky habitually overestimated the strength of the opponent.[25]

The eastern portion of Johnston's line was defended by the aggressive Brig. Gen. Felix Zollicoffer, who took the attitude that a good defense would be a good offense. In October, Zollicoffer, with a movement up the Wilderness Road, set his sights on Camp Dick Robinson. On October 21, 1861, the general was turned back by Union troops in an encounter known as the Battle of Camp Wildcat.[26] The engagement convinced both sides the Wilderness Road was not a viable route for a campaign. Zollicoffer retreated south into Tennessee and moved the center of his operations approximately one hundred miles west to Mill Springs.[27]

In mid-November two key commanders arrived on the scene for the North. Brig. Gen. Buell took command of the newly formed Department of the Ohio on November 15, 1861. Maj. Gen. Henry Wager Halleck took command of the newly formed Department of the Missouri on November 19, 1861.[28] Both men immediately bemoaned the sorry state of the organization of troops in their departments. Buell made perfecting the organization of his army, rather than confronting the enemy, his first priority, and he made no aggressive moves that could result in a Confederate response. He had this luxury because Johnston had no designs for significant offensive action.[29]

Halleck had a different problem: an insurgency racked Missouri, and an invading army occupied the southwestern area of the state. The overworked general brought order from chaos in Missouri, improving the organization of his forces, directing troops against areas under rebel insurgent control, and putting together a large enough force to drive out of the state the Missouri State Guard of Maj. Gen. Sterling Price.[30]

As 1861 waned, President Lincoln faced numerous problems and badly needed some positive results; but Union armies showed no ambitions to deliver any. Halleck's forces were tied down in Missouri, which constrained him from advancing. Buell identified Nashville as the desired objective but believed he needed to deal with Bowling Green first. He wanted Halleck to prevent rebel reinforcements moving from Columbus to Bowling Green. However, Halleck identified the true line of operations as the Tennessee and Cumberland Rivers.[31]

As the Army of the Potomac languished in camp, the Battle of Ball's Bluff took place on October 21, 1861, with far-reaching consequences for the Union war effort. Union troops were routed by rebel forces. Furious at the fiasco, Radical Republicans questioned the integrity of the army and formed the Joint Committee on the Conduct of the War, which plagued Lincoln and high-ranking officers until the fighting ended.[32]

Union activity west of the Mississippi mostly concentrated in Missouri, but even in the Department of Kansas there were efforts to control Kansas and the Indian Territory. Lincoln's administration pressured the military to send a force to invade Texas, but the idea proved impracticable and was abandoned.[33]

Lack of progress fighting the war was not Lincoln's only dilemma as 1861 entered December. A diplomatic row erupted with Britain when the USS *San Jacinto* removed two Confederate envoys from the British mail packet RMS *Trent*. Britain demanded the representatives' immediate release, and Lincoln eventually complied, to the chagrin of national pride. The president concluded it was best to fight just "one war at a time."[34]

Union loyalists were hanged in Eastern Tennessee, but entreaties for Buell to provide them aid and arms fell on his deaf ears. McClellan kept his plans to himself during the good months of fall, and the war entered the winter months, making large-scale movements difficult. Lincoln struggled to placate the Joint Committee on the Conduct of the War and explain why the armies did not advance.[35]

The president's woes increased when the commanding general of the Union armies caught a case of typhoid fever. McClellan took to his bed in mid-December just as Lincoln pushed for the army to do something.[36]

President Lincoln complained to Quartermaster Montgomery C. Meigs, "The bottom is out of the tub." However, rather than stand idly by, Lincoln inserted himself into a process to induce Union armies to advance. He naively believed that Generals Buell and Halleck were communicating with each other to hatch an ingenious scheme to take down Johnston's defensive line. But the two officers informed Lincoln that they had never discussed a campaign, that each of them had no idea what the other was doing, and that McClellan bore responsibility for any concerted action between them.[37]

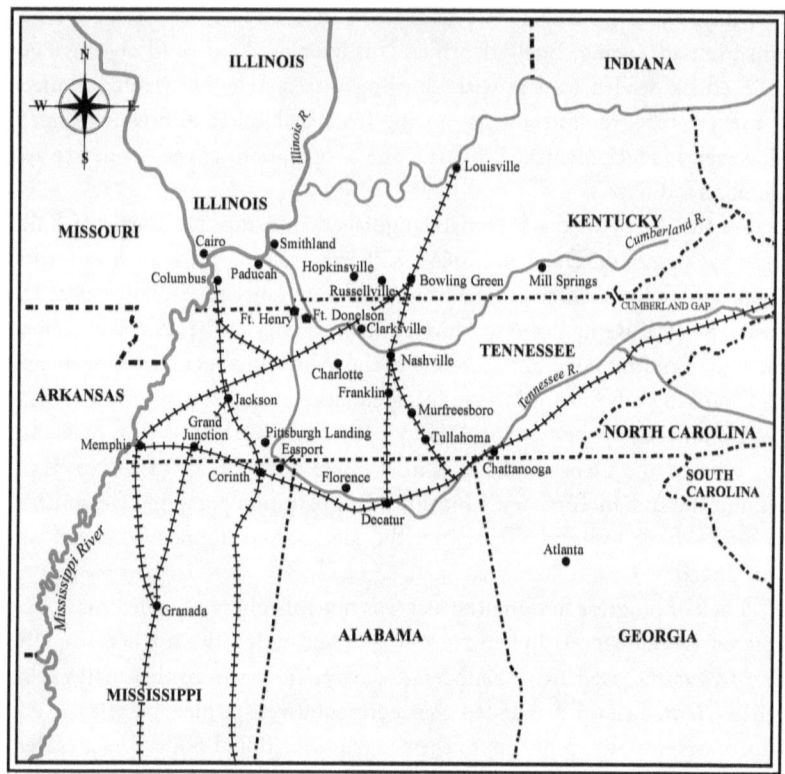

Western Theater

This response put Lincoln in the doldrums, but history shows that his inquiries made Buell and Halleck communicate. A concept of a plan grew that had Buell move against Bowling Green while Halleck prevented Confederate reinforcements from leaving Columbus. While Buell complained about not having enough men and transportation to make a move, Grant and Flag Officer Andrew Hull Foote were making do with what they had at Cairo.[38]

Rebel defeat at Mill Springs finally alerted the Confederacy to the fragile condition of Johnston's defensive line through Kentucky and Tennessee. Fortunately, Grant had Foote's new ironclad gunboats and a fleet of steamboats to transport his army and supplies via the rivers.

Forts Henry and Donelson were prime targets for the initial thrust of Union troops into Tennessee. President Lincoln's prodding of Generals Buell and Halleck as McClellan lay disabled with typhoid fever advanced the timetable for invasion up the Tennessee and Cumberland Rivers.

CHAPTER 1

BEFORE THE BATTLES

As 1862 started, President Lincoln pressured Maj. Gen. Henry Halleck to cooperate with Brig. Gen. Don Carlos Buell in a movement against Bowling Green. Halleck confronted insurgency in Missouri and perceived threats to Cairo and Paducah from rebel forces at Columbus, and he had to decide how to respond to the president's entreaties. In response to information about the vulnerability of Fort Henry and the anticipated arrival of reinforcements for the Confederate army, Halleck had to determine a plan of action for the Tennessee and Cumberland Rivers. With two critical decisions in January, Halleck set in motion the Battles for Forts Henry and Donelson.

Halleck Orders Demonstrations into Kentucky,
January 10–22, 1862

Situation

Halleck graduated from West Point in 1839 and stayed on as a French instructor for one year. Gen. Winfield Scott sent him to Europe for six months to study war and defenses. Upon his return to America, Halleck published *Elements of Military Art and Science*. During the Mexican War, he served in California as secretary of state to the military governor. After leaving the army he started a profitable law firm in 1854 and was successful in land speculation and mining. With the outbreak of the Civil War, Halleck offered his

Maj. Gen. Henry Halleck.

services to the government and arrived in Washington, DC, in August 1861 with a reputation as one of the most brilliant military minds in the country.[1]

The United States Army changed commanders and reorganized departments in mid-November 1861. Replacements were needed for Maj. Gen. John C. Frémont in St. Louis, Missouri, and Brig. Gen. William Sherman in Louisville, Kentucky. Two new departments were formed with the Cumberland River in Kentucky as a boundary.[2]

Halleck got the difficult assignment to replace Frémont and command the new Department of the Missouri that covered Missouri, Illinois, and the part of Kentucky west of the Cumberland River. Frémont left behind a disorganized situation, rebellion in Missouri, and risk from Confederate forces in Kentucky. The command of the new Department of the Ohio went to Buell and included Tennessee and Kentucky east of the Cumberland River.[3] The boundaries of the two departments put Forts Henry and Donelson on the exterior ends of each of them. Although a thrust up the Tennessee and Cumberland Rivers would shatter Johnston's defensive line, both Halleck and Buell focused on problems in their departments and away from the river forts.[4]

Halleck struggled to improve the organization of his command amid insurrection, and his priority became saving Missouri for the Union. Once the state was secure, Halleck could strike rebel strongholds outside it.[5] After about two weeks in command, Halleck sent reports to McClellan outlining the sorry state of affairs and the steps taken to bring order to the department. The forces were disorganized and suffered from a lack of arms and equipment. Enemy troops numbered more than expected, as rebellion raged in northern Missouri, and Price led a large force of insurgents in southwestern Missouri.[6]

On December 2 McClellan telegraphed Halleck and requested a report on the situation in Missouri, including information on the gunboats. Halleck referred to his previous correspondence and stated that he had no information about the vessels. Another telegram from McClellan on December 5 alarmed Halleck by informing him that the commander intended to withdraw troops from Missouri.[7] Protesting strongly, Halleck pointed out that it would be madness to remove men from the state. On December 10 McClellan replied that he would not strip troops from Halleck if the soldiers could not be spared. But if Halleck had troops available, McClellan proposed that he work in concert with Buell on a very important movement against Bowling Green.[8]

With receipt of McClellan's letter, Halleck relaxed. He sent a long letter to the commander on December 16 detailing success against the insurgents. There were enough men and thousands of weapons on the way to arm the Federals. In mid-December, Halleck looked forward to ending the insurrection in Missouri and then turning his attention to rebel strongholds outside the state.[9]

When the time came for an advance, Halleck identified the true line of operations to be the Tennessee and Cumberland Rivers. However, McClellan, Buell, and, most important, President Lincoln pinpointed Bowling Green and Nashville as the prime targets. Since the objectives were in Buell's department, that put Buell in charge of the advance with Halleck expected to render support.

During the last half of December, Halleck received no information from McClellan concerning a joint move with Buell. He sent two reports to the Union commander detailing more success against the rebels. Halleck ended his December 26 report with the prediction that by the first part of February he should be able to reinforce Cairo and Paducah with the goal of carrying out operations outside Missouri.[10]

However, the Lincoln administration wanted a military success somewhere and quickly. When McClellan took sick with typhoid fever in mid-December, the president chafed under the delay and finally wielded his authority on the first day of 1862. Lincoln sent telegrams to Halleck and Buell asking whether they were working together regarding Buell's move on Bowling Green. He prodded Halleck by observing that a simultaneous movement on Columbus would prevent rebel reinforcements from there reaching Bowling Green.[11]

Lincoln was surely disappointed when Halleck informed him he had never contacted Buell to plan anything; he could not cooperate with him at present; but he had discussed the subject with McClellan. Buell repeated to Lincoln that no arrangement between him and Halleck existed, as McClellan handled that. The president then sent both generals terse telegrams demanding they communicate with each other at once.[12]

Halleck quickly sent a message to Buell pointing out that he had received no instructions concerning their cooperation. Regardless, all available troops were in the field in Missouri, except for those at Cairo and Paducah. He hoped to be able to assist Buell in a few weeks.[13] Buell sent a long response to Halleck on January 3, 1862. He declared that the strength of Johnston's forces lay along the line from Columbus to Bowling Green through Forts Henry and Donelson on the Tennessee and Cumberland Rivers. Halleck already had the idea from Lincoln that Buell was about to move against Bowling Green. Now, Buell wrote anxiously of a movement requiring Halleck to distract the rebel troops at Columbus and send two gunboat expeditions up the Tennessee and Cumberland Rivers to take out railroad bridges. Buell closed his message with an urgent plea that Halleck act within a few days.[14]

Halleck's subordinate Ulysses S. Grant, stationed at Cairo showed readiness to advance and fight, as evidenced by the Battle of Belmont. The rebel insurgency in southeastern Missouri was under control, so most of the Union troops at Cairo and Paducah were available for action.[15] However, Halleck believed there were more rebels at Columbus than he had men to assault them. The ironclad gunboats were not ready for service, and he had no word from McClellan as Buell proclaimed something must be done posthaste. Taking Buell's letter as an immediate request for support, Halleck had a decision to make.

Options

Halleck considered his options when confronted with misleading messages from McClellan, Buell, and Lincoln. He could wait until he had a direct order from a senior commander to make a movement, or he could aid Buell with the limited forces he could muster the first week of January.

Option 1

Halleck could take no action even though Buell's message of January 3 indicated something needed to be done speedily. Halleck did not receive a direct order to make a demonstration, but the president had ordered Halleck and Buell to collaborate on an advance against Bowling Green. While Halleck was not in position to attack Columbus and the gunboats were not ready for service, it would be unwise to completely ignore Lincoln's expectations.

Option 2

Halleck believed he was expected to mount expeditions up the Cumberland and Tennessee Rivers while Buell moved against Bowling Green and Nashville. But he surmised Grant had only enough men to make two demonstrations into Kentucky with orders not to risk a battle with rebel forces. While avoiding combat, the demonstrations could be conducted to confuse the Confederates as to the Union's intentions and gather important information for future operations up the Tennessee and Cumberland Rivers.

Decision

Halleck ordered Grant to immediately assist Buell by launching two demonstrations into Kentucky, one from Cairo and the other from Paducah.

Results/Impact

On January 6, 1862, Grant received the order to make demonstrations in force and target Mayfield, Kentucky. His instructions were to feign an attack on Columbus and act like the objective was Dover, Tennessee, and then an attack on Nashville. Just ten thousand men were available in Cairo and Paducah to make movements toward Columbus and the Tennessee River. Serious engagements were to be avoided because the purpose of the exercise was to prevent rebel reinforcements from entering Bowling Green from Columbus.[16]

Grant acted immediately and sent Brig. Gen. John McClernand forward to Fort Jefferson, located across the Mississippi River in Kentucky, approximately five miles south of Cairo. A Union cavalry detachment approached Columbus (about eighteen miles south of Cairo) on January 12, and the rebel pickets retreated behind the fortifications. McClernand's approach bewildered Polk, who pleaded for reinforcements.[17]

On January 14 McClernand set up camp near Blandville, Kentucky, which blocked roads from Columbus. Grant met the column and instructed the Federals to move toward Milburn, Kentucky, on January 16 to deceive the rebels as to their destination. The men then backtracked, and by January 19 the objectives of the demonstration were met. On January 21 the column returned to Cairo.[18]

Brig. Gen. Charles Ferguson Smith left Paducah on January 15 to use subterfuge to convince the rebels he was headed toward Dover and then on to Nashville. He traveled down the west side of the Tennessee River while the *Lexington*, commanded by Lieut. James Shirk, and the *Conestoga*, commanded by Lieut. Seth Phelps, supported the expedition and approached Fort Henry via the river.[19]

Smith's movements caused the Confederate commander at Forts Henry and Donelson, Brig. Gen. Lloyd Tilghman, to guess at the motive of the Federal advance. A couple of feints by Smith kept Tilghman off balance. By January 21 Smith was at Calloway, Kentucky, approximately twenty miles downriver from Fort Henry. That night Tilghman concluded that the Union troops would cross the river and attack one or both of the forts.[20]

January 22 became an eventful day for the Union cause when Smith boarded the *Lexington* and went upriver to make a reconnaissance of Fort Henry. Upon making his survey, the officer wrote a sentence that reverberated through Union command all the way to Halleck in St. Louis: "I think two iron-clad gunboats would make short work of Fort Henry." Smith arrived back at Paducah on January 25.[21]

The demonstrations Halleck ordered have not received sufficient recognition for the value of the information they supplied. Historian Benjamin Franklin Cooling writes, "What would start as a simple, limited, and minor demonstration in force became the first stage of a more serious advance." The operations revealed weaknesses in the Confederate defensive line, including a lack of manpower at Forts Henry and Donelson.[22]

Union leadership noted the Confederates' lack of aggressive response in the face of the blatant intrusion into their territory. This raised confidence that Federal forces could successfully assault Columbus and the forts.[23]

In addition, Smith's column encountered such bad roads that the officer concluded an army could not be supported by a wagon train of supplies during the rainy season, which was expected to start later in January. This was important information for planning an advance against the rebels in winter.[24]

At the time of the maneuvers little had been accomplished at Fort Heiman, and Smith made no mention of it. Low water prevented gunboats from approaching Fort Donelson, so recent information was not available. As the end of January approached, the Union command's general consensus was that Fort Henry presented a more formidable problem than Fort Donelson.[25]

Johnston viewed the demonstrations with growing alarm, and by January 20 he concluded Grant was headed to Nashville. The rebel general subsequently ordered the transfer of eight thousand men in Kentucky from Bowling Green to Russellville. From Russellville they could move in the direction of either Columbus or Bowling Green, depending on where the hammer fell.[26]

Grant did his job well. The Confederates panicked, as they lacked enough

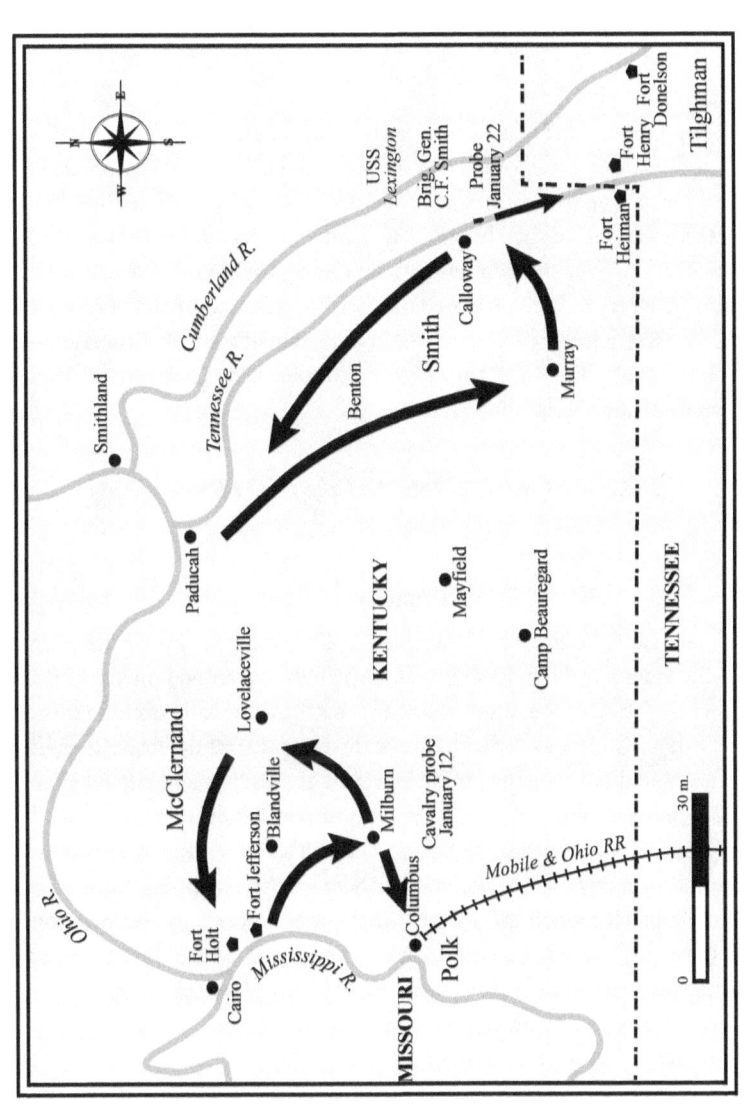

January 1862 Demonstrations

men to cover all threatened areas, and the Tennessee and Cumberland Rivers provided an avenue into Tennessee.

Alternate Decision and Scenario

If Halleck had not sent out demonstrations in support of Buell, there might never have been a battle at Fort Henry because Buell would not have moved on Bowling Green. Until Buell was ready, McClellan would not have given Halleck a direct order to move. As of February 4, when Grant's forces set sail for Fort Henry, Buell was not ready. The demonstrations revealed weakness at Fort Henry and gave the Union army confidence it could take the stronghold quickly. Without the demonstrations Grant would not have taken Fort Henry on February 6. By February 8 the fort was defeated by the floodwaters of the Tennessee River. The Union would have gained control of the Tennessee River without a fight and turned its attention to the Cumberland River, Fort Donelson, and Nashville.

Halleck Orders Grant to Take Fort Henry, January 30, 1862

Situation

As President Lincoln stewed in Washington, DC, apparently unaware he had indeed stirred up some activity out west, he penned a letter on January 13, 1862, to Halleck and Buell. The letter illustrates that Lincoln had correctly identified the military strategy needed to break the Confederate defensive line. The president pointed out that the Union had greater numbers and should simultaneously threaten Johnston's line with superior force at different locations.[27]

On January 15 McClellan requested Halleck's views on proposed movements and how many men he could contribute without stripping troops from Missouri. Halleck replied on January 20 that he opposed an advance down the Mississippi. Instead, he emphasized proceeding up the Tennessee and Cumberland Rivers with Nashville as the objective. Halleck estimated that the move required sixty thousand men. Currently, there were but fifteen thousand men at Cairo, Paducah, and Smithland.[28]

The time frame Halleck contemplated for the movement was the middle or end of February, when he hoped to have fifteen thousand more men available. The major general accurately predicted it would be mid-February before Brig. Gen. Samuel R. Curtis would drive Price out of Missouri. But when Halleck wrote the January 20 letter, he did not know that the Battle of Mill Springs had shattered Johnston's defensive line in Kentucky. The Confederates' response to their disaster at Mill Springs meant serious ramifications for Halleck's schedule for proceeding up the rivers.[29]

Johnston called on the Confederacy for immediate assistance. On January 22 he wrote the War Department, proclaiming that the defense of Tennessee required all the resources of the government. He warned officials that any thought the Union would not advance in the winter was a delusion. Johnston wanted more troops. What he got was Gen. Pierre Gustave Toutant Beauregard.[30]

Grant returned to Cairo on January 20, read the letter from Smith depicting the weakness of Fort Henry, and forwarded it to Halleck. Grant requested permission to visit Halleck in person in lieu of submitting a written report on the findings of the demonstrations. Halleck agreed, and Grant left for St. Louis the night of January 23. Meanwhile, Foote busily worked to locate crewmen for the fleet of seven ironclad gunboats. Sailors were in short supply, and there were just enough to put four ironclad gunboats on the water.[31]

Events had moved quickly, and the victory at Mill Springs broke Johnston's right flank. Perhaps it was time to attack Johnston's center?

Grant's trip to St. Louis ended in disaster. Halleck rattled Grant with a rude greeting and after just a few sentences cut him off and dismissed him. Grant left with the impression his plan was preposterous and returned to Cairo very much crestfallen on January 28.[32] Despite the disappointing meeting, he showed optimism and confidence the day he returned, asking Halleck's permission to attack Fort Henry and establish a large camp there. The next day, January 29, Grant pointed out that now was the time to strike, as rebel defenses on the rivers would only get stronger.[33]

With gunboats ready to go, the navy could cooperate with the army. In a telegram to Halleck, Foote backed Grant's play, stating his and Grant's opinion that they could carry Fort Henry with four ironclad gunboats and troops. He asked Halleck for authority to attack Fort Henry and permanently occupy it as soon as they were ready.[34]

Halleck read these telegrams as he perused the president's General War Order No. 1, issued on January 27. Lincoln's patience at a lack of progress had worn thin, and he ordered U.S. land and naval forces to advance against the insurgent forces on February 22. Sure to catch Halleck's attention, the president clearly stated that the army and navy at Cairo must move. Fortunately, Lincoln's desperate order coincided with Halleck's statements that it would be mid-February before he could make movements outside Missouri.[35]

But fate was not yet finished with Halleck, for McClellan sent him a startling telegram on January 29. The message contained information from a deserter who had overheard officers say Beauregard received orders to go to

Kentucky with fifteen regiments. Halleck totally believed the false intelligence from McClellan and contemplated his reaction to it.³⁶

Options

Halleck weighed his options after receipt of McClellan's low-grade intelligence that Beauregard was due to arrive with fifteen regiments. He could maintain his timetable of an advance in mid-February, or he could order Grant and Foote to make an immediate advance up the Tennessee River against Fort Henry.

Option 1

For weeks Halleck postulated he had insufficient forces to make a movement outside Missouri. Lincoln's General War Order No. 1 did not require an advance until February 22, and neither McClellan, Buell, nor the president expected action by Halleck. Halleck received no orders to make an advance and could wait until he did, but a delay would allow the Confederacy to strengthen Fort Henry's defenses.

Option 2

Halleck's judgment that it would be mid-February before he could use troops from Missouri elsewhere was accurate; but Fort Henry was reported vulnerable now. Although not fully prepared with more troops and more manned gunboats, Halleck could order an immediate attack on Fort Henry with the forces available before the Confederacy could reinforce it. Grant and Foote stood ready to move quickly to take Fort Henry if given authority.

Decision

Despite misgivings that it was not time for a forward movement, Halleck sent Grant one of the most important telegrams of the war: "Make your preparations to take and hold Fort Henry."³⁷

Results/Impact

Halleck's decision to attack Fort Henry brought an ecstatic reaction from Grant and his staff. The reactions from McClellan and Buell were much more muted. Halleck informed McClellan on January 30 that he had received the telegram about Beauregard and acted on it. Grant and Foote were ordered up the Tennessee River to take Fort Henry.³⁸

Buell received the startling news from Halleck that a Union advance on

Fort Henry and Dover was underway. Since Halleck had claimed inability to help Buell until mid-February, the sudden movement up the Tennessee River left Buell perplexed and angry. He inquired whether forceful cooperation was essential for Halleck's success; but Buell could not do anything for several days. Halleck assured him support was not needed at present.[39]

Grant stressed secrecy in orders to McClernand and Smith. McClernand's First Division would leave Cairo on February 2, while Smith's Second Division would depart from Paducah following McClernand's troops. Foote gathered enough crewmen to send four ironclad gunboats on the expedition: the *Essex, Carondelet, Cincinnati*, and *St. Louis*. They were joined by the timberclads *Lexington, Conestoga*, and *Tyler*. The expedition commenced, and fifteen thousand men converged on Paducah.[40]

McClernand steamed through Paducah the evening of February 3, and Grant issued him orders for the attack on Fort Henry. The flotilla picked up Col. John Cook's brigade of Smith's division, but the rest of the men watched the transports pass them by. Only thirteen transports were available, which was insufficient to take both divisions at the same time. At 4:30 a.m. on February 4 McClernand's division disembarked eight miles north of Fort Henry at Itra Landing. The Union troops were in enemy territory not knowing how many rebels opposed them.[41]

But Grant wanted McClernand's division nearer to the fort, so he boarded the *Essex* for a closer look at Fort Henry and to test the range of the fort's guns. The first shots from the stronghold fell far short, but suddenly a shell from the rifled 24-pounder crashed through the *Essex* at a distance of two and a half miles. The range of the fort's guns established, Grant ordered McClernand to re-embark and locate his camp north of Panther Creek at Bailey's Landing. This put the camp approximately four miles north of the fort. As McClernand's men commenced laying out their camp, Grant and the transports returned to Paducah for the rest of Smith's division.[42]

In less than one week after the go-ahead, Grant positioned fifteen thousand troops and a fleet of four ironclad gunboats and three timberclads within three miles of Fort Henry. The Confederates did not realize the Federals' presence until McClernand's men walked down the ramps of the transports. During February 5 Smith's division landed on the west side of the river to move against unfinished Fort Heiman. Grant returned with the lead transports, while the rest of Smith's unit trailed and did not reach the staging area until the early morning hours of February 6.[43]

Halleck's critical decision to order Grant to take Fort Henry started the campaign leading to the capture of Forts Henry and Donelson. But the department commander's influence on events waned once Grant and his army steamed out of Cairo. Grant felt relief as his troops and Foote's gunboats moved into position to attack Fort Henry. He was beyond the telegraph should Halleck decide to call off the assault, so the next critical decision was his own.[44]

Grant's advance sent a shiver through the Confederates' defensive line. Back in Bowling Green, Johnston and Beauregard contemplated what they would do upon the fall of Fort Henry. Grant pondered what he would do next once he had Fort Henry in his possession.

CHAPTER 2

BATTLE FOR FORT HENRY
THURSDAY, FEBRUARY 6, 1862

On this day ironclad gunboats attacked an earthen fort for the first time in history. For two days Union troops landed north of Fort Henry while the gunboats sat and waited. At the same time, the bastion's defenders observed the growing host against them. Each commander had a critical decision to make. Grant had to determine when to proceed with the attack, even if the fort was not fully invested. Tilghman observed the threatening gunboats and knew his force was badly outnumbered. He had to decide whether to defend Fort Henry against such odds or abandon the fort and save the entire garrison.[1]

Grant Attacks Fort Henry

Situation

Grant received written instructions from Halleck on January 30, 1862, outlining how he should attack Fort Henry. However, Halleck made an unrealistic assumption that Grant could fully invest the garrison and cut off its escape. Reports of the possible arrival of rebel reinforcements made Grant move rapidly to reduce Fort Henry.[2]

Grant graduated from West Point in 1843 without distinction, except as an excellent horseman. He won two brevets during the Mexican War while

Brig. Gen. Ulysses S. Grant.

learning the role of a quartermaster. After marrying in 1848 and having two children, Grant took an assignment to the West Coast, away from his family. The separation caused him to drink and led to his resignation from the army in 1854. When the war broke out, Grant was working at his father's leather store in Galena, Illinois, and he helped raise a rifle company and then escorted it to Springfield.[3]

Illinois Governor Richard Yates needed a new mustering officer, and Grant fit the bill. He spent a month traveling the state to muster in Illinois regiments and then returned to Galena. In June, Grant attempted to secure an assignment to McClellan's staff but failed. The same month, Yates offered Grant the colonelcy of the Twenty-First Illinois. In late July the Illinois congressional delegation provided a list of men to be commissioned brigadier generals from Illinois. Not only was Grant's name on this list, but the date of his commission was also retroactive to May 17. Frémont put Grant in command of all troops in southeastern Missouri and southern Illinois. Fortunately for the new general, he was in place at Cairo when Halleck replaced Frémont in November, because Halleck would never have put Grant in that position.[4]

Halleck instructed Grant to cut off retreat of the garrison by a rapid movement to occupy the road to Dover and totally invest the fort. But Halleck's information lacked the fact that the Confederates could use several routes between Fort Henry and Dover. The "road to Dover" was labeled the Telegraph Road and was located north of the fort. Another road, the Ridge Road, ran south of the Telegraph Road to Fort Donelson. Farther south there were rough tracks the rebels could use. To completely invest Fort Henry required more forces than Grant had available, and making the attempt would delay the attack.[5]

Grant and Foote were confident they would make short work of Fort Henry, but Grant was concerned about Fort Henry being reinforced. Grant would decide when he would attack Fort Henry, but time was of the essence because he expected Johnston to send men to the stronghold from Columbus, Bowling Green, or both.[6]

On February 5 McClernand probed the territory between the Union camp and Fort Henry. While McClernand learned details of the terrain, creeks, and roads between his camp and Panther Creek, he could not get close enough to estimate how many troops defended Fort Henry. Nor could he assess the road system south of Panther Creek. Union intelligence west of the river also was lacking, and the number of troops defending Fort Heiman was unknown, as was the status of the fortifications and artillery placements.[7]

The possibility of additional men for the assault was good, as Halleck scrounged through Missouri and surrounding states for more troops. But that would take time, and it had already been over a week since Grant and Foote convinced Halleck they would take Fort Henry with what they had.

Smith's division took all of February 5 and into the night to arrive at Bailey's Landing. Finally, the last piece of the attack force was falling into place. Beyond recall by Halleck, Grant was buoyed by aggressive subordinates eager to strike at the Confederacy.

The question was when would Grant attack Fort Henry?

Options

Grant's options were to attack Fort Henry immediately, or delay the offensive to give McClernand's division time to invest the garrison and cut off its retreat to Fort Donelson. Waiting for reinforcements was not considered a choice.

Option 1

Grant could launch an immediate attack, as he had his entire force deployed and expected no additional gunboats or men in the next few days. Despite not knowing the number of defenders and possessing inadequate knowledge of escape routes for the rebel garrison, Grant felt confident of success, and the army and navy were poised for battle.

Option 2

Grant could delay the attack while he tried to get troops in position to capture the garrison, but it would take time to reconnoiter and get into position. Any delay could result in the arrival of reinforcements for the fort.

Decision

Grant did not waver when in sight of his objective. Whatever the number of defenders in the fort, Grant had authority to take it, and that was what he was going to do. Even if he did not capture the whole garrison, waiting would only benefit the Confederates. Thus there would be no delay. Grant ordered the attack to commence once the troops on the last transports were unloaded.

Results/Impact

The attack on Fort Henry had a late start at 11:00 a.m. on February 6 to allow the last troops of Smith's division time to arrive. Foote would engage the fort, and Smith would start the approach to Fort Heiman. McClernand would seize the Telegraph Road to block the garrison's escape, and then his men would attack the fort from the landside.[8]

Rain came in torrents during the night but did not sway Grant's determination to move quickly. Watercourses that had flowed tranquilly the day before became obstacles to rapid movement. Foote cautioned Grant to move his troops earlier than the gunboats to give them time to get in position before the

Fort Henry. Star-shaped outline of fort in 1937 aerial view prior to filling of Kentucky Lake. Courtesy of National Park Service.

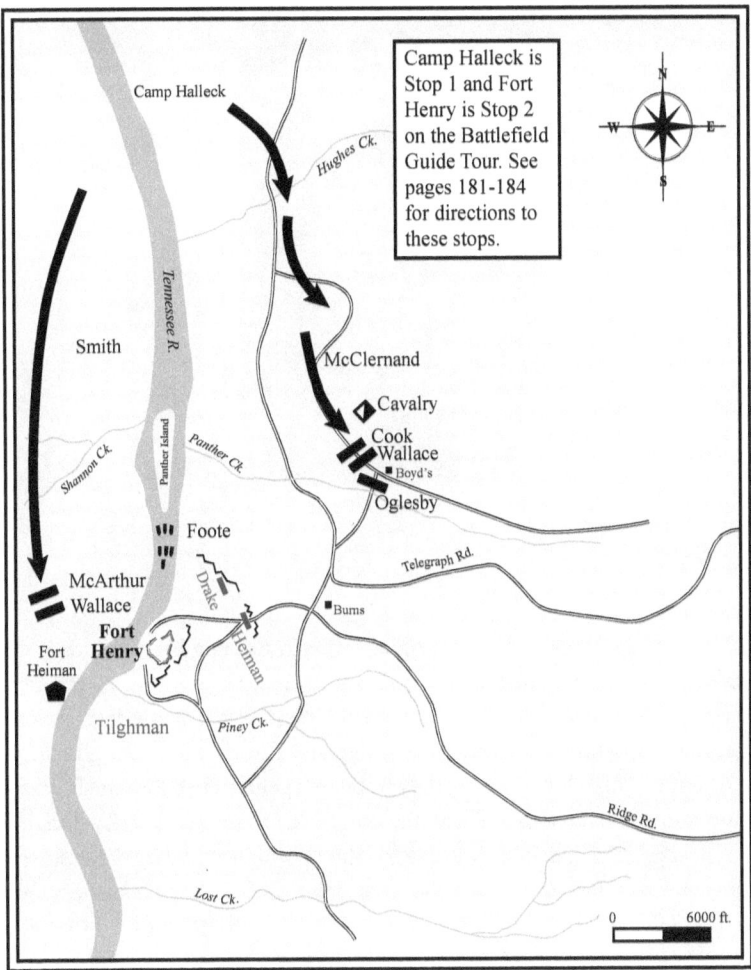

Attack on Fort Henry, February 6

bombardment started. At this point in the war the army was in charge of the river watercrafts, while the navy provided officers and men. Grant and Foote cooperated well with the same goal of taking Fort Henry. But Grant would not delay the gunboats' attack to give McClernand's troops more opportunity to approach Fort Henry before the vessels opened fire. The confident Foote told Grant the navy would take the fort before the army could get there.[9]

While McClernand struggled through flooded creeks, the fleet sailed forth with the four ironclad gunboats in front, followed by the three timberclads in support. Foote's gunboat attack on Fort Henry was the first of

Flag Officer Andrew Foote.

its kind in the history of naval warfare. Ironclad floating batteries were used in the Crimean War, but Foote's gunboats came with propulsion systems to move them forward under their own power. Neither the fort's defenders nor the attacking sailors knew what would happen. But they soon found out.[10]

At approximately 12:30 p.m. the gunboats opened fire when the boats got within range and huge mounds of dirt erupted from the fort's walls. The rebel cannoneers responded, and shots rattled the pilothouses and casemates. After almost an hour the *Essex* took a shot that burst through the boilers. The boat was disabled and drifted with the current out of the fight, but the other gunboats continued to close the gap with the fort. As Foote predicted, the navy took Fort Henry before the Union infantry was even close. The surrender flag was hoisted aloft at approximately 1:50 p.m.[11]

Two brigades of Smith's division found Fort Heiman empty as the defenders had fled upon their approach. McClernand got his column moving on time, but it took approximately three hours just to reach the Telegraph Road. His orders were to block the road to keep the garrison from escaping, and prevent reinforcements from Fort Donelson from reaching Fort Henry. Grant's instructions did not recognize there were rough trails to the south for the garrison's exodus to Fort Donelson.[12]

McClernand understood he was to stop once he reached the Telegraph Road. The anxious soldiers waited and heard the gunboats duel it out with the fort. McClernand finally advanced on the citadel because there were no de-

USS *Essex*, which was heavily damaged at Fort Henry.

fenders in front, and rebel troops were not on the move from Fort Donelson to Fort Henry.[13]

Not until 3:30 p.m. did Grant and Union troops take possession of Fort Henry. Federal cavalry pursued the rebels but were in no position to block the column. They picked up stragglers and recovered abandoned rebel artillery until nightfall.[14]

Grant decided to attack the fort before the roads leading from the area were blocked. He identified poor road conditions as a factor in the escape of the garrison, reasoning the rebels commenced their retreat early in the morning. But Tilghman did not order troops to start evacuating until around 11:00 a.m., when the gunboats came into view and commenced fire at fifteen minutes before noon. The garrison soldiers used a route south of the Ridge Road to lessen the chance of Union troops getting ahead of them.[15]

Today the remains of Fort Henry sit below the waters of Kentucky Lake. The fall of Fort Henry was a pivotal episode in the Civil War because it split the Confederate defensive line and opened the Tennessee River to Union exploitation. Johnston had limited assets to counter Grant's army on the Tennessee River. The weakness of Tennessee and the Confederacy in defense of the Tennessee River was evident, with the unforeseen result that after almost seven months of effort to construct Fort Henry, the bastion did not last two hours against Foote's gunboats.

There were no rebel gunboats to confront those of the Union. The day

USS *Tyler*, a timberclad.

after Fort Henry fell, Foote sent the timberclads up the Tennessee River to Florence, Alabama. During the excursion Lieut. Phelps rendered the Danville railroad bridge inoperable, severing the railroad connection between Columbus and Bowling Green. Phelps returned to Fort Henry on February 10, and the Union had free rein of the Tennessee River to conduct military expeditions from Kentucky to Florence, Alabama.[16]

For some unfathomable reason Johnston never visited the twin forts and projected the rapid destruction of Fort Henry onto Fort Donelson. If he had visited the forts, perhaps he would have recognized the difference in the defensive situation at each one. Instead, Johnston concluded Fort Donelson was indefensible against gunboat attack and would fall without need of a land assault. He informed the government in Richmond of this belief, which was a factor in his response to the fall of Fort Henry.[17]

The disaster at Fort Henry prompted a war council at Bowling Green on February 7 attended by Generals Johnston, Beauregard, and Hardee. Beauregard pushed for an aggressive response to force Grant out of Tennessee, but Johnston believed he lacked the manpower to drive Grant away and also prevent Buell's advance to Nashville. The risk was more than Johnston would take.[18]

As Halleck predicted, the capture of Fort Henry caused Johnston to withdraw from Bowling Green to Nashville and consider the abandonment of Columbus. Johnston ordered Brig. Gen. John Floyd's Brigade and Brig. Gen.

Simon Buckner's Division to Clarksville. The Union field of operations moved to the Tennessee River as Johnston waited to see what Grant would do next.[19]

The surprising ease with which Fort Henry fell to the gunboats caused consternation throughout the South. Indeed, Tilghman was pilloried in the Southern press for loss of the fort. Yet in the North there was great rejoicing. Foote's report of the victory was read in the halls of Congress, bringing him much acclaim.[20]

Tilghman Defends Fort Henry

Situation

The Confederacy did not recognize the importance of defending the Tennessee River until it was too late. While Polk's citadel at Columbus boasted a total of 142 cannon, the poor cousin at Fort Henry mustered just seventeen, with twelve facing the river.[21] Engineer officer Maj. Jeremy Gilmer joined Johnston's army in late October to improve the defenses of the river forts and build fortifications at Clarksville and Nashville. In early November Gilmer reported Fort Henry in good defensive shape, but not Fort Donelson.[22]

Johnston ordered Tilghman to take command of Forts Henry and Donelson on November 17. Tilghman was a graduate of the West Point class of 1836 who had worked as a civil engineer on railroads throughout the East and South, as well as in Panama. He had also served in the Mexican War. Having lived in Paducah since 1852, Tilghman was familiar with the territory. He

Brig. Gen. Lloyd Tilghman.

also held a prominent role in the Kentucky State Guard and commanded the Confederate Third Kentucky. Johnston became aware of the lack of progress at the forts and instructed Tilghman to complete the works and arm them as quickly as possible. For the next two months Tilghman struggled to improve the ramparts at Fort Donelson and obtain additional ordnance.[23]

In mid-January Johnston got word little had been done at Fort Heiman. A terse note to Tilghman increased soldiers' efforts. Near the same time, Smith's demonstration heightened urgency to bolster the defenses of Forts Henry and Heiman in anticipation of the Union army's and navy's imminent arrival.[24] But time was running out for Fort Henry. First, it was not possible to change the location. In addition, the need for additional strong cannon that could damage gunboats went unanswered, as did calls for more troops with adequate weapons. And while Fort Henry had an extensive length of fortifications, there were no available troops to fill them.

Tilghman and Gilmer were at Fort Henry on January 31, 1862. Just a few more days' work would ready that stronghold for defense, but no cannon had arrived for Fort Heiman. Tilghman lamented a lack of artillerists to man the guns at Fort Henry. His greatest fear was a gunboat attack, and he did not have long to wait for one.[25]

On February 3 the two officers moved to Fort Donelson to work on defenses there. As McClernand's division approached Paducah, Tilghman got word from his pickets that no enemy was in sight, and he and Gilmer departed for Fort Donelson, leaving Col. Adolphus Heiman in command.[26] At 4:30 a.m. on February 4 rocket signals from rebel pickets at Bailey's Landing brought ill tidings to Col. Heiman. Union gunboats and transports loaded with troops, cavalry, and artillery were steaming up the Tennessee River. Heiman immediately ordered pickets and cavalry vedettes forward to take positions between Bailey's Landing and the fort.[27]

In addition, Heiman sent couriers to Fort Donelson to keep Tilghman advised of the growing threat to Fort Henry. Around 1:00 p.m. gunboats fired shells at the fort, and the two sides exchanged missiles for about thirty minutes. The cannonade was heard at Fort Donelson. After the gunboats withdrew, Heiman rushed another courier to inform Tilghman that Union troops were arriving at Bailey's Landing, and that the general was needed at Fort Henry. Tilghman issued orders for the defense of Fort Donelson and then left for Fort Henry, where he arrived at 11:30 p.m.[28]

Upon reaching the fort, Tilghman learned a sizable Union force had landed on the east and west banks, about four miles north, accompanied by gunboats. Tilghman ordered the two regiments at Fort Heiman across the river to Fort Henry and moved two small regiments up from the Danville, Tennessee area to Fort Henry. His defenders numbered 2,610, but only a third of them were disciplined and armed with decent weapons. The infantry were placed in the outer works, in the area of the camps and out of range of the gunboats.[29]

A message sent to Johnston on February 5 claimed that Tilghman could win a glorious victory with reinforcements. A hopeless dispatch was sent to Columbus, as Polk had no intention of sending any infantry troops to Fort Henry. Tilghman knew it was now too late to reinforce the stronghold, and he would have to make do with the men he had.[30]

During the night of February 5 transports unloaded Union troops on the west side of the river to assault Fort Heiman. With each passing hour Tilghman's position became more dire. Lieut. Col. Milton Haynes commanded Tilghman's artillery and rode to Fort Henry from Fort Donelson the night of the fifth. In the morning he examined the works and declared the fort untenable, saying it should be immediately abandoned.[31]

It became clear the Union troops were preparing to strike. By 10:00 a.m. on February 6 it was certain the Federal gunboats were going to attack. Tilghman knew the Union troops on the east bank would attempt to cut off the garrison from escape. On the west bank, Fort Heiman was abandoned.[32]

The time had come for Tilghman to decide his course of action in the face of overwhelming odds.

Options

Tilghman had several options when it became clear the attack was coming. He could make a resolute defense against the gunboats and ground forces, or he could abandon the fort immediately without a fight. A third option involved a compromise: the artillerists would defend Fort Henry against the gunboat attack, but the garrison would abandon the fort and retreat to Fort Donelson.

Option 1

Tilghman could fight in the fortifications until forced to surrender. This would result in the loss of all the defenders. If the gunboats reduced the fort, there was no point in a land fight. If the vessels were defeated, there were not enough rebel defenders to hold the fortifications.

Option 2

Tilghman could abandon the fort and spare all the defenders to fight another day. Lieut. Col. Haynes recommended this option, but giving up the fort with no effort to defend it might result in morale problems in the army and civilian outrage against the government. Tilghman's sense of duty required that he make the best defense his limited resources would allow.[33]

Option 3

Tilghman could sacrifice the artillerists but allow the garrison to retreat to Fort Donelson. He knew the rain that had fallen during the night would delay advance of the Union land forces, but he concluded the gunboats had to be held off long enough for the garrison to escape. While the gunboats were engaged, Grant's army could not approach the fort for fear of shells from their cannons. Grant greatly outnumbered Tilghman, so even if, by chance, the artillerists were able to beat back the gunboats, the fort would fall to the land forces.[34]

Decision

Regardless of the odds, Tilghman was not going to give up the fort without a fight. He knew Fort Henry was lost, but it was imperative that the garrison be saved and the Confederates retreat to Fort Donelson to bolster its defense. Once Tilghman concluded that Grant intended to attack with the gunboats and all the Union's land forces, he would order the garrison to start for Fort Donelson. A sacrificial artillery battalion of fifty-four men under command of Capt. Jesse Taylor would stay at the guns to cover the withdrawal of the garrison.[35]

Results/Impact

Fort Henry's cannons were inadequate in power and number to take on ironclad gunboats. Eight of the guns were 32-pounders. The main threats to Foote's boats were the single 24-pound rifled cannon that pierced the *Essex* at two and a half miles and a 10-inch Columbiad. But as the gunboats got closer disaster struck. First, the rifled 24-pound cannon burst, and then the crew on the 10-inch Columbiad broke the priming wire in the vent, putting the gun out of action. The artillery crews gamely fought on with the 32-pound guns.[36]

As rebel artillerists engaged Foote's advancing gunboats, the land forces monitored McClernand's lumbering approach through the flooded waterways and quagmire roads. Tilghman estimated accurately that Grant had ordered about twelve thousand troops to advance on Fort Henry. Once the chance was dispelled that some, or all, of those men might be headed for Fort Donelson, Tilghman knew his approximately 2,600 troops should retreat to Fort Donelson via the route farthest from McClernand's column.[37]

When the Federal gunboats approached Fort Henry, Tilghman ordered the infantry to take position in the outer works, away from shells fired by the

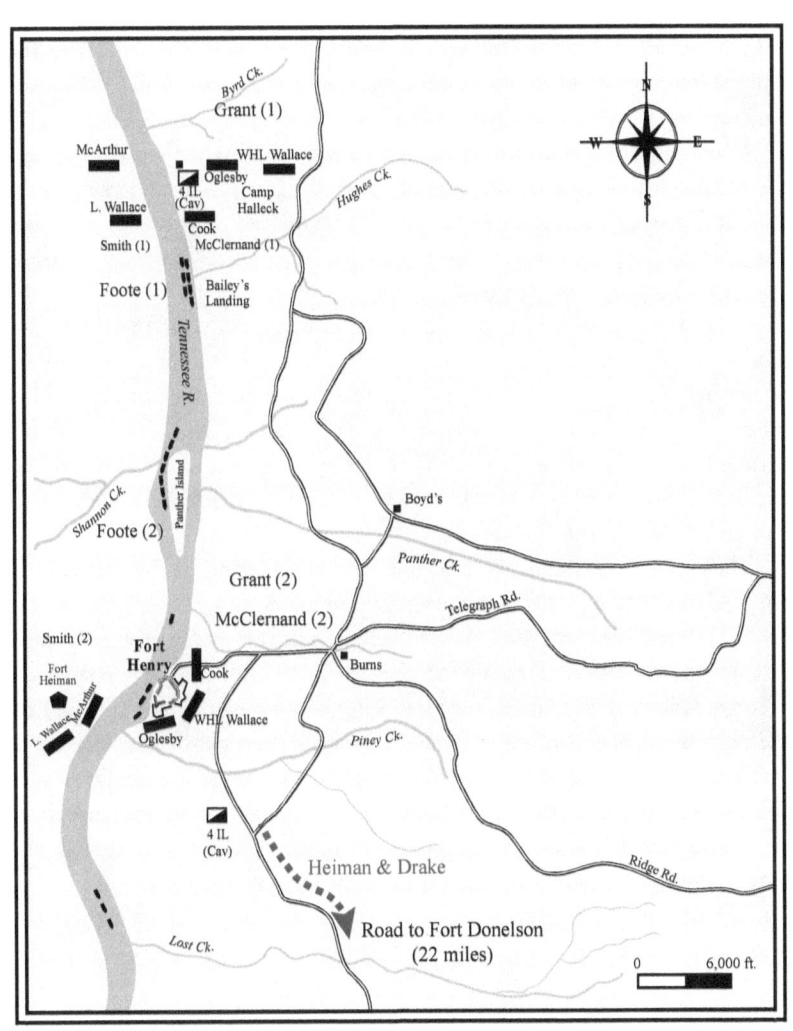

Escape from Fort Henry

gunboats. As the gunboats bombarded the fort, rebel pickets reported that McClernand's column was approximately one-half mile away from the advanced works and marching toward them. The rebel infantry withdrew from the fortifications and passed behind Fort Henry headed for Fort Donelson. The last of the Fort Henry defenders were beyond the vicinity of the fort when Tilghman raised a white flag and surrendered. Union cavalry pursued the Confederates but stopped after capturing a few stragglers and abandoned enemy artillery.[38]

When Fort Henry struck its colors, the end of the retreating column was not too distant when the rebel flag was lowered. Garrison defenders marched to Fort Donelson via a route south of the Ridge Road that crossed Standing Rock Creek five times. It was a twenty-two-mile exodus, with the men straggling into Fort Donelson throughout the night.[39]

Tilghman neglected his responsibility as commander of the forces defending Forts Henry and Donelson when he surrendered himself. Regardless of his belief he should stay in the fort to support the stout defenders, his bigger obligation was to the defense of both citadels. Tilghman justified his actions by referencing his duty to stay with the brave men who had fought the gunboats. His presence inspired the men to continue the contest, but staying had no bearing on the outcome.[40]

The capture of Tilghman put a void in rebel leadership at the crucial time when Grant was a major threat only twelve miles away from Fort Donelson. Tilghman's loss resulted in command chaos at Fort Donelson, as there was no general officer in command there after the fall of Fort Henry. Col. Heiman was ranking officer, but he did not assume command, anticipating the arrival of general officers. Bushrod Johnson received orders just before midnight on February 6 at Nashville to take command at Fort Donelson, and he arrived the evening of February 7. Pillow took command on February 9 and then Floyd on February 13. Having three different leaders in the space of a week did not bode well for the defenders of Fort Donelson.[41]

The decision to engage the gunboats allowed both sides to witness the results. For the Union the success of the gunboats at Fort Henry buoyed the confidence of Foote and Grant in their preparations to attack Fort Donelson. They believed what worked at Fort Henry would work at Fort Donelson. The Confederates thought the same, and the troops in Bowling Green immediately headed for Nashville.

Tilghman's defense of Fort Henry saved the garrison, but it also damaged the gunboats sufficiently that Foote had to travel back to Cairo for repairs and replacements. This bought additional time for the rebels at Fort Donelson to receive more reinforcements and strengthen the earthworks.

CHAPTER 3

BETWEEN THE BATTLES

Between the fall of Fort Henry and the Union advance against Fort Donelson, four different commanders made five critical decisions. A nervous Halleck had to decide whether to support Grant's move against Fort Donelson or rein him in. Disgruntled Buell had to determine whether he would send aid to Halleck. Johnston faced a command crisis and twice had to choose which brigadier general should command at Fort Donelson as the situation developed. Grant was delayed by rain and a rising Tennessee River that threatened supplies and equipment. He had to conclude whether to wait for reinforcements and gunboats before he ordered an advance against Fort Donelson.

Halleck Supports Grant's Attack on Fort Donelson

Situation

Halleck declared expeditions up the Tennessee and Cumberland Rivers should not be attempted with fewer than sixty thousand men. Grant had just fifteen thousand men when he took possession of Fort Henry, and he made no complaints about needing reinforcements. He would take Fort Donelson, without delay, with what he had.[1]

Halleck had informed Buell on January 30 that Grant was ordered to take Fort Henry. Buell inquired whether the advance would be successful without his own active support, but Halleck confidently replied on February 1 that no assistance was required now. However, once Grant got within range of Fort Henry, Halleck's outlook changed in response to reports of rebel troop movements in Grant's direction. He increased efforts to get reinforcements to Grant from his own department and appealed to McClellan for more troops.[2]

Halleck had ordered Grant to sail his force deep into enemy territory. The situation changed rapidly on Grant's end, and Halleck could not keep current with developments at the front. While Grant intended to engage the enemy with his available force, Halleck worried he did not have enough manpower. The departmental commander thus sent additional troops toward Grant that were en route when Fort Henry fell.[3]

Buell sent a message to Halleck on February 3 with erroneous intelligence about rebel troop movements. First, he reminded Halleck that Beauregard was on the way with fifteen regiments. Second, Buell stated that ten thousand rebel troops had left Bowling Green on January 22 for Paris, Tennessee, but they stopped at Russellville, Kentucky. The soldiers were never destined for Paris, but Halleck believed they were.[4]

Halleck's transformation from confidence to panic is reflected in the messages he sent on February 5 to Buell, McClellan, and Thomas Scott, assistant secretary of war, clamoring for reinforcements. He wanted Buell to mount a diversion by threatening Bowling Green. From McClellan, Halleck called for infantry regiments from Ohio. Scott was beseeched to send to Cairo all the infantry regiments he could. Halleck told each of them Johnston had sent ten thousand men from Bowling Green to reinforce Fort Henry.[5]

Buell replied that he could not do a diversion, saying it would be twelve days before he could approach Bowling Green. But McClellan responded to Halleck's entreaty with a message to Buell asking whether Buell could assist Halleck and make a demonstration on Bowling Green. Buell reluctantly agreed to send a brigade if Halleck really needed it.[6]

On February 6 Halleck, Buell, and McClellan waged war with telegrams while Grant and Foote subdued Fort Henry. At least four hours after the Stars and Stripes were raised over Fort Henry, Halleck informed McClellan that Fort Henry was largely reinforced. If he did not get more men, he might fail to take it.[7] Halleck's dire predictions for Fort Henry were mooted with a short telegram from Grant on February 7 starting with "Fort Henry is ours." A relieved but still anxious Halleck passed the electrifying news to McClellan, along with confirmation that the fort would be held at all costs as the commander desired.[8]

On February 7 Grant made his intentions known to Halleck that, since Fort Henry was in his possession, he would cross over to the Cumberland River to "take and destroy" Fort Donelson on February 8. Grant would then return immediately to Fort Henry with his forces. He expected to carry out operations from that location, and he wanted to remove any Confederate threat from Fort Donelson.[9]

Halleck considered Fort Henry under threat of counterattack by Johnston and expected Grant to fortify it. Instead, Grant behaved aggressively with the intent to advance at once on Fort Donelson. If Halleck thought Grant's army was undersized to strike Fort Henry, he surely was concerned when Grant declared he was going to assault Fort Donelson. However, as he pondered a response to Grant's audacious plan, Halleck acknowledged the general in the field had the best grasp of existing conditions.[10]

Options

The options available to Halleck were halting Grant's movement to the Cumberland River or allowing him to attack Fort Donelson while supporting him with additional troops.

Option 1

Halleck could order Grant to stay at Fort Henry and not continue with an attack on Fort Donelson. Grant was deep in enemy territory, with Confederate troops to the northwest and northeast of Fort Henry. Halleck believed Johnston would concentrate troops to take back the citadel and reestablish his defensive line. It was more important to the Union high command to hold Fort Henry than to take Fort Donelson.[11]

Option 2

Halleck could approve and support Grant's quick move toward Fort Donelson, although he feared the Confederates were moving troops toward Fort Henry. Grant needed more men, and Halleck could enhance efforts to send them his way.[12]

Decision

Halleck did not hamper Grant's determination to attack Fort Donelson. He allowed Grant to move on the stronghold even when Grant's assault was delayed—the general lacked gunboats, and heavy rains caused the Tennessee River to rise, flooding the low areas around Fort Henry. The rains also made the roads muddy and too wet for infantry and artillery to move. While Grant set the schedule for the attack, Halleck sent all the men he could from his department and alerted McClellan and Buell that the army was in peril and needed more troops.[13]

Results/Impact

Halleck had instructed Grant to make his force as large as possible with support from the men at Cairo and Paducah. To aid in the attack on Fort Henry, Halleck also dispatched more troops from Missouri to augment Grant's army. He sent a message to Grant on January 31 that three regiments and artillery would head for Cairo in the next few days. Another communication dated February 5 alerted Grant that three more regiments were on the way. This support arrived after Grant captured Fort Henry.[14]

Halleck confessed to McClellan on February 6 that he was not ready for an advance, but he moved in anticipation of Beauregard's arrival. Upon receiving word of the capture of Fort Henry on February 7, Halleck informed Buell that Missouri had been stripped of every available man, and if the rebels rose up, he would just put them down again. Grant had fifteen thousand men, and eight thousand more were on the way. Eight infantry regiments, cavalry, and artillery landed at Fort Henry the night of February 8.[15]

Halleck sent nonchalant messages to McClellan and Buell that Grant expected to take Fort Donelson on February 8. Instead, Halleck received notice of delays caused by rain and a rising Tennessee River. Foote was at Cairo working to replace the damaged gunboats, leaving Grant with just one gunboat at Fort Henry. The capture of Fort Donelson did not occur, and Halleck heard that Beauregard was going to attack either Paducah or Fort Henry out of Columbus.[16] On February 10 Halleck sent a plaintive message to McClellan declaring he could not do anything more for Grant and asking McClellan to send him more troops. It was a crisis. The army was in peril because the enemy could come down the Cumberland River from Nashville and strike Grant in the rear.[17]

By February 11 the weather had improved, and Grant was anxious to advance on Fort Donelson. More men from Halleck's department had arrived, enabling Grant to march a column of fifteen thousand men toward Fort Donelson while leaving a sufficient force to garrison Forts Henry and Heiman. The same day, transports arrived at Fort Henry with reinforcements from Halleck and a brigade from Buell. Rather than having them march with the advance, Grant ordered these soldiers to steam back to Paducah and go up the Cumberland River to Fort Donelson. Grant assumed the troops would arrive at Fort Donelson the evening of February 12, but the transports did not arrive until around midnight of February 13, along with other regiments from Illinois, Ohio, and Indiana.[18]

Reinforcements flowed to Grant from Halleck's and Buell's departments, and the states of Illinois, Ohio, and Indiana quickly sent forth new regiments.

Halleck's efforts paid off, and Grant made a bold move against Fort Donelson. The Confederates had rushed enough additional troops to the fort, so that Grant approached with approximately the same number of soldiers defending it.[19]

The Union reinforcements supported Grant's plan to attack Fort Donelson as soon as possible. The added troops gave him the confidence that he would successfully capture the bastion. Even though he misjudged when help would arrive, he knew it was coming and adjusted his plans accordingly.

For Confederate commanders the Union reinforcements had the opposite effect. As more Union troops arrived, the Confederates despaired of defending the fort and planned an attack on February 14 to keep the escape routes open. But the plan was aborted. On February 15 the assault took place to open the routes, but at the end of the day the rebels were back in their trenches. That night word of more Union soldiers arriving was a key factor in the decision to surrender the fort.

Halleck doubled the size of Grant's army from the fall of Fort Henry to the surrender of Fort Donelson. Historians disparage Halleck for taking too much credit for Grant's success at the Battles of Forts Henry and Donelson, but Grant needed every man Halleck sent him. Without that support, Grant would have lacked enough men to thwart the rebel breakout attempt and convince the Confederate generals to surrender.

Buell Sends Reinforcements to Halleck

Situation

During January 1862 McClellan, Lincoln, and Buell assumed any forward movement would be done by Buell with Halleck in a supporting role. The president and McClellan considered the most important objective to be sending a force into East Tennessee. Buell disagreed and wanted to attack Bowling Green and then Nashville. In early January the Union high command focused on the Department of the Ohio and Buell's preparations to advance. Halleck had let it be known he lacked the manpower for a serious forward movement, as his forces were still heavily engaged in Missouri.[20]

Buell graduated from West Point in 1841 and was sent to fight in the Seminole War but saw no major action. He served on Maj. Gen. Zachary Taylor's staff in the Mexican War and was brevetted three times for bravery. In 1859 Buell started a special assignment for Secretary of War John Floyd and played a part in the Fort Sumter drama when he visited Charleston, South Carolina, and left a written memorandum to Union commander Maj. Robert Anderson. The document was interpreted as permission to move the garrison to Fort

Sumter. Buell had stayed in the army and held the rank of lieutenant colonel when the war erupted. He hoped for a high command, but when his friend George McClellan became commander in chief, Buell toiled in Washington, DC, to help organize the army. He was promoted to brigadier general and appointed to command the new Department of the Ohio in November 1862.[21]

Pressure on Buell made him possessive of his men, and he wanted more. In late December Adjutant General Lorenzo Thomas asked Buell whether he needed additional regiments. Buell responded that he could use additional soldiers if available, but he did not want raw troops. He suggested to the adjutant general that new troops ordered in from Illinois be sent to garrison Cairo and Paducah, letting men who had been in service longer take the field. Buell wanted the more experienced troops from Halleck's command, leaving Halleck with the new recruits.[22]

On January 30 Buell sent a message containing information from a contact in Paducah describing the ease with which vessels could steam up the Tennessee and Cumberland Rivers due to the present high water. Buell encouraged Halleck to promptly send gunboats up the rivers to destroy the bridges and ease the Federals' way into Bowling Green. Halleck sent the perplexing response that gunboats and fifteen thousand troops had already been ordered up the Tennessee River to take and hold Fort Henry.[23]

Angry at the development that put Halleck in command of a forward movement, Buell protested to McClellan on February 1. Buell raged that early in January, at the behest of the president, he had proposed a cooperative

Brig. Gen. Don Carlos Buell

effort. Halleck replied that he could do nothing, but that Buell should name a day for a demonstration. Buell was confused and did not ever designate a day for a demonstration, but Halleck moved ahead anyway. Now, Buell protested his comrade's prompt advance on Fort Henry, which he himself was expected to aid. But as of February 1, Halleck had not requested assistance from Buell.[24]

However, on February 5 Halleck asked Buell to mount a diversion, but Buell refused, as he was in no position to approach Bowling Green. He warned Halleck of Confederate reinforcements headed toward Fort Henry, including ten thousand men from Bowling Green. Halleck made no request for troops from Buell, but on February 5 he appealed to McClellan for regiments from Ohio. In response, McClellan sent Buell a message to assist Halleck if possible. Halleck's request for aid had reached Buell through the Union commander.[25]

Options

Buell could either support Halleck by any means available, as McClellan asked, or he could not provide any assistance.[26]

Option 1

Buell had discussed operations with McClellan. When Buell was ready to advance, he assumed Halleck would then send supporting expeditions with gunboats up the Tennessee and Cumberland Rivers. Now Halleck had advanced, and Buell was not ready to move. But Buell considered Halleck's attack on the center of the Confederate defensive line a decisive action of utmost importance that must not fail. Buell had warned Halleck about Confederate reinforcements headed toward Fort Henry, which caused Halleck to request more troops from McClellan, who asked Buell whether he could assist Halleck. Buell was too far from Bowling Green to make a diversion, but he could send reinforcements to boost Halleck's force in the attack on the center of the Confederate defensive line.[27]

Option 2

At first Halleck informed Buell his assistance was not required. Five days later, Halleck wanted help. Buell was then perturbed that Halleck made a quick movement toward Fort Henry without any coordination with him. Pressured by McClellan to send an expedition into East Tennessee, Buell committed a part of his force to that objective. Buell had use for every man in his department, and sending reinforcements to Halleck would further disrupt his plans. McClellan did not order Buell to help Halleck, so Buell could decide it was impossible to send additional troops at this time.[28]

Decision

McClellan asked Buell to assist Halleck with a demonstration on Bowling Green. The Union commander let Halleck know that eight regiments had just moved from Ohio to western Virginia, and further troops from Buell's department could not be spared unless absolutely necessary. Knowing that a diversion on Bowling Green was impracticable, Buell decided to send Halleck reinforcements.[29]

Results/Impact

Buell responded quickly to McClellan's message to aid Halleck. On February 5 Buell informed Halleck he would send him a brigade providing it was truly needed. Buell subsequently dispatched a good unit from Calhoun, Kentucky, on the Green River; commanded by Col. Charles Cruft, it had been organized in December and consisted of four infantry regiments. Cruft's brigade arrived at Fort Henry on February 11 as Grant prepared to advance on Fort Donelson. Rather than have Cruft join the column and march the twelve miles between the forts, Grant ordered Cruft to stay on the boats and travel to Fort Donelson by water. The trip was expected to take a day, but the brigade did not arrive at the landing downstream from the fort until around midnight on February 13. At approximately midday on February 14, Cruft's brigade of 2,150 men became the First Brigade of the newly formed Third Division commanded by Brig. Gen. Lew Wallace.[30]

When Halleck asked for help, Buell was being pressed by McClellan to aid the Unionists in East Tennessee. Halleck wanted more troops from McClellan, but the Union commander prioritized Buell, whom he telegraphed the governors of Ohio and Indiana to aid so as not delay a move into East Tennessee. On February 6 McClellan wrote Buell and told him to get what he needed from Ohio and Indiana.[31]

But the roads into East Tennessee and in front of Bowling Green were practically impassable. Since land travel was near impossible, Buell could not use any new regiments from Indiana and Ohio. But movement by river was feasible, so Buell sent Halleck messages on February 6 notifying him that he could send Cruft's brigade, two regiments from Indiana, and six regiments from Ohio. Buell directed Governor David Tod of Ohio to form that state's six inexperienced regiments into two brigades and dispatch them to Halleck. Buell also warned Halleck the troops were raw and unorganized.[32]

It took over a week before the impact of Buell's choice reached Grant at Fort Donelson. Then Buell's reinforcements played key roles in four critical decisions made on February 14 and 15. Details of the decisions' influence are found under the "Results/Impact" headings in discussion of the subsequent critical decisions. A small sample of the effect of Buell's reinforcements follows to provide an inkling of the contributions of the men from his department at Fort Donelson.

On February 14 Grant made a critical decision and ordered Lew Wallace to Fort Donelson to command a new division formed from regiments that arrived during the night. Cruft's brigade became the First Brigade of Wallace's division, while Col. John Thayer from Nebraska was designated to command a brigade that included Thayer's First Nebraska out of Missouri. But the balance of the brigade consisted of three Ohio regiments—the Fifty-Eighth, Sixty-Eighth, and Seventy-Sixth—that came from Buell. Of the eight regiments that formed Wallace's force on February 14 and took position in the center of Grant's line, seven were sent by Buell. In addition, from Buell; the Fifty-Second Indiana reported at Fort Henry and joined Cook's brigade; the Twentieth Ohio disembarked at Fort Donelson and was assigned to Wallace's division.[33]

On February 15 the first critical decision made by Lew Wallace was to send Cruft's brigade to McClernand's support. Later, Wallace made a second critical decision when he ordered Thayer's brigade to advance to the right to put the unit between the Confederates and McClernand's retreating men. Finally, when Grant made the critical decision to mount a counterattack, Cruft's brigade occupied the far-right flank of the Union line and ended the day holding that key position.

Of twelve regiments from Indiana and Ohio, nine made it in time to join the fight for Fort Donelson. The forces received from Buell's department were extremely important to the success achieved. Reinforcements not only strengthened the combat power of Grant's army, but they also discouraged the resilience of the Confederate defenders.

Johnston Orders Pillow to Fort Donelson, February 9, 1862

Situation

With the loss of Tilghman there was no general officer at Fort Donelson after the fall of Fort Henry. Department commander Johnston had four brigadier generals in theater he could put in command. The lowest-ranking brigadier was Bushrod Johnson, who was at Nashville. His promotion to brigadier had occurred less than two weeks earlier on January 25. Simon Bolivar Buckner was third in rank and was in Russellville. Pillow, second highest in rank, commanded at Clarksville, where he arrived on February 5 to strengthen the city's defenses. The highest-ranking officer was Floyd from Virginia, who was also at Russellville.[34]

Albert Sidney Johnston was born in Kentucky in 1803, and he attended West Point two years ahead of his friend Jefferson Davis. After graduating in 1826 and participating in the Black Hawk War in 1832, Johnston resigned to care for his ailing wife until her death in August 1835. In July 1836 he cast his lot with Texas, where he served as army commander, secretary of war, Indian fighter, and bought a large plantation. Moreover, Johnston led a volunteer Texas regiment for six months in the Mexican War. He participated in the Battle of Monterrey and then returned home to Galveston.

In 1850 President Zachary Taylor put Johnston back in the army as a paymaster in Texas. After five years Johnston secured the command of the Second Cavalry in Texas and was chosen to head the Mormon expedition from 1857 to 1859. He went to California in January 1861 to command the Department of the Pacific. Johnston resigned from the army in April and followed his adopted state of Texas out of the Union. Over three months, he made a perilous overland journey from San Francisco to Richmond and offered his services to the Confederacy in early September 1861. Davis appointed Johnston full general and gave him the monumental task of defending the Confederacy west of the Appalachians through the Indian Territory, an area designated Department No. 2. Johnston immediately set up his headquarters at Nashville.[35]

Gen. Albert Sidney Johnston.

John Floyd served as secretary of war in the Buchanan administration prior to the Civil War. When Johnston took charge of the Mormon expedition in September 1857, he did so under orders from Floyd. In Utah, Johnston constructed and operated out of Camp Floyd from July 1858 through February 1860. After an extended leave of absence, he requested assignment to California in November 1860. Floyd approved the transfer, but after six months Johnston resigned his commission when Texas left the Union. Johnston served under orders from Floyd for over three years, and he did not hesitate to delegate responsibility to Floyd for defense of the Cumberland River.[36]

Gideon Pillow resigned from the army just after Christmas over perceived mistreatment by Polk. He went home but recanted his resignation on February 2, traveled to Bowling Green, and requested an assignment back in the army. Johnston lacked experienced high-ranking officers and was happy to have Pillow return. He knew of Pillow's high rank in the Mexican War and told Confederate senator Gustavus Henry he had a high opinion of Pillow as a military man.[37]

When Johnston arrived at Nashville on September 14 and decided to extend the defensive line north to Bowling Green Simon Buckner was already there. Johnston needed a brigadier general to command the force that was to occupy and defend Bowling Green. Buckner was awaiting a commission from Richmond, but Johnston went ahead and made Buckner a brigadier general, assuming the government would approve. The two officers would work closely together over the next five months.[38]

Bushrod Johnson graduated from West Point in 1840, but his military

Brig. Gen. Bushrod Johnson.

career ended in 1847 when he resigned rather than be dismissed because he attempted to use his position in the commissary department for profit. Johnson had a history with Fort Donelson that included approving its location. In late January 1862 he spent a week in command of the stronghold while Tilghman was at Fort Henry. When he returned to Nashville, Johnson learned his promotion to brigadier general was approved on January 25.[39]

Johnston needed information from Fort Donelson to plan a response to Grant's invasion. Since Floyd and Buckner were at Russellville and Pillow was in command at Clarksville, Johnston chose the most expedient option, which was ordering Bushrod Johnson from Nashville to Fort Donelson to take command. Johnson received the order between 11:00 p.m. and midnight on February 6.[40]

A flurry of telegrams on February 7 revealed Johnston's uncertain strategy for defense of the Cumberland River. Pillow had alerted Johnston that a stand could not be made at Clarksville without more troops. Johnston ordered Floyd and Buckner to transfer their forces from Russellville to Clarksville, and the two generals quickly had their men in motion. When Floyd reached Clarksville, he would be the ranking officer. His instructions were to move his force across the Cumberland River in order to support Fort Donelson but leave the route to Nashville open.[41]

The same day, a steamer from Nashville brought Bushrod Johnson to Clarksville on his way to Fort Donelson. Pillow reiterated Johnston's order to Bushrod Johnson to take command at Fort Donelson. The Second Kentucky had arrived from Clarksville and boarded the steamer; and the entourage arrived at Fort Donelson that night. Pillow intended to forward any Confederate reinforcements that arrived at Clarksville to Fort Donelson.[42]

Johnston struggled to understand what was happening on the Cumberland River. He sent a telegram to Pillow at Clarksville on February 7 that indicated Pillow was to take command at Fort Donelson. If the fort fell, Pillow would retreat and join Floyd's Command. But with no one else available to take command at Clarksville, and knowing that Bushrod Johnson was on his way to Fort Donelson, Pillow did not immediately go to Fort Donelson.[43]

By the evening of February 7 Johnston acknowledged he did not know the best path to pursue and had to depend on the local commanders to make decisions. He sent a telegram at 10:00 p.m. telling Pillow to do the best he could because the reports received were so contradictory. Johnston left the matter of command at Fort Donelson to Pillow, stating, "If your service or Buckner's or both are most important at Donelson, go there." When Johnston sent this telegram, Buckner was still at Russellville.[44]

While Johnston concentrated on the evacuation of Bowling Green, he transferred his responsibility for the defense of the Cumberland River to Floyd. On February 8 Floyd reported he had reached Clarksville with most of his force, a large part of which had been forwarded to Fort Donelson. Johnston then sent a telegram stating he could not give specific instructions and placing Floyd in command of the entire force. Floyd requested Johnston to come to the Cumberland River to determine objectives and defense lines. Currently, Johnston did not know the location of all his troops and the number of men at Clarksville and Fort Donelson.[45]

Because Pillow sent reinforcements as they arrived in Clarksville, Floyd's Brigade and Buckner's Division were split. Two of Floyd's five regiments were at Fort Donelson. Five of Buckner's eight regiments were either at the fort or on the way. Brig. Gen. Charles Clark's brigade, with approximately 1,700 men, arrived at Clarksville from Hopkinsville on February 7. Clark refused to recognize Pillow's authority, and Johnston had to settle the dispute. Johnston ruled in favor of Pillow, and Clark turned over the brigade to Col. Thomas Davidson. As February 8 ended, Pillow and Clark's Brigade were still in Clarksville.[46]

At the end of February 8, the Confederate forces and generals destined to defend the Cumberland River stretched from Fort Donelson to Clarksville. Thousands of rebel reinforcements arrived at Fort Donelson, and by February 10 Bushrod Johnson commanded over half the force on the river. Over half of Buckner's men were headed for Fort Donelson, but he trailed his division and had not yet arrived at Clarksville. Part of Floyd's Brigade was at the stronghold, but he was now the commanding officer at Clarksville in charge of defending the Cumberland River. When Floyd arrived, Pillow was no longer the ranking officer. Johnston surely knew Pillow was still at Clarksville due to the dispute with Clark, and Pillow had sent no reports from Fort Donelson.

By February 9 Johnston knew that the safety of the army retreating from Bowling Green to Nashville depended on Fort Donelson holding out against the gunboats. The situation had become clearer over the last couple of days. Grant was still at Fort Henry, and no gunboats had appeared at Fort Donelson. Johnston still had the opportunity to put the general in charge of Fort Donelson who he thought would best defend the Cumberland River from that location.[47]

Options

While the threat to Fort Donelson increased, Johnston remained fixed on Buell and Bowling Green as the most serious threat. Giving no thought to commanding Fort Donelson himself or having Maj. Gen. William Hardee do so, Johnston limited his options for command to one of the four brigadier generals. These men were Johnson, Buckner, Pillow, and Floyd, in ascending order of rank.

Option 1

By February 9 Bushrod Johnson, a brigadier general for just over two weeks, had been in command at Fort Donelson for two days. Johnston showed confidence in Bushrod Johnson by promptly ordering him to assume control of the stronghold upon learning of the fall of Fort Henry. Johnston could leave Bushrod Johnson in command. Johnson had been involved with the fort since the beginning and was familiar with its construction and surrounding terrain.[48]

Option 2

Johnston's telegram to Pillow on February 7 stated that Buckner should go to Fort Donelson if there was a need. Johnston had made his respect for Buckner evident by requesting him to take command of the troops that would advance to Bowling Green. On February 8 Buckner let Johnston know he was still in Russellville, putting his troops on trains for Clarksville. By February 9 over half of Buckner's Division was headed for Fort Donelson, and the balance of his men were headed to Clarksville, but Buckner lagged behind his soldiers. He had a large division, and Johnston could order him to take command at Fort Donelson.[49]

Option 3

February 9 found Pillow still in Clarksville, and Johnston had put Clark's Brigade under his authority. For four days Pillow had forwarded reinforcements and supplies to Fort Donelson, including regiments from Floyd's and Buckner's Commands. Johnston's good opinion of Pillow became noticeable when Pillow showed up in Bowling Green looking to rejoin the army in early February. Pillow was immediately reinstated, and Johnston assigned him the command at Clarksville. Johnston's first impulse on February 7 was to send Pillow to Fort Donelson, but he later left the decision to Pillow's discretion. When Bushrod Johnson passed through Clarksville, Pillow concurred that Johnson should lead at Fort Donelson while Pillow stayed in Clarksville. Now, Floyd was in command at Clarksville, and Pillow was available to go to Fort Donelson.[50]

Option 4

Late on February 6 Floyd got orders to move his brigade to Clarksville. He traveled quickly, and by daylight on February 8 he and most of his command

Brig. Gen. Gideon Pillow.

were at Clarksville. Two of his regiments were already forwarded to Fort Donelson. Since Johnston was at Bowling Green and fixated on Buell, he delegated defense of the Cumberland River to Floyd and offered no specific instructions. Johnston thought enough of Floyd to immediately give him control of the forces in closest contact with Grant's invading army. With Confederate reinforcements strengthening Fort Donelson, Johnston could order Floyd to station himself there and take command.[51]

Decision

By February 9 Johnston had received the disturbing news that there were no defenses constructed at Clarksville. Reinforcements were sent to Fort Donelson, but Bushrod Johnson was still in command. Buckner trailed his division, and Floyd was at Clarksville, where he was expected to improve the defensive works, with three of his regiments. Pillow was at Clarksville with Clark's Brigade. Johnston had confidence in Pillow, a Tennessean with an aggressive attitude, and ordered him to take command at Fort Donelson. Pillow arrived there on February 10 along with Clark's Brigade sans Clark.[52]

Results/Impact

Johnson arrived at Fort Donelson late on February 7 and was in charge until Pillow took over on February 10. Pillow's and Floyd's time in Clarksville had overlapped for a day; then Pillow was off to make a stand at Fort Donelson. When Pillow left Clarksville and arrived at Dover, he gave speeches at both locations stating he did not expect to surrender. He was a Tennessean and intended to defend Tennessee soil. He had already forwarded five regiments of Buckner's Division and two regiments from Floyd's Brigade to Fort Donelson. Pillow also brought with him the four regiments of Clark's Brigade. With eleven fresh regiments, Pillow and Bushrod Johnson believed a decisive battle could be fought at Fort Donelson. Pillow issued a special order stating that he would rely on the defenders to maintain the post, and that the battle cry was "Liberty or Death."[53]

Upon arrival at Fort Donelson, Pillow conducted an inspection with engineer officer Gilmer, who had laid out a portion of the outer trenches in January that encompassed the fort proper and the town of Dover. Only about a third of the line had been completed. Pillow got the men busy working to finish and strengthen the fortifications, along with the river batteries. They cut trees to clear fields of fire for land batteries and laid abatis. Urged on by Pillow, the morale and confidence of the troops increased.[54]

On February 10 Pillow touted Fort Donelson to Johnston, Floyd, and Governor Harris as a stronghold that could be maintained and would not be surrendered. Johnston had chosen Pillow to be the general at the fort. The Union army could not move on the bastion immediately, so Johnston was given time to absorb information from the Cumberland River. There were no defenses at Clarksville, so when Pillow declared his belief he could hold Fort Donelson, thirty-five miles downstream of Clarksville, Johnston took note and started to think that the fortification could hold until the rest of his army retreated to Nashville.[55]

On February 10 the Confederate force at Fort Donelson numbered approximately 13,500 men, with additional men at Clarksville. Pillow put Grant's numbers at 10,000 to 15,000 soldiers. The fortifications were being constructed, and Pillow had confidence he could defeat a land attack, considering Grant did not have a large numerical advantage. Moreover, the rebels would be fighting in trench works. The river batteries were being finished, and Pillow thought the gunboats could be defeated. He sent communications about Fort Donelson's preparations to Floyd, asking Floyd to forward the information to Johnston because he was too busy. Pillow requested Floyd to send Buckner as soon as possible, as he was badly needed.[56]

Engineer officer Gilmer expressed confidence to Johnston that the earthworks being constructed could resist a land attack, and hopefully could stop a water attack. Johnston put a lot of value into Gilmer's opinion, as he was an experienced officer. The general was loath to give up Fort Donelson without a determined attempt to hold it. At this point he knew Nashville had no means to resist an attack. Reports from Fort Donelson indicated its defenses were being quickly improved.[57]

Pillow wanted Buckner to command Buckner's Division holding the right flank of the fortifications. What Pillow did not know was that Buckner and Floyd had concluded Cumberland City would be a better location to confront the Union army. When Buckner arrived at Fort Donelson late on February 11, he had an order for Pillow from Floyd. Pillow was to allow Buckner to remove his and Floyd's troops from Fort Donelson and fall back to Cumberland City.[58]

Floyd had been designated by Johnston to command all the forces defending the Cumberland River. But Pillow refused to follow the order until he had talked to Floyd at Cumberland City. Early the next morning, on February 12, Pillow boarded a steamer for Cumberland City. He left Buckner in command with orders not to fight a general engagement that required troops to leave the trenches should Union forces approach the fort. Unbeknown to Pillow, Grant chose this day to advance on Fort Donelson.[59]

Col. Nathan Bedford Forrest entered the Fort Donelson area the morning of February 11 and brought needed aggressive cavalry to Pillow's Command. He immediately went out on a reconnaissance toward Fort Henry. On the morning of February 12 Pillow ordered Forrest out again before he left for Cumberland City.[60]

Pillow was unsuccessful in his quest to talk to Floyd. Instead, he was at Cumberland City when the *Carondelet* bombarded Fort Donelson around

Brig. Gen. Simon Bolivar Buckner.

11:30 a.m. Hearing the shots, Pillow rushed back to Dover only to find Union troops starting to encircle the fort. He immediately called for rebel troops from Cumberland City and told Buckner he could not leave with his men. The fight for Fort Donelson was on.[61]

In four days, the number of defenders at Fort Donelson rose from 7,000 to near 13,500, with more nearby at Cumberland City and Clarksville. Johnston had believed Fort Donelson was untenable, but on February 10 he received encouraging messages from Pillow and Gilmer that they could defend it. As a result, Johnston thought Fort Donelson would hold while he evacuated the rest of the army and all the supplies from Bowling Green to Nashville. If the time came when the fort could not be held, the army there would retreat to Nashville. Johnston later claimed in a letter to Davis, "I determined to fight for Nashville at Donelson and gave the best part of my army to do it."[62]

The selection of Pillow to take command at Fort Donelson was the first critical decision in a series of Confederate command decisions leading to the surrender of Fort Donelson and most of the army. Pillow was so confident he would hold the fort that he gave no thought to contingency plans to extricate the rebels should the enemy show up with overwhelming force. His enthusiasm caused Johnston to change his judgment about how many troops should be used to defend Fort Donelson. Pillow's selection caused Confederate command chaos because he was able to push his view even though it contrasted with those of his superior officers.

Grant Orders an Immediate Attack on Fort Donelson, February 12, 1862

Situation

Grant knew the Confederates at Fort Donelson would be in disarray, and he was impatient to attack the citadel. There was no discussion with Halleck because there was no time, and Grant recalled Halleck did not approve or disapprove the move. Grant correctly concluded that the enemy would reinforce Fort Donelson and delay would only benefit the Confederates. He believed he would be more effective with fifteen thousand men on February 8 than fifty thousand later. Reinforcements that arrived on February 7 enabled Grant to add one brigade each to the divisions of McClernand and Smith.[63]

Grant showed impetuosity on February 7 when he ordered McClernand to be ready to move with infantry and cavalry at any hour the next morning. As Grant explained it, the roads were impassable for artillery and baggage; therefore, if a move was made it would not be encumbered with wagons. Men were to have two days' rations. The results of a reconnaissance would determine whether the movement was to be conducted that day.[64]

Albert Richardson, a *New York Tribune* reporter, stopped by Grant's office to say goodbye on February 7. Grant told him he should stick around for another day or two, as he would attack Fort Donelson tomorrow. Richardson asked the officer whether he knew how strong the fort was. Grant replied, "Not exactly; but I think we can take it; at all events, we can try." The journalist noted that the general considered attacking a fort he knew little about with just cavalry and infantry and no artillery. Grant was going to charge Fort Donelson with the army he had, not the army he wished he had.[65]

A report from a cavalry patrol dispelled the idea of moving on Fort Donelson without artillery. Capt. Warren Stewart of McClernand's staff led a patrol on February 7 that met rebel pickets and drove them in. A captured rebel boasted that Fort Donelson had more cannon than Fort Henry, adding that reinforcements were headed for the fort. Whether this was true could not be verified, but Capt. Stewart gave the opinion that the enemy would make a stand at Fort Donelson. He further contended that any advance should include artillery.[66]

But Grant had other problems besides impassable roads because the Tennessee River continued to rise. The army was locked in by flooded lowlands that endangered the troops' supplies, which had to be moved to higher ground. Foote had left for Cairo with three ironclad gunboats, and the three timberclads were sent up the Tennessee River, all without known return dates. This left Grant with just a single gunboat, which was insufficient to attack Fort Donelson.[67]

Brig. Gen. George W. Cullum, Halleck's chief of staff, was sent to Cairo to facilitate operations on the rivers. Grant wrote Cullum of his woes concerning high water and no gunboats on February 8 with the request Cullum forward the information to Halleck. Grant complained the situation prevented him from taking the offensive as he wanted to. The same day Halleck asked Grant to destroy the bridge at Clarksville, if possible. He must have thought Grant would keep his promise to take Fort Donelson on the eighth and could also advance thirty-five miles upstream to Clarksville. Halleck alerted Grant trenching tools were on the way because it was vital Fort Henry be strengthened. But most important, he informed Grant reinforcements would arrive daily and said Fort Henry must be held at all costs.[68]

A frustrated Grant saw days slip by as the conditions were unfavorable. Smith received a note from Grant on February 8 to move one of his two brigades across the river the next day. The shift was to occur because Grant might move to Fort Donelson if reports from a reconnaissance were favorable. Grant intended for one of Smith's brigades to stay behind and protect Fort Henry, but high water prevented Smith's other brigade from reaching the steamers in order to cross.[69]

On February 9 Grant headed up a cavalry patrol and made a reconnaissance to within four miles of Fort Donelson. He informed McClernand the roads were good and hard once the horsemen left the river bottom. This improvement in conditions buoyed Grant's spirits, and he wrote a letter to his sister that night ending as follows: "G. J. Pillow commands at Fort Donaldson [sic]. I hope to give him a tug before you receive this."[70]

Grant wanted help from the navy when he attacked Fort Donelson. Because he did not feel justified in attacking Fort Donelson without gunboats to assist, Grant asked Foote on February 10 to send two boats up the Cumberland River immediately. The same day, Grant instructed Commander Henry Walke to steam the *Carondelet* to Fort Donelson.[71]

Despite being encamped in enemy territory between two rivers and remaining ignorant of how many Confederates had reinforced Fort Donelson, Grant prepared to attack. He knew Union reinforcements were coming, yet he did not know how many and when. Anxious to keep the momentum gained by capturing Fort Henry, but wondering what his officers thought, Grant called a meeting with division and brigade commanders at his headquarters aboard the *New Uncle Sam* at 3:00 p.m. on February 10. The question under discussion was whether to move on Fort Donelson immediately or wait for reinforcements.[72]

The officers gathered around a table, and without preliminaries Grant turned to Smith for his view. Grant heard that not a day should be lost, and that McClernand was for immediate movement. Lew Wallace stated, "The sooner the better," but he later expressed anxiety to his wife because the Federals knew so little about the circumstances of the enemy.[73]

Grant had heard the responses of his officer corps. Now he had to decide what to do.

Options

Grant considered either waiting for reinforcements or attacking Fort Donelson immediately.

Option 1

Union reinforcements had arrived after Fort Henry fell, and Halleck confirmed that more were coming. Daily reconnaissance revealed the enemy was increasing their numbers and preparing to meet an attack. Grant could wait for more assistance, but that would give Johnston extra time to strengthen the defenses and send additional soldiers to the bastion. Grant could expect the fort would only get stronger every day.

<u>Option 2</u>

Grant's numbers had increased, so he could send the same number of men against Fort Donelson that he did against Fort Henry and leave a sizable garrison at Fort Henry. He did not know when, and how many more, reinforcements he would get. But Grant knew the Confederates were going to fight. He could order a movement straightaway and attack Fort Donelson with the men he had.

Decision

In the four days since Fort Henry fell, the rising river and poor roads had hemmed Grant in. Now the conditions had improved, and the general would tolerate no more delay. He decided to attack Fort Donelson at once.

Results/Impact

At the end of the meeting on February 10 Grant declared, "Very well, gentlemen, we will set out immediately. Orders will be sent to you. Get your commands ready." McClernand and Smith were to be ready to move as early as practicable on February 12, but no tents or baggage would be taken except that which the soldiers were willing to carry. Wagons could follow the expedition but not impede the progress of the march. The men were to have two days' rations and forty rounds of ammunition. Along with cavalry and artillery, one brigade from Smith's division and two regiments from McClernand's would be left at Forts Henry and Heiman.[74]

On February 11 Grant set February 12 as the day to march toward Fort Donelson. Two brigades of McClernand's division would advance on the Ridge Road, while one brigade would start on the Telegraph Road. This plan would allow McClernand's brigades to arrive together, deploy in a continuous line approximately two miles in front of Fort Donelson, and await further orders. Union intelligence was so lacking that Grant recognized details for the attack could not be given, and orders would be issued in the field. Smith's two brigades would follow McClernand's brigades on the Ridge Road.[75]

On the afternoon of February 11 McClernand decided to get a head start and move past the flooded lowlands. Starting around 4:00 p.m., the men marched out on both the Ridge and Telegraph Roads four to five miles and

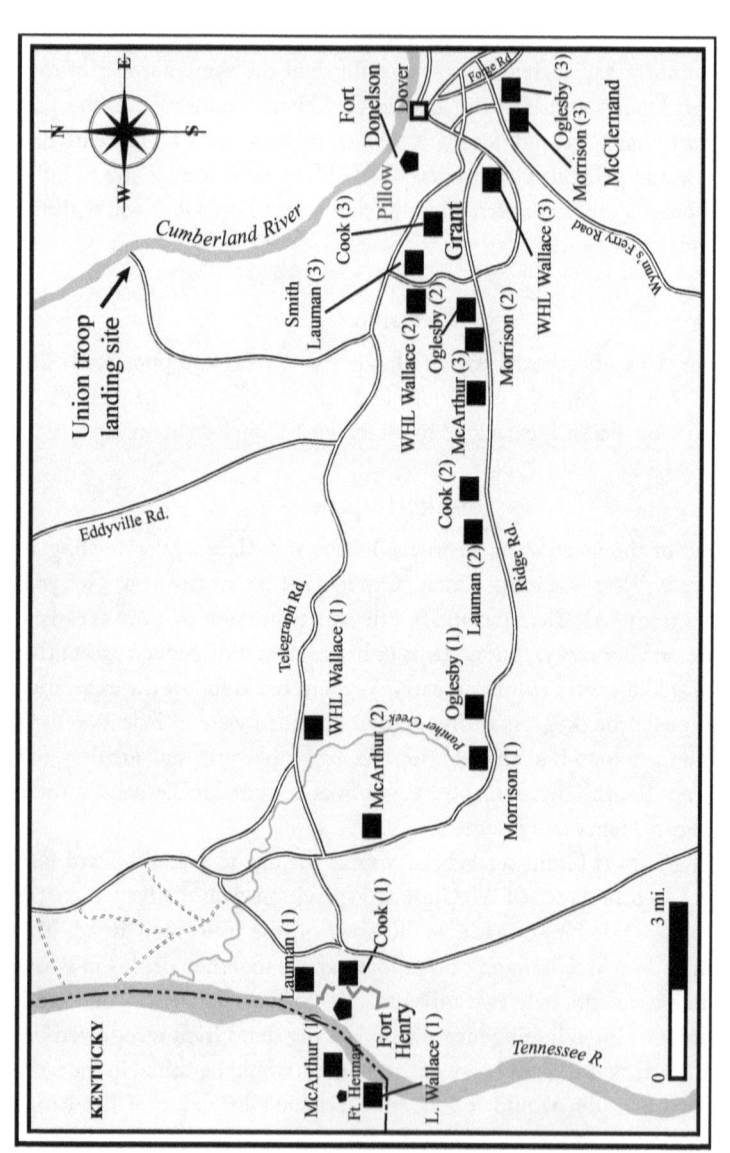

Union Movement to Fort Donelson

bivouacked for the night. They moved again at 8:00 a.m. on February 12, a warm and sunny day. Cavalry detachments probed the way on both roads.[76]

Before Pillow left for Cumberland City, he ordered Forrest out on a reconnaissance toward Fort Henry. The cavalry leader recalled that Pillow did not expect the Federals to advance against Fort Donelson that day and gave orders not to confront any Union troops in a general engagement. The opposing cavalry units collided about two miles in front of the fort. Forrest attempted to block the enemy advance, but Federal infantry in large numbers drove the rebel cavalry toward their entrenchments. Forrest appealed to Buckner for reinforcements, but he was instead ordered to retreat inside the trenches. This was the only attempt to fight the Union advance.[77]

After Union cavalry and infantry drove Forrest's horsemen off the field, there was no Confederate resistance to Union advance and encirclement. As expected, Grant issued orders in the field based on circumstances. Grant caught up to McClernand around 2:00 p.m. in the vicinity of the Widow Crisp cabin, which he used for his headquarters. Smith's division approached, and Grant ordered the unit to take position opposite the right flank of the enemy's line. McClernand was sent toward the town of Dover, which necessitated crossing the Indian Creek Valley and extending his line along the Wynn's Ferry Road. Smith had to cover three thousand feet of line, and he had enough men to do that. However, McClernand's assigned deployment was over two and a half miles long, and he did not have enough personnel. As McClernand lengthened his line to the east, the gap between the two divisions grew.[78]

Henry Walke, commander of the USS *Carondelet*.

USS *Carondelet*.

Around 11:20 a.m. Commander Walke arrived north of Fort Donelson with the *Carondelet*. Walke made his presence known by aiming ten booming shots at the fort, which seemed evacuated and did not return fire. While Pillow searched for Floyd in Cumberland City, he received a dispatch reporting Union forces advancing on Fort Donelson. He left for the stronghold immediately after writing Floyd and Johnston about the artillery fire he had heard, and informing them that he would suspend the order from Floyd to Buckner to transfer troops from Fort Donelson to Cumberland City.[79]

By nightfall Col. Richard Oglesby's and Col. William Morrison's brigades of McClernand's division encamped on the east side of Indian Creek Valley. Col. William Hervey Lamme Wallace's brigade occupied a hill just west of the valley, and Smith's division partially invested the rebel entrenchments toward Hickman Creek. Grant noted that the Federals approached and surrounded the enemy's fortifications with only slight skirmishing. In the center, McClernand described how the Confederates were enclosed in a continually shortening line, and after crossing the Indian Creek Valley the Federals were able to close the distance between the two armies. Oglesby proudly pointed out that by nightfall his brigade occupied the last main road out of the rebel fortifications. Grant's gambit had paid off. At small cost, his troops had invested a portion of the works and gotten batteries in place, and reinforcements and gunboats were expected to arrive the next day. The Confederates seemed content to stay inside their fortifications.[80]

Grant's insistence on attacking Fort Donelson with little delay had tremendous impact because he arrived the day the commanding officer, Pillow, was away and left Buckner with orders not to bring on a general engagement. In the morning, Forrest informed Buckner the enemy was approaching in force with intent to envelop the Confederates' defensive line. Buckner sent no aid to Forrest while the cavalry skirmished with McClernand's column. Pillow was aggressive and had earlier advocated attacking Grant's force after the fall of Fort Henry. Had Pillow been present when Grant moved toward Fort Donelson, he could have ordered troops out to contest the advance. If the rebels could not stop Grant, they could then fall back into their fort and entrenchments.[81]

But Grant was allowed to approach within two miles of the Confederate position without meeting any resistance. This was the case because the rebel command was splintered with differing ideas of where most of its forces should be stationed. Owing to bad timing, Floyd's decision to withdraw his and Buckner's troops to Cumberland City made Pillow leave Fort Donelson just hours before Grant's divisions approached. When Pillow returned, rather than confronting Grant, he spent his time sending messages to Johnston to overrule Floyd on removing troops from the fort. Pillow ignored Floyd's authority and called for more men from Cumberland City while the men continued work on the fortifications.[82]

Grant was pleased with the first day's results. In an overconfident message to Commander Walke the next day, he claimed he had succeeded in "almost entirely investing the enemy's works." While Smith's division ended the day fronted on the rebel right wing, and McClernand's division was spread out in front of the rebel works east of Indian Creek Valley, there were large gaps in the center of the Federal formation, and McClernand's line did not reach Lick Creek.[83]

Grant recognized the importance of building on the success at Fort Henry. He kept the initiative by approaching Fort Donelson as quickly as possible without waiting for reinforcements. Grant expected the arrival of more gunboats and reinforcements, but he did not want to lose the momentum of his attack by waiting.[84]

Alternate Decision and Scenario

Had Grant delayed, he would have faced a different situation. Reinforcements bolstered the defense, and the rebels worked on the trenches and fortifications to strengthen the earthworks. Fort Donelson's defenses got stronger each day. But on February 12 the command situation was in chaos, with Pillow preparing to hold Fort Donelson while Floyd and Buckner wanted out. Grant's arrival that day caused Johnston to order Floyd and the last available troops to Fort Donelson. Had Grant delayed a couple of days, he would have allowed Johnston to analyze the situation more clearly and realize Fort Donelson and Nashville could not be held.

The Union preponderance of forces made Fort Donelson untenable. The Confederates would have had to abandon the fort and move south to await reinforcements to give Johnston enough men to strike back against the Union armies, but the army would have survived. Had Grant waited to attack Fort Donelson, Johnston might have arrived to take command as Floyd so much wanted him to. If Johnston had been on site and in command, he would have made decisions to save the garrison since that was the most important objective. Johnston would have been in sole command and unhampered by the differing views of subordinate generals.

Johnston Orders Floyd to Fort Donelson, February 13, 1862

Situation

When Fort Henry fell, Johnston sent telegrams to Pillow and Floyd that separated the two officers in location and responsibility. On February 7 Pillow, who was at Clarksville, was ordered to take command at Fort Donelson. Floyd, who was in Russellville, was ordered to move his brigade to Clarksville, where he arrived the morning of February 8. Early on February 7 Johnston assigned Pillow to Fort Donelson, while Floyd would set up in Clarksville and offer support to the stronghold. But the situation kept changing, and Johnston grew frustrated with contradictory reports. By nightfall on February 7 Pillow received another telegram telling him to use his best judgment as to whether it was most important for Pillow, or even Buckner, to go to Fort Donelson. Floyd was given authority to determine his future movements in regard to the enemy once he and his men arrived in Clarksville. By the end of the day on February 7, Johnston abrogated strategy on the Cumberland River to Pillow and Floyd. Floyd had overall command, but Pillow ended up in contact with the Federals. Johnston did not know his commanders differed in opinion as to where the main battle should be fought.[85]

Johnston believed that Fort Donelson would fall quickly, as evidenced in his instructions to Pillow to reunite with Floyd if the bastion could not be held. But it would be five days before Union forces arrived at Fort Donelson on February 12. During that time, most of the Confederate soldiers on the Cumberland River were sent to the fort. Johnston finally ordered Pillow there on February 9, and he arrived the next day. Pillow subsequently alerted Johnston that Fort Donelson could be defended on land and river. On February 11 Johnston sent two messages to Floyd giving him full authority to use his judgment and deploy all troops for defense of the Cumberland River, Fort Donelson, and Clarksville. Floyd replied that he would do all he could with what he had. The most serious threat to Johnston's department was not met by the commanding general, but by a quartet of brigadier generals with different strategies on how to confront Grant's army.[86]

Much is made of why Johnston put the trio of Floyd, Pillow, and Buckner in command of the most critical portion of his defensive line. Insight into this question is found in a comment in Johnston's letter to President Jefferson Davis dated March 18, 1862: "And the generals—Floyd, Pillow, and Buckner—were high in the opinion of officers and men for skill and courage, and among the best officers of my command." Johnston assumed these men were competent, or else the Confederacy would not have made them brigadiers.[87]

When Pillow returned to Fort Donelson from Cumberland City on February 12, the differences between his strategy and that of Buckner and Floyd had not been resolved because Pillow and Floyd had not met. For four days Pillow had worked on the fortifications and batteries and sent messages informing Johnston and Floyd that he could hold the fort. Now Grant had unexpectedly advanced and commenced investing Pillow's trenches. Pillow suspended Floyd's order for Buckner to remove troops and fall back to Cumberland City. He also informed Johnston that he had delayed obeying an order from Floyd, whom Johnston had put in charge. Now Pillow bypassed Floyd with an urgent message to Johnston. He began, "If I can retain my present force, I can hold my position. Let me retain Buckner for the present. If now withdrawn, will invite an attack." Pillow ended the communication by stating, "With Buckner's force, I can hold my position. Without it, cannot long." Pillow asked Johnston to overrule Floyd. Johnston had been concentrating on the evacuation of Bowling Green, but he was now thrust into the command dispute at Fort Donelson, a place he had never been.[88]

Johnston was too remote from the situation and did not understand what was happening. He wondered why Pillow wrote about the disposition of troops when Johnston had placed that authority with Floyd. At 3:00 p.m. Johnston telegraphed Floyd a copy of Pillow's dispatch, along with a terse endorsement showing his vexation: "I do not know the wants of General Pillow, nor yours, nor the position of General Buckner. You do. You have the dispatch. Decide. Answer."[89]

Floyd sent a message that should have raised a red flag that he disagreed with Pillow. Floyd wrote that he was moving troops as fast as possible, but he did not tell Johnston where he was moving them to. Johnston had to be confused, as Floyd included the following remark: "The force, except what is absolutely necessary for the fort, I think (General Buckner concurs), ought to be at Cumberland City, whither we go from all directions." There was command confusion on the Cumberland.[90]

Floyd's plan to remove troops from Fort Donelson and station them at Cumberland City came too late. Grant's approach to Fort Donelson froze the defenders in place, and they could not easily be withdrawn in the face of the enemy. There were no defenses or batteries at Cumberland City, leaving Fort Donelson the only option to stop the gunboats.

A message conflicting with Floyd's strategy arrived from Pillow. Pillow telegraphed Floyd at Clarksville, directing copies to Johnston and Governor Harris, that there would be a battle at Fort Donelson in the morning including an attack by gunboats. Bypassing Floyd again, Pillow wrote that he ordered two of Buckner's regiments at Cumberland City to go to Fort Donelson. Pillow admitted he was not fully ready, but he remained sanguine about victory. Johnston was not sure where Floyd was sending troops, but Pillow's message confirmed a large Union force was set to attack Fort Donelson, and Pillow wanted reinforcements.[91]

At 10:30 p.m. Johnston sent a message to Floyd that started, "My information from Donelson is that a battle will be fought in the morning." Johnston realized the two top-ranking generals were not in agreement. The second-in-command disagreed with the general Johnston had put in command on the Cumberland River. The situation needed to be resolved, and quickly.[92]

Options

Johnston was aware that Pillow called for reinforcements and wanted to keep Buckner's forces at Fort Donelson, while Floyd thought Cumberland City

Brig. Gen. John Floyd.

was a better location to concentrate soldiers. Johnston considered his options. He could overrule Floyd's order to remove troops from Fort Donelson in face of the enemy and leave Pillow in command. Alternatively, he could let Floyd's order stand, but it would be up to Floyd to decide future actions against Grant's forces investing Fort Donelson. Finally, Johnston could order all remaining available Confederate forces, including Floyd, to Fort Donelson for the expected battle to come.

Option 1

Pillow wanted Johnston to prevent Floyd from removing any troops from Fort Donelson. In view of a pending battle, Johnston could concur with Pillow that the soldiers should remain in place. Pillow would keep command at Fort Donelson, but Floyd would decide what to do with forces not yet at the fort.

Option 2

Johnston had given Floyd the authority to deploy Confederate forces on the Cumberland River. Pillow decided to bypass Floyd and appealed to Johnston directly. Johnston could ignore Pillow's entreaties to not remove any men from Fort Donelson, then leave it up to Floyd to decide troop positions in response to Grant's arrival at the citadel.

Option 3

Pillow told Johnston he could hold Fort Donelson with the troops he had. Johnston could not only order that all the forces then at the fort remain there, but he could also direct all available Confederate forces on the Cumberland River to be positioned at Fort Donelson to maximize the opportunity to defend it.

Decision

Johnston decided to give all the support he could to hold Fort Donelson. He ordered Floyd to take all the force available, including Floyd, to Fort Donelson, except for a small garrison at Clarksville. Floyd was to move through the night in order to be in time for the coming battle.[93]

Results/Impact

Once Johnston accepted Pillow's claim that a battle would be fought the next day, he decided to concentrate all available forces at Fort Donelson. The remaining available troops were three regiments of Floyd's Brigade. Johnston could hardly send the rest of this brigade to Fort Donelson without Floyd. Johnston had put Floyd in charge of the defense on the Cumberland River, not knowing the major battle would be fought at Fort Donelson. With Floyd having the highest rank, the sequence of events dictated he would be in command when the Union army invested Fort Donelson.

Johnston had shown confidence in all four brigadier generals at Fort Donelson and let their ranks determine who gave orders to whom. The concentration of forces put all four officers at the fort at a crucial time. Johnston did not send Floyd to Fort Donelson because he wanted him in command at the fort. But Johnston was apparently unconcerned by the fact that Floyd would be the commanding officer when he arrived with the rest of his brigade.

Pillow wanted all the troops he could get at Fort Donelson, but he did not want Floyd. When Pillow got back to the bastion on February 12, he sent orders to Cumberland City for the rest of Buckner's Division. He bypassed Floyd and did not call for his remaining regiments. He made no mention of needing Floyd at Fort Donelson. Instead, Pillow let Johnston know that if he could retain his present force, he could hold the fort. Pillow added that he had ordered up the rest of Buckner's Division from Cumberland City. It was Johnston who sent Floyd to Fort Donelson, ignoring the latter's declaration that the main force should concentrate at Cumberland City.[94]

Before daylight Pillow found out he was no longer the commanding general at Fort Donelson. Buckner led the right wing and Bushrod Johnson the left wing, leaving Pillow without a command. The new leader was unfamiliar with Fort Donelson. After eating breakfast with Pillow, Floyd toured the defenses while Pillow supervised the placement of Floyd's regiments.[95]

As morning dawned on February 13, Pillow wanted to hold the fort. Floyd wanted to keep Union troops and gunboats from passing on to Nashville before the remnants of Johnston's army from Bowling Green crossed the Cumberland River, and Buckner just wanted to be somewhere else.[96]

Floyd's arrival at Fort Donelson negatively affected the command structure. Pillow was a Tennessean and well known to the defenders, approximately one-third of whom were Tennessee troops. Pillow vowed to the men, Gen. Albert Sidney Johnston, and Governor Harris that he would defend the fort and never surrender it. Floyd took command having declared to both Pillow; by his order to remove troops from Fort Donelson to Cumberland City; and Johnston in a letter that Floyd felt Fort Donelson was a trap and that the best location to confront the Union invaders was at Cumberland City. Pillow had a clear objective and exercised firm command control. Floyd held a different perspective but exercised inadequate command control, resulting in confusion between the commanding officers.

The command friction between Floyd and Pillow was compounded by Floyd's lack of leadership. Floyd made command decisions but then delegated the crucial task of carrying them out to Pillow. He did not stay close enough to the action to observe that his orders were executed. The result was that in some cases Pillow failed to follow Floyd's directives and even countermanded them.

At 9:50 a.m. Floyd sent an optimistic message to Johnston that even though gunboats were advancing, and the Union army was in force around the works, the field defenses were good, and he thought they could sustain themselves against the land force. But there was just one gunboat at the time, and Grant's expected reinforcements had not yet arrived. The Union forces spent the day extending their line, while the Confederate troops were content to just play defense. Rebels did not attempt to impede Grant's investment, except with artillery and sharpshooters.[97]

On February 13 the Federals probed the challenging Confederate defenses. Smith tested Buckner's Division with an attack on the Confederate right and found the rebel resistance and abatis daunting. After several hours and numerous casualties, Smith withdrew, concluding that any attack across his front would result in an enormous loss of life. McClernand tried to silence a rebel battery east of the Indian Creek Valley and failed with heavy casualties. The rebels' confidence rose with the repulse of the two Union sorties. Floyd determined that Grant was so badly beaten he would not attempt to charge the rebel lines again.[98]

As Floyd's first day in command drew to a close, he telegraphed Johnston to say that the fort had maintained itself against attacks on land and river, and that a battle would be fought tomorrow. The Confederates would hold the position if possible. But Union reinforcements were on the way; Floyd let Johnston know there was information circulating that fifty thousand men or even more were concentrating on the Tennessee River. Floyd concluded, and assumed Johnston did also, that Fort Donelson could not be held against the increasing numbers of forces the Union army could throw against it. It was just a matter of time before the fort would have to be evacuated.[99]

Johnston sent Floyd and almost all of his force on the Cumberland River to defend Fort Donelson, expecting that the commanders would withdraw the army once the fort could no longer be held. Even though Floyd recognized the stronghold would eventually be lost, he spent the crucial day of February 13 inspecting the fortifications, observing the attacks by Smith, McClernand and the *Carondelet*, and writing telegrams to Johnston. Floyd, Pillow, and Buckner gave no consideration to how the army would retreat from the fort when necessary.[100]

The aggressive moves by Grant put a command strain on the Confederates.

Floyd's presence made no impact on the events of February 13. He issued no orders to obstruct the extension of Grant's line from blocking the Forge Road escape route. He let Pillow direct the defense to the Union attacks. With Grant pounding against the fort, Floyd took measure of the fort's defenses. He devoted no thought to saving the army because the defenses had held, and Floyd did not think Grant could take the fort with the force he had.

But all that changed around midnight, when a Union convoy of gunboats and transports laden with troops arrived at the landing downstream of the fort. This information reached Floyd early on the morning of February 14, and he recognized the increased threat from the gunboats and Union reinforcements. To compound the rebels' dilemma, the weather turned to blizzard conditions, with wind, snow, and temperatures plummeting to twelve degrees above zero. The nasty weather hampered movement, and the rebels needed to move. Johnston's critical decision to send Floyd to Fort Donelson put Floyd in command. Floyd's reaction to the arrival of the Union convoy is discussed with respect to his critical decision to mount the breakout attack.

Alternate Decision and Scenario

Floyd was at Cumberland City with three regiments of his brigade; the other two were already at Fort Donelson. Johnston could have left Floyd at Cumberland City, which would have left Pillow in command at Fort Donelson. Had Johnston done so, he would have left the fort in command of a general who had vowed never to surrender, instead of one who had no qualms about deserting the men he led and condemning them to the rigors of Northern prisons.

Floyd's final three Virginia regiments could have been sent to Fort Donelson without Floyd. While Pillow made mistakes, he vowed he would die first before he would relinquish the fort. Grant did not have overwhelming numbers with which to bottle up Pillow and the rebel defenders. Forrest showed there was an escape route for those willing to chance it.

Floyd was not up to the challenge of extricating the garrison from the fort. While it is doubtful all the men could have escaped, a large portion of them might have been able to if given the choice. Pillow stated at the surrender conference that he wanted to stick with the plan to evacuate the fort, which would have given the soldiers an opportunity to flee. Yet Floyd and Buckner chose to surrender rather than proceed with the withdrawal.

CHAPTER 4

DAY OF DECISIONS

FRIDAY, FEBRUARY 14, 1862

After two days of skirmishes, sniping, and artillery fire, the combatants awoke in a frozen winter landscape on Valentine's Day, February 14, 1862. Four different commanders faced critical decisions today. Grant needed to get more troops into the investment. Foote arrived at the fort in the early morning hours and rushed to formulate a plan of attack. Floyd strove to decide how to save the army from the encircling Union lines. McClernand was pressed to find a way to strengthen his right flank and get troops closer to Lick Creek.[1]

Grant Orders Lew Wallace to Fort Donelson

Situation

The easy conquest of Fort Henry gave Grant momentum and the belief the Confederates were already whipped. Circumstances delayed his advance for six days, during which the rebels strengthened the river batteries and entrenchments around the fort and Dover. But Grant's efforts to maintain pressure on the rebels kept them playing catch-up to his movements.[2]

Grant understood the concept of momentum. In the Mexican War he had witnessed outnumbered American armies led by Zachary Taylor and Winfield Scott take the fight to the Mexican armies and prevail. Grant intended to do

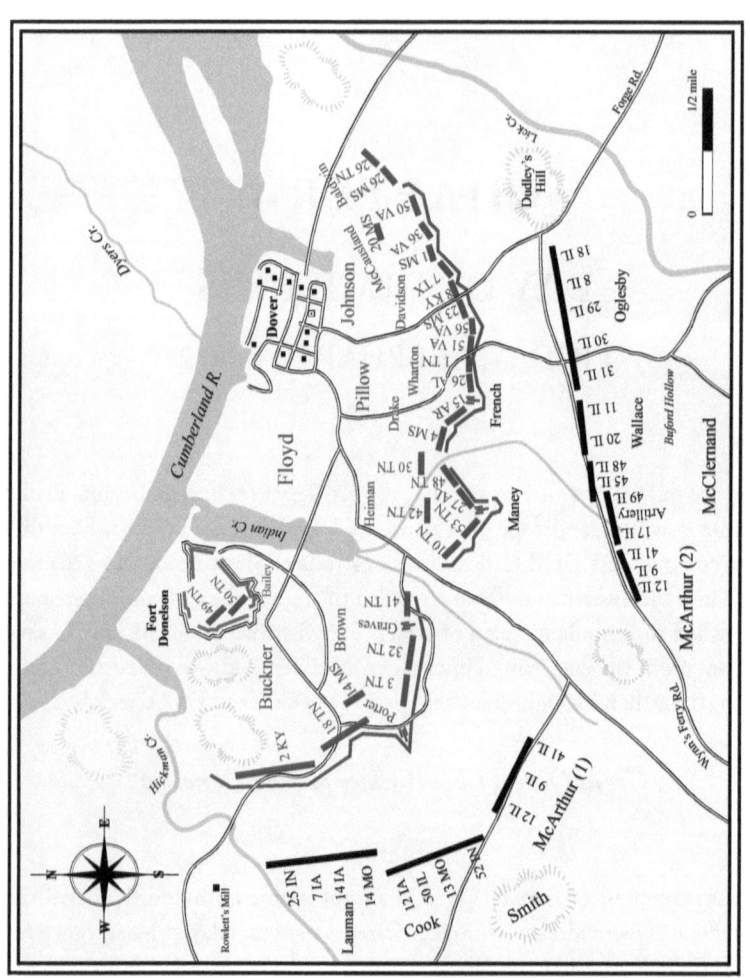

End of February 13

the same to the Confederates. He attacked Fort Henry with twenty infantry regiments, but by February 11 he had twenty-eight. A third brigade joined McClernand's division, which was encamped at Fort Henry. Smith's division received a fourth brigade, with two brigades at Fort Henry and two, under command of Lew Wallace, across the river at Fort Heiman.[3]

Grant issued General Field Orders No. 11 on February 11, 1862, for the attack on Fort Donelson. Due to the lack of information on the terrain, number of Confederates, strength of the enemy's fortifications, and location and number of Confederate artillery pieces, Grant intended to improvise his attack as circumstances developed. He showed ignorance of the terrain and distances by suggesting that a brigade of Smith's division enter Dover and cut off retreat if possible. This feat was not possible, but Grant was confident of success and took most of his army to Fort Donelson.[4]

McClernand left two regiments at Fort Henry, while Smith designated Wallace's brigade, including artillery and cavalry, to remain at Fort Heiman. This did not sit well with Wallace. He venomously wrote his wife that he was sick with rage and felt abused because Smith left him behind. Like most volunteers, Wallace had enlisted with a strong ambition to fight and yearned to participate in a great battle. Now, he led a brigade in the army commanded by an aggressive general who needed every man for a fight that could end the rebellion in the West. Wallace and his brigade watched in dismay as Grant's army marched off while they were left behind.[5]

Grant's bulldog mentality paid off again because the weather was mild during the advance to Fort Donelson on February 12. Within twenty-four hours the weather turned cold, windy, and snowy, but Grant's army was in position around Fort Donelson by then. Had the general waited, he might not have commenced an advance movement in the cold and snow, as the men were not equipped for such weather. Grant described the weather change in a message to Halleck on February 14: "Last night was very severe upon the troops. At dusk it commenced raining, and in a short time turned cold and changed to snow and sleet. This morning the thermometer indicated 20° below freezing."[6]

In Special Field Order No. 6 of February 11, Grant verified that Brig. Gen. L. Wallace had "been designated to remain behind during the expedition against Fort Donelson." Grant declared that Wallace would take "command of all the forces at Fort Heiman and Fort Henry," and that any troops arriving would be encamped and positioned "for self-defense." When Wallace protested, Capt. William S. Hillyer of Grant's staff tried to soothe him and asked him to be patient. Hillyer's note of February 11 to Wallace lends credence to the notion that Grant expected to take Fort Donelson with just the men who marched the next day. Hillyer explained that Grant intended to give Wallace a division organized from regiments expected to arrive in the next few days. The brigadier general would have a position in the next fight, and Fort Donelson was just the first skirmish.[7]

Cruft's brigade, along with the First Nebraska and Fifty-Seventh Illinois, arrived at Fort Henry the evening of February 11, but Grant ordered them to travel by river to a landing north of Fort Donelson. This 150-mile trip had an uncertain time frame, as the troop transports were to join the gunboats from Cairo and not precede them to Fort Donelson. Grant assumed the reinforcements would arrive the night of February 12 in time to cooperate with the troops from Fort Henry. Thayer of the First Nebraska would assume command of regiments that arrived on river transports.[8]

Wallace and his staff watched from the deck of a steamer at Fort Henry as the army left for Fort Donelson. Lieut. James Ross stated Grant did not have enough men, and he expected him to return. Wallace asked Ross the basis of his opinion, and Ross noted that Grant was moving with fifteen thousand troops, while the estimate of rebel strength was twenty thousand. The Confederates also had the advantage of fortifications. Based on this information, Wallace contended Grant would call for the brigade within twelve hours, meaning the force must be ready to move at once. Wallace ordered four boats to be under steam so the men could move quickly across the river. He ordered Col. Morgan Smith to have troops stack arms and receive three days' rations. The artillery soldiers were to put, and keep, their horses in harness. After making preparations for an immediate movement, Wallace waited.[9]

Grant's troops skirmished with Confederate pickets and Forrest's cavalry, which yielded a few prisoners who claimed there were twenty to twenty-five thousand rebel defenders at Fort Donelson. Grant believed he was outnumbered, but he nevertheless ordered his forces to advance in line of battle and complete as much of the encirclement as possible. By the end of the day on February 12, Smith's brigades commanded by Col. Jacob Lauman and Col. John Cook were in position, while Col. John McArthur went into reserve. William Wallace's brigade went into camp west of Indian Creek Valley and maintained close proximity to Smith's division. Oglesby's brigade stretched McClernand's line far enough to block the Wynn's Ferry Road, where the route turned north toward Dover. Morrison's small brigade of two regiments trailed, and at nightfall Oglesby and Morrison were east of the Indian Creek Valley, which left a gap between them and William Wallace's brigade. Grant needed more men.[10]

Messages from Grant to Halleck on February 13 show Grant's concern with a lack of manpower and a possible rebel attack back at Fort Henry and

Widow Crisp farm, Grant's headquarters during the battle for Fort Donelson. From *Battles and Leaders of the Civil War* edited by Robert Underwood Johnson.

Fort Heiman. Grant wrote Halleck that reinforcements should be sent to Fort Henry rather than up the Cumberland River. He also kept his focus on Fort Donelson, where he looked hourly for more gunboats and men.[11]

On February 13 McClernand continued to slide his division to the right to cut off the escape routes. William Wallace moved to the right first thing on the morning of February 13 to catch up with the left of McClernand's line. This left the heights along Indian Creek unoccupied and created a large gap between the divisions of Smith and McClernand that the Indian Creek Valley bisected. Grant had a hole in his line but no available troops to fill it. Meanwhile, Lew Wallace sat at Fort Henry waiting for the call from Fort Donelson.[12]

On February 13 Smith tested the rebel fortifications when he ordered Lauman to advance toward the rebel works and, if the opportunity presented itself, carry the trenches with the bayonet. Lauman's regiments moved down from the ridge and then ascended the hill, but they encountered a wide swath of fallen trees that prevented further advance. The two sides skirmished for a couple of hours, then the men of Lauman's brigade retired to their original positions after suffering near one hundred casualties.[13]

Cook's brigade advanced to a ridge six hundred yards from the rebel fortifications. From this vantage point, Cook noted the large expanse of abatis in front of the rebel trenches. Based on the experiences of Lauman's and Cook's brigades, Smith concluded the rebel works could only be carried with an enormous loss of life.[14]

As McClernand's line extended eastward, its soldiers received cannon fire from a rebel battery on high ground just three hundred yards from Oglesby's line. McClernand attacked across the hollow to take out the battery. Morrison led the assault with his two-regiment brigade and a third regiment from

William Wallace's brigade. The assault failed with heavy casualties and confirmed what Smith saw on the Union left flank. The rebels had a strong line with thousands of defenders that would make an offensive very costly for Grant's army.[15]

Grant finally received information on Foote's progress, and on February 13 he informed McClernand of a dispatch stating that four gunboats and ten steamers were bound for the Cumberland. That afternoon, Grant alerted Commander Walke that four gunboats would probably arrive the next morning. The general added that the army was doing well.[16]

The rebel left flank extended a little over half a mile beyond Oglesby's right flank. This put Oglesby in a precarious position, as the rebels could move to block further advance. Oglesby needed more men to extend his line farther toward Lick Creek. McArthur's brigade was detached from Smith's division at 4:00 p.m. and moved to bolster McClernand's line east of Indian Creek. This left a larger gap in Grant's line on the heights west of Indian Creek.[17]

Grant's assumption the troops sent by transports would arrive the evening of February 12 was wrong. By nightfall on February 13 the expected reinforcements had not appeared. Grant needed to fill the gap in the center of the line and provide for efficient command of the reinforcements that would probably arrive in the morning.

Options

By the evening of February 13 Grant needed reinforcements. The nearest troops were those in Wallace's brigade, anxiously waiting at Fort Henry while other regiments were steaming toward Fort Donelson. Grant could order Wallace to Fort Donelson or leave him at Fort Henry.

Option 1

Grant could leave Wallace and his brigade at Fort Henry. By nightfall on February 13, Grant found the fortifications at Fort Donelson strong and the arrival time of the gunboats and reinforcements uncertain. There was a large gap in the center of Grant's line that needed to be filled immediately. Wallace's brigade was just twelve miles away, while other reinforcements were somewhere on the Cumberland River. Even though Wallace's brigade had fewer men than were on the river, Grant needed soldiers immediately. Grant had envisioned distributing the six regiments sailing from Fort Henry to McClernand and Smith. However, additional transports from Cairo had joined the flotilla in Paducah with other troops that had to be organized.

Option 2

Grant could order Wallace to come to Fort Donelson with his brigade. McClernand's and Smith's divisions were already large and separated by a significant distance. They had their hands full, and it would be inefficient to assign more regiments to them. Grant had planned to form a third division with Wallace as commander, and he could decide to do that now.

Decision

By the evening of February 13, the perceived threat at Fort Henry had vanished. Grant wanted as many troops as possible, and he ordered Wallace to Fort Donelson with two regiments of his brigade. A third division with Wallace in command would be formed from the regiments arriving at Fort Donelson.[18]

Results/Impact

Wallace predicted Grant would call for him before February 12 was over, but no order came. Though Wallace fretted, he kept up the vigil of being ready. February 13 passed with only unconfirmed rumors arriving from Fort Donelson, and Wallace went to bed with his boots on. Around midnight he received an order directing him to Fort Donelson with two regiments. Within five minutes Wallace and his staff awakened, mounted, and rode off the steamer onto shore.[19]

Brig. Gen. Lew Wallace.

Wallace chose his Eleventh Indiana and the Eighth Missouri to march to Fort Donelson. He left his cavalry, and the transports brought Wallace's regiments and artillery over from Fort Heiman. The temperature dropped to a brutal twelve degrees, and as dawn broke Wallace's column started the twelve-mile hike to Fort Donelson. A cavalry unit met Wallace and guided him to Grant's headquarters. The cavalry leader told of heavy fighting the day before, and Grant encountered a much more difficult "Johnny's nest" than expected, plus rebel reinforcements continued to arrive. Wallace took comfort from news that Foote's gunboats and a large number of transports had arrived with men designated for his new division.[20]

Wallace reached the Widow Crisp's clapboard cabin around 11:00 a.m. and found Grant inside. The reinforcements for Wallace's division were in motion from the landing to headquarters. Wallace's First Brigade was Cruft's, and Thayer's was designated Third Brigade. The Second Brigade included the Forty-Sixth, Fifty-Seventh, and Fifty-Eighth Illinois regiments, but these units did not report on February 14 because they were in transit from the landing. In addition, troop movements slowed because of the inclement weather. Wallace had to return his brigade to Charles Ferguson Smith's division, and Morgan Smith led the Eighth Missouri and Eleventh Indiana to rejoin Smith's division.[21]

Grant apprised Halleck that five gunboats and twelve transports arrived in the morning, adding greatly to the Federals' strength. Wallace estimated he had six thousand men in the First and Third Brigades who finally appeared, marching up the road around 2:00 p.m. First in line was Cruft's brigade, followed by Thayer's. Wallace and Cruft were acquainted from Indiana, and Wallace had confidence in Cruft and was glad to have him command the First Brigade.[22]

With Capt. John Rawlins, Grant's aide, as guide, Wallace set out for his assigned position in the center of the line. His orders were to keep the rebels from escaping without being aggressive. After about an hour, Rawlins told Wallace to deploy his men in this area. Wallace asked Rawlins how far away Smith's and McClernand's lines were, and the answer stunned him. Rawlins replied that McClernand was approximately one-half mile away, while Smith was probably a quarter mile distant. Now Wallace understood why Grant had sent for him. Wallace's brigades were serenaded with sounds of the gunboat battle. Hearing rebel cheers as the gunboats drifted downstream, Wallace added more men to his picket line in case the rebels followed up their gunboat victory with a land attack.[23]

Wallace's six thousand men closed the gap west of Indian Creek, yet they remained separated from McClernand's division east of Indian Creek. Smith had ten regiments with over five thousand men in Lauman's and Cook's brigades to cover approximately three thousand feet of ridgeline. He had sufficient manpower to cover his area, but McClernand needed more men. McArthur's brigade crossed Indian Creek Valley the night of February 13 to a position on the left of McClernand's line. The small brigade of Morgan Smith remained as a reserve behind Smith's troops. Indian Creek Valley was covered with undergrowth and blackjack, so both sides considered the valley unsuitable for operations and were satisfied to cover the area with artillery. As darkness fell on February 14, approximately a half mile separated Wallace's right flank and McClernand's left.[24]

Grant found the rebels in a stronger position than expected. He stripped defenders from the Tennessee River forts to bolster the attack on Fort Donelson, and he made plans assuming the Confederates would not attack him at Fort Donelson, Fort Henry, or Fort Heiman. Grant believed he would dictate whatever fighting occurred on the rivers.

When Grant saw a large gap in the center of his line and the reinforcements from Fort Henry had not yet arrived, he sent for Wallace. However, a lack of urgency to complete Wallace's division is evident because the regiments assigned to the Second Brigade did not report on February 14. They did not join Wallace's command until the morning of February 15, as the Confederate breakout attempt crushed the Union right flank.[25]

Nevertheless, two brigades of Wallace's division made it into position by the night of February 14, providing much-needed support to McClernand's division during the fierce fighting that raged on February 15. The importance of Grant's decision to order Wallace to Fort Donelson was shown the next day, when Lew Wallace made two critical decisions. The next chapter describes Wallace's choices to use his command to aid McClernand and stop the rebel attack along the Wynn's Ferry Road.

Foote Attacks Fort Donelson

Situation

Flag Officer Foote arrived at Cairo the morning of February 7 to cheers from a raucous crowd. The easy victory enhanced confidence for the North and filled the South with dread. Rebel major Jeremy Gilmer warned that the victory at Fort Henry would embolden the enemy to quickly attack Fort Donelson.[26]

Andrew Hull Foote, aided by an influential father who served Connecticut as a US representative and senator, received a midshipman appointment in 1823 at age sixteen. His career started in the age of wooden sailing ships, but promotions came slow in an overstocked officer corps. Foote served about one year in the Caribbean fighting pirates, three years in the Pacific squadron off the coast of South America, and thirty months with the Mediterranean squadron. He subsequently served on a two-year cruise around the world, then took shore duty and completed another two-year stint with the Mediterranean squadron. Foote's Mediterranean assignment was followed by service at the Charleston Navy Yard. Finally, Foote got command of his own ship, *Perry*, and spent two years chasing slave traders off the coast of Africa. In May 1856 he joined the East India squadron and showed aggression by taking and destroying four barrier forts at Canton, China (now Guangzhou). Foote positioned his ship within five hundred yards of his opponent and came under enemy fire for the first time in his career. He returned to the Brooklyn Navy Yard in October 1858. On August 30, 1861, Foote's boyhood friend Gideon Welles, secretary of the navy, appointed him to take command of naval operations on the western waters.[27]

At this time in the war the army was in charge of the gunboats. The navy provided officers and crews, but Foote was under the command of the army. Fearing a rebel counterstroke, on February 9 Halleck ordered Cullum to talk to Foote and find out how many gunboats could go and when. The army applied pressure to send vessels up the Cumberland River immediately, but Foote answered that he could not.[28]

On February 10 Halleck increased pressure to send gunboats, ostensibly only to escort troop transports destined for Fort Donelson. However, the same day, Halleck telegrammed Foote and Grant to send some boats up the river at once and destroy the railroad bridge at Clarksville. In response to Halleck's directive, Foote planned to send gunboats to attack Fort Donelson and then demolish the bridge at Clarksville. Foote regretted that the lack of men for the vessels would make the expedition inefficient, but he hoped to accomplish what Halleck wanted.[29]

Also on February 10, Grant wrote Foote that he did not feel justified to attack without ironclad gunboats. He asked whether Foote could send at least two gunboats up the Cumberland immediately, and he offered steamers to tow the watercrafts and an artillery company to serve on them. The army put heavy pressure on Foote to move quickly.[30]

The pressure hit a crescendo on February 11, when Halleck wrote that gunboats should attack Fort Donelson with the least possible delay because the stronghold must be taken immediately. Time was everything, and Foote wasn't to delay one instant. Halleck cajoled Foote to make his name famous in history with the capture of Fort Donelson and Clarksville because their possession was a military necessity. Foote must act boldly and quickly even if he was just half-ready. Foote responded that he would move up the Cumberland River the next day.[31]

Foote vented his frustrations to Gideon Welles the evening of February 11. He explained that Halleck wanted him to attack Fort Donelson, so he reluctantly prepared three gunboats even though he was short of men. If the attack could wait ten days, he would go with eight mortar boats and six ironclad gunboats, providing he had enough men, "and conquer." Foote's vessels at Fort Henry had been undermanned, and he did not want to go into another fight without a full complement of crewmen. But no mortar boats were ready, and he could man just three ironclad gunboats. Nevertheless, Foote responded to Halleck's urgency and departed for Fort Donelson at 8:30 p.m. that evening.[32]

Halleck informed Foote there would be troop transports waiting for escort at Paducah. A *New York Herald* reporter expressed surprise that eleven transports full of troops were added to the gunboat flotilla. He had thought Grant would only have the troops that came from Fort Henry. The reporter hopped aboard the *Louisville* for a front-row seat for the impending action.[33]

The gunboats reached Paducah on February 12 and then left, fighting the fierce current. At Canton, Kentucky, approximately thirty-five miles below Fort Donelson, the steamer *Alps* joined the flotilla around 3:00 p.m. on February 13 to tow gunboats upriver. Foote was disconcerted that Union troops had assaulted the rebel lines and the *Carondelet* had engaged the fort's batteries, because he had understood Grant would wait for him before making any offensive moves. The sailors pressed forward, and as Foote approached Fort Donelson he ordered the gunboats to prepare for action. Sailors went to their battle stations, and guns were run in, loaded, and placed in battery. The flotilla arrived at the landing around midnight.[34]

An anxious Grant met Foote at 9:00 a.m. on February 14 aboard the *St. Louis* to strategize. They agreed the navy would open the ball, and Grant expected the gunboats would silence the water batteries, take position opposite the town of Dover, and shell the rebels in their trenches. McClernand's forces would then attack the rebels' left flank and drive them westward against the divisions of Smith and Wallace, who would prevent their escape. Grant thought he had the works well invested, and the Confederates did not seem inclined to come out. He expected to capture every man.[35]

The army pushed Foote for a quick victory. He had to plan an attack with the gunboats available and then issue instructions to the captains of the boats.

Options

Foote had the option to close with the fort's guns or subdue them with a slower, long-range bombardment that kept the gunboats beyond range of the 32-pound guns in the fort.

Option 1

Foote could repeat the attack plan of Fort Henry and engage the water batteries at short range. Grant's army was already in place. Foote was expected to immediately sail past the fort's guns and then shell the Confederates in their trenches while Grant assaulted the fortifications. For a quick victory as at Fort Henry, Foote could have the gunboats steadily advance toward the fort with bows forward, firing on the enemy at close quarters.

Option 2

Foote could hold the gunboats out of range of the 32-pound guns and bombard the fort with the bow guns. The barrage would continue until the gunboats silenced enough of the fort's guns to let the gunboats close with the fort and finish the job. However, the day before Foote's arrival, the *Carondelet* expended 139 shells and managed to dismount just one of the fort's guns. A long-range bombardment would be time consuming, and Foote wanted a resolution by nightfall.[36]

Decision

Foote decided the same plan of attack that produced victory in little over an hour at Fort Henry would be successful at Fort Donelson. He would confidently lead the gunboat flotilla to close-quarters combat with the fort's water batteries.

Results/Impact

Foote summoned the gunboat captains around noon to receive orders for the attack. The gunboat crews protected the vulnerable areas of boilers and decks using hard materials such as sacks filled with coal, chains, and lumber. This methodical preparation ate up time, and it was 1:45 p.m. before Foote guided the flotilla forward for the attack.[37]

The gunboats were designed to fight head on. The two-and-a-half-inch iron cladding only protected the front casement and the sides in front of the engines and boilers. Rebels' batteries could hit the gunboats with plunging fire, and the pilothouses and chimneys were inviting targets, as Foote found out.[38]

Lieut. Col. Milton Haynes, a West Pointer and chief of the Tennessee Corps of Artillery, arrived at Fort Donelson on January 16 to train rebel gun crews. Troops set range markers and practiced with varying powder charges. The upper battery consisted of a 6.5-inch rifled cannon and two worthless carronade pieces. The lower battery had eight 32-pounders and one 10-inch

Columbiad. Amazingly, the rebels' two long-range guns were readied for action only on February 11. On February 13 the long-range guns sparred with the *Carondelet*.[39]

Foote's deployment was the same as at Fort Henry. From right to left the gunboats were the flagship *St. Louis*, the *Louisville*, the *Pittsburg*, and the *Carondelet*. The timberclads *Conestoga* and *Tyler* took position and kept a quarter mile in rear of the ironclads. Foote gave the signal to advance, and at 2:35 p.m. the gunboats rounded the bend and came in view of the fort's gun crews. The distance from the bend to the stronghold was approximately one and a half miles. The fort's Columbiad opened with a shot that fell short. Then the 6.5-inch rifled gun joined in, and large splashes of water showed where shells were landing. The four gunboats ascended the river to within one mile of the water battery. Foote opened fire, and the other boats soon joined in. As the combatants continued to exchange their "iron valentines," the gunboats crept closer.[40]

The rebels had constructed a barricade of logs and tree limbs across the river nine hundred yards from the battery, but the river rise allowed the gunboats to pass over the obstruction. The barricade marked the range of the 32-pounders, and when the vessels crossed over, the 32-pound guns opened fire. Approximately forty-five minutes after rounding the bend, the gunboats closed to within three hundred yards of the fort, and the battle raged.[41]

Present day photo of Fort Donelson's Upper Battery. Photograph by the author.

Present day photo of Fort Donelson from downriver. Photograph by the author.

On the *St. Louis* a 32-pound shell smashed into the pilothouse. The civilian pilot was killed, and Foote received a painful injury to his left ankle that had dire consequences the next day. More shells smashed into the *St. Louis*, and the vessel would not respond to the helm. Attempts to steer with the relieving tackle failed in the swift current. Foote reluctantly allowed the boat to drift downstream.[42]

The *Louisville*, on the left of the flagship, received even more deadly fire. A projectile from the Columbiad demolished the gun carriage of an 8-inch Dahlgren gun, killing three of the crew. Then the coup de grace shot passed aft after killing one crew member, wounding two others, and severing the tiller cables, making the boat unmanageable. In quick succession half the gunboat fleet was floating down the river.[43]

The *Pittsburg* steamed closer to the batteries as the flagship and *Louisville* drifted out of range. The gunboat had suffered just two wounded crewmen, but two well-placed solid shot balls penetrated the hull in the bow between wind and water. Crew members ran the bow guns aft to lessen the water gushing into the boat, and reversed the engines as they fought to get the vessel out of range before she sank.[44]

The *Carondelet* managed to hold its own against the rebel guns, despite being the most damaged and suffering more dead and wounded than the other three gunboats combined. One bow gun exploded, wounding a dozen men. Walke continued to advance toward the fort until he noticed the three companion gunboats were drifting down the river. He had no option but to withdraw from the fight. The *Carondelet* kept firing its bow guns as the Union gunboat fleet drifted back down around the bend and out of sight of Fort Donelson.[45]

During his naval career Foote commanded the capture of six forts and participated in several naval engagements. He told a reporter that he had never been under so heavy a fire as what he had just endured. But naval warfare had changed due to increased firepower of the guns and exploding shells. In the past, ships closed with the batteries in a fort in order to silence them. Foote had successfully silenced the guns in four Chinese barrier forts near Canton (now Guangzhou) in 1856 with just two wooden ships that were towed into position. The wooden vessels were struck forty times without serious damage, as the Chinese used only solid shot. Foote proved to be an aggressive commander who believed in close combat with the enemy.[46]

Rebel artillery officers considered Commander Walke's lone gunboat engagement on February 13 more formidable than the attack by four gunboats on February 14. On the thirteenth, Walke stationed the *Carondelet* beyond the range of the 32-pound guns, and the gun crews could take their time and fire with deliberation and better results. The February 14 attack, with orders to close with the fort as rapidly as possible, put the gunboat crews under fire

Present day photograph of Fort Donelson's Lower Battery. Photograph by the author.

and stress. This resulted in hurried shots that went wild. Not a single rebel gun was disabled.⁴⁷

The gunboats were not invincible. The *New York Herald* reporter who jumped on the *Louisville* to witness the fight up close left his readers with his observation as to the gunboats' vulnerability to cannon shot: "The fact is, our boats are proof against ordinary shot, even as large as a sixty-four; but this trial has demonstrated the fact that rifled thirty-pounders, even, will penetrate our iron sides, while one hundred and twenty-pounders nearly laughed at the obstruction."⁴⁸

Foote learned a hard lesson. He yielded to the pressure from Halleck and Grant for a quick victory at Fort Donelson and steamed right up to the batteries to silence them, but what worked at Fort Henry failed at Fort Donelson. Foote was chastened by the rough treatment his gunboats received, and he mourned the death and wounding of men he led into battle. He was troubled that he acquiesced with Halleck's and Grant's plans to attack before he felt ready. He regretted the close approach to the fort's batteries. He claimed the Union sailors were close to victory; just fifteen minutes more and they would have had it. While Foote exaggerated how close the gunboats came to success, if they came close at all, he recognized the mistake of getting within range of the 32-pound guns.⁴⁹

Foote noted in his official report to Gideon Welles that he had made the assault at the request of Halleck and Grant because it was a military necessity, but he was not properly prepared. Foote also wrote his wife and told her of his wounded foot, assuring her he would not go so close again. He explained the attack order had come from Halleck; Foote had acted against his own judgment, and he was not to blame.⁵⁰

Lieut. H.L. Bedford served on the crew of the 10-inch Columbiad and gave his opinion as to the strategy Foote should have used against Fort Donelson. Bedford noticed the gunfire from the *Carondelet* the day before was more accurate when the gunboat stayed out of range of the 32-pound guns. He concluded that had Foote remained beyond the range of the 32-pound guns, the Union fleet could have concentrated on the two long-range pieces. Upon silencing them, Foote could then have destroyed the 32-pounders. Bedford concluded Foote was overconfident, stating, "Flushed with his victory at Fort Henry, his success there paved the way for his defeat at Donelson."⁵¹

On May 16, 1861, Commander John Rodgers had reported to McClellan in regard to the design and construction of a new type of gunboat suitable for river combat. It had to be constructed from the keel up and clad in iron to protect men and machinery. Rodgers worked with naval constructor Samuel M.

Pook to develop the design for seven ironclad gunboats, affectionately known as Pook's turtles. Rodgers oversaw the construction of the gunboats and made recommendations for armament and design features. His early involvement included much thought as to how the vessels should be tactically handled in a fight, but Rodgers would not lead them into battle. On August 30, 1861, he was replaced by Capt. Andrew H. Foote.[52]

When Rodgers heard of the repulse of the gunboats at Fort Donelson, he concluded Foote should have at least tried to knock out the guns of the fort while staying outside the range of the 32-pounders. Foote was a courageous officer of the old school that called for rapid fire at close range, but advancing within range of the stronghold's 32-pound guns negated a large part of the advantage of the iron armor on the boats. Rodgers summed how to take advantage of the new factor of iron armor: "Iron Clad vessels are to fight wooden vessels and forts, at distances which leave the Iron Clads impenetrable to the artillery opposed to them."[53]

Foote was game to try again, but not until he returned to Cairo and had the damaged gunboats repaired, the other gunboats manned, and the mortar boats in tow. Then he would return "and conquer." Crews worked feverishly through the night to make repairs and plug holes. By morning the gunboats had their steering mechanisms functioning, and all the boats could get underway, but another assault on the fort was out of the question except for long-range bombardment.

The army's expectation of an easy conquest vanished as Foote's fleet drifted downstream and the guns fell silent. The defeat of the gunboats saddened Grant, and he went to bed thinking he would have to entrench his position and bring in tents, or build huts, to shelter the men against the winter weather. In a letter to his wife, the general mused that the taking of Fort Donelson would be a long process, but he was confident of success. When it would end was hard to predict. He wrote to Halleck on February 15 that it appeared the Federals were in for a protracted siege. Grant feared the result if he stormed the formidable breastworks with raw troops, but he believed he would ultimately prevail. Grant had not yet placed his batteries in siege position, anticipating the gunboats would have made it unnecessary. He acknowledged his line did not extend to the river above Dover as he wanted because of high water. However, he was looking into sending a force around the high water to the riverbank above Dover. Grant thought he had all the time he needed to complete his investment of Fort Donelson and Dover. He was thinking only offensively because he did not anticipate the rebels would come out from behind their fortifications and attack him.[54]

Floyd Orders Breakout Attack against the Union Right Flank

Situation

Floyd arrived at Fort Donelson before daylight on February 13 and took over command from Pillow. Buckner was third in line, followed by Bushrod Johnson. At the point of contact, the Confederate command consisted of four brigadier generals functioning like a committee, while Johnston and Major Generals Hardee and Beauregard sat at Bowling Green. The most experienced officers were at Bowling Green when military leadership was most needed at Fort Donelson.[55]

John Buchanan Floyd was born into an influential family in western Virginia on June 1, 1806. His father served in the US Congress (1817–29) and as governor of Virginia (1830–34). Following his father Floyd became a lawyer and entered public life in 1843, and he was elected to the Virginia House of Delegates in 1847 before serving as governor from 1849 to 1851. He spoke for Buchanan as a Democratic elector in the 1856 presidential election, after which Buchanan appointed him secretary of war. Floyd served a tumultuous term in this office ending on December 29, 1860, with his resignation. Counties in western Virginia did not support secession, and the Confederate government searched for an influential man to keep those counties in the fold. Floyd fit the bill and was commissioned brigadier general in the Confederate army on May 23, 1861, despite having no military background. He raised a brigade and confronted Union intrusion into western Virginia. The new officer acknowledged his inexperience and used councils of war to discuss operations. After five months of unsuccessfully jockeying with Union forces to take back the western counties of Virginia, Floyd and his brigade were ordered in mid-December to join Johnston's army in the West at Bowling Green, Kentucky.[56]

During his tenure as secretary of war Floyd got embroiled in a scandal for using Indian trust bonds to pay costs to contractors during the Mormon Utah expedition. He ordered the transfer of military arms from northern arsenals to southern ones as tensions between the two regions intensified. Suspicion was cast on Floyd that he had made a calculated move to aid the South should war come. Floyd considered Maj. Robert Anderson's nighttime switch from Fort Moultrie to Fort Sumter in Charleston Harbor on December 26, 1860, to be against orders. He pressured Buchanan to order Anderson out of Fort Sumter and back to Fort Moultrie. When Buchanan refused, Floyd resigned.[57]

A review headed by Attorney General Edwin Stanton found no nefarious reason for the transfer of arms. In the case of the Indian bonds Floyd was indicted by a District of Columbia grand jury in January 1861, but the charges against him were quashed in March 1861 for lack of evidence. Thus, on February 13, 1862, Floyd was not under any indictments. Even so, suspicion of Floyd was rampant in the North, where he was considered a traitor. In his memoirs Grant wrote that Floyd betrayed his oath to maintain the Constitution of the United States, and that he was unfit for command because he feared the North would try him for treason if he was captured.[58]

The failed attacks by Smith and McClernand on February 13 bolstered the rebels' confidence they could hold the fort. Floyd sent Johnston a telegram noting the day's events: "The day is closed, and we have maintained ourselves fully by land and water. . . . We will endeavor to hold our position if we are capable of doing so." But Floyd's outlook changed when Foote arrived around midnight with five gunboats and twelve transports full of troops. As February 14 dawned, the Confederates braced for a gunboat attack and renewed ground attacks and skirmishing.[59]

With McClernand's line extended to the vicinity of the Forge Road, Floyd feared a trap and held a council of general officers the morning of February 14. The meeting concluded that the rebels should make an immediate attack on the Union right in response to the reported arrival of an estimated fifteen thousand reinforcements during the night. If the sortie was successful the army would retreat, and Buckner's Division would form the rear guard. Troop dispositions were made, but Floyd canceled the attack at the insistence of Pillow.[60]

Participating officers confirmed that a movement with Pillow leading Col. William Baldwin's brigade did start. Forrest joined the movement, but the size of the force was inadequate for such an important task. At noon Pillow directed Baldwin to form the Twentieth and Twenty-Sixth Mississippi and Twenty-Sixth Tennessee in the open ground to the left of his position on the Confederate left flank. The brigade advanced in a road located about two hundred yards past the end of the trenches and approached the right flank of McClernand's line. Baldwin reported that after less than a quarter mile Pillow suddenly ordered him to return to the rebel lines, claiming it was too late in the day for success.[61]

Maj. William Brown of the Twentieth Mississippi wrote that he received an order at one o'clock p.m. to form his regiment in an open field on the extreme left and assault the enemy. A short time later the regiment advanced, and a small amount of firing was heard from the Federals. After advancing approximately one hundred yards a Confederate private was shot, and after another one hundred yards an order came to halt. Brown believed the command emanated from Floyd, saying that it came "with the explanation that we did not have time to accomplish what he wanted." The Twentieth Mississippi's troops marched back and retook their position. Forrest confirmed the sortie had opposition to its advance from Union soldiers, probably cavalry. Forrest was ordered out past the line of entrenchments, but after a short time the Confederates exchanged shots with the enemy, and he was ordered back to the trenches.[62]

The rebel commanders are criticized for not offering more resistance as Grant's army extended their line toward Lick Creek. But Floyd ordered an attack, as noted in the reports of Buckner, Baldwin, Brown, and Forrest. Neither Floyd nor Pillow mentioned the aborted assault in his report. The attack, if carried out, would have struck McClernand's line at right angles near the Forge Road with Lew Wallace's division not yet in place.

Maj. Peter Otey of Floyd's staff claimed the idea of the attack was entirely Floyd's. Pillow was ordered to lead the charge while Floyd attended to other duties, and Otey accompanied Pillow as Floyd's representative. A shot from a Union sharpshooter brought down a man toward the front of the column. Pillow told Otey the movement was discovered, and it would not do to move out of the trenches. Otey protested because he thought the shot came from sharpshooters far away. Pillow sent him to report to Floyd that it would be best to defer the attack till morning.[63]

Otey found Floyd and gave him Pillow's assessment. Floyd exploded in anger and wailed, "In the name of God, Captain, what does this mean? My orders were to move out and attack." Floyd first ordered Otey to ride back and tell Pillow to make the attack, but he soon realized crucial time had been lost, meaning Pillow should return the troops to the trenches. Years later Otey gave the opinion that aborting the sortie on February 14 was "the fatal mistake at Donelson." If Floyd considered the assault so vital, he should have seen that it was carried out.[64]

The arrival of Foote's flotilla in the middle of the night caused Floyd to send a message of ill tidings the morning of February 14. Johnston got the ominous news that gunboats and transports had arrived near the fort, bringing twenty thousand more troops for the enemy. Floyd estimated the Union army's strength at forty thousand men and stated he would fight them that day. A skeptical Johnston responded with a short telegram to Floyd: "If you lose the fort, bring your troops to Nashville if possible." Realizing that time might be short, Johnston also instructed Hardee to expedite the evacuation of Bowling Green.[65]

Union army activity almost ceased as Grant waited for the results of the gunboat attack. Floyd sent conflicting reports to an anxious Johnston. First, he reported that gunboats advanced with a heavy cannon fire, and they would make the best defense they could. Next, Floyd asserted the fort couldn't last twenty minutes. Finally, he said the gunboats were driven back and the fighting was over for the day. However, a relieved Johnston was still in the dark, as Floyd sent no word on what his next move would be. February 14 was a day of contrasts for Floyd. The attack on the Union right flank was aborted after minimal effort, but the water batteries defeated Foote's gunboats. As night fell, McClernand's right flank had shifted just one hundred yards east from where it started the day.[66]

The gunboats' defeat did not change the dilemma faced by Fort Donelson's defenders. Thousands of reinforcements were marching toward the fort, which would allow the Union line to extend eastward toward Lick Creek and the river. As darkness fell on another bitter evening, Floyd called a meeting in his room at the Dover Hotel just after dark to discuss what to do next. The attendees were Floyd, Pillow, Buckner, and Gilmer.[67]

Options

Floyd had options to continue to hold the fort, the water batteries, and the fortifications in front of Dover, or attempt another breakout attack similar to the aborted sortie.

Option 1

The appearance of the gunboats threatened the Bowling Green army's retreat to Nashville. Floyd would state later that he thought Fort Donelson had to be held until the Bowling Green army crossed the Cumberland River. Considering the successful defense made against the gunboats, as well as his access to an ample supply of food and ammunition, Floyd could hold the fort and fortifications for additional time to ensure Johnston's arrival at Nashville.[68]

Option 2

Grant's investment line was significantly strengthened with the placement of Lew Wallace's Third Division in the center. Additional reinforcements were on the march, which could allow McClernand to move closer to Lick Creek. Floyd assumed even more troops would arrive at any time. The Union army would only get stronger, so Floyd could decide to make another breakout attempt as soon as possible.

Decision

Floyd was the commander, and the decision was his, but every member of the council agreed that a breakout attempt should be made. Floyd ordered an attack against McClernand's division starting at daylight the next morning, February 15, 1862.[69]

Results/Impact

Floyd concluded the Union high command would send Grant as many troops and gunboats as necessary to reduce Fort Donelson. Floyd saw but one hope to save the garrison, or at least a part of it, and that was to attack the Union right flank, drive the enemy from their position, and pass into the open country and head for Nashville. Floyd had no delusions about striking Grant's army such a devastating blow that the rebels could remain at Fort Donelson. Unfortunately, Floyd let Pillow present a confusing plan lacking details about what would happen if the attack was successful.[70]

Gilmer confirmed the confusion when he wrote that the enemy might be dislodged to allow the garrison to escape, but that it might also be possible to destroy the Union army. However, the most important objective was to withdraw the rebel forces from their peril. It was mission creep to think the Confederates might be able to devastate Grant's army. What would have devastated Grant most was an enemy escape.[71]

Buckner's interpretation of the plan was to fight through the Union lines and retreat to Nashville via Charlotte. His division would take position on the Wynn's Ferry Road to cover the army's retreat and then serve as the rear guard. Buckner ordered his men into combat carrying knapsacks, blankets, and rations so they could retreat from the field. However, Pillow understood the troops would open the path to escape and return to the fort for their equipment and rations and leave later.[72]

Floyd commanded the army, but Pillow devised the plan. Pillow visualized the Union army concentrated in four separate encampments. One encampment commanded the Wynn's Ferry and Forge Roads leading to the interior. Opposite the center of the left wing was another encampment along the Wynn's Ferry Road. A third site was in front of the left of the rebels' right wing, and the fourth was where the steamboats deposited troops. Pillow assumed dense foliage of brush and blackjack would hamper Union support units' movement between encampments.[73]

Pillow's plan concentrated all left-flank brigades and Forrest's cavalry in the open ground beyond the end of the entrenchments. The estimated total of six thousand men formed approximately one-third of the rebel force. Pillow's attack would strike the right flank of the Union line and drive the bluecoats along the Wynn's Ferry Road toward Buckner's Division. Buckner would attack the Union line on the road and rout the Union forces. The result would be a stunning victory for Confederate arms while opening up the escape route to Nashville.[74]

Pillow proposed to lead the attack with his troops, but he also wanted Buckner's Second Kentucky because its soldiers were more experienced and better armed. The greatest amount of fighting would be by the flank attack. Success depended on driving the Union forces west along the Wynn's Ferry Road, where Buckner could attack the Union troops in flank and rear. Pillow was not just thinking of opening an avenue of escape; he also hoped to rout the investing force. Yet Buckner objected. Pillow recalled that Buckner proposed to keep the Second Kentucky, remarking, "He [Buckner] should attack the enemy simultaneously with my [Pillow] attack." Buckner surmised this strategy would "lessen the labors" for Pillow's forces and "strike the enemy in a more vital point." Pillow agreed to this change as an improvement to his plan. Floyd approved the plan with Buckner's change and ordered it carried out at daylight.[75]

The brigades of Col. Joseph Drake, Col. Gabriel Wharton, and Col. Davidson held the entrenchments where the Wynn's Ferry and Forge Roads passed through the rebel line. During the early morning hours of February 15, Buckner was to move his division of six regiments on the Confederate right into the area vacated by the aforementioned three brigades. Col. John Head would fill the trenches vacated by Buckner with 450 men of the Thirtieth Tennessee. Col. Heiman's brigade, positioned around Capt. Frank Maney's battery east of Indian Creek, was to remain in position and protect Buckner's right flank when Buckner left the trenches to attack the Union line.[76]

Baldwin's Brigade was split between Buckner's and Pillow's Divisions. Baldwin himself was assigned to Pillow's Division, and he received orders to form his brigade at 4:00 a.m. on February 15. He was to do so on the same ground and in the same order as the day before for the aborted sortie. The men took knapsacks, blankets, and rations in anticipation of making their escape. Baldwin led the advance brigade toward the right of the Union line, which was reported to be one and a half to two miles away and not deployed for battle in the direction the Confederates would approach.[77]

Buckner's Division consisted of Col. John Brown's brigade of three regiments augmented with three regiments of Baldwin's Brigade. Brown's oversized brigade had to wait for the arrival of Head's regiment from the fort before moving to the area vacated by Pillow's brigades. The men marched with knapsacks, blankets, and three days' rations. Brown understood the objective was to drive back the enemy's right wing and then retreat to Nashville.[78]

Head voiced concern that he had to defend three-fourths of a mile of trenches with just 450 men. Buckner instructed him to retreat back into the fort if he was attacked and overpowered. Heiman feared for Head and himself should their positions be attacked, and when he confronted Floyd with this worry, he got a disheartening reply. If Heiman was pressed, he should retreat to the fort or act as circumstances required. The plan did not sit well with Col. Randall McGavock of the Thirtieth Tennessee. He saw plainly that Heiman's Brigade, Head's regiment, and the regiments in the fort were to be sacrificial lambs for the rest of the army.[79]

Bushrod Johnson assisted Pillow in the assault on the Union right. He was not at the generals' conference, but he attended the council where instructions were given to the brigade commanders. He stated that the Union right would be rolled back, allowing the Confederates to retreat. When and how the retreat would start was not determined at the conference, but it would be decided later. Johnson claimed the plan was detailed to the point that a rallying site was designated far beyond the enemy's lines should the attack fail. This provision indicated that if the plan failed, the army would be ordered to escape as best they could and meet at the rallying point.[80]

In their reports, Gilmer, Forrest, Heiman, Col. John McCausland, and Wharton made no mention of what would happen after the escape route was opened. Johnson and Brown also remained silent as to when the troops would head for Nashville. The plan left out crucial details about rations, knapsacks, blankets, and other equipment. Buckner assumed his men would withdraw from the field. Pillow fought with the goal of defeating Grant's army to such an extent that the rebels could return to the entrenchments, gather up their equipment and rations, and then leave at a time of their choosing. Floyd included no description of the plan in his reports.[81]

Floyd and Buckner agreed that the objective of the attack was to open the pathway of escape and get away from Fort Donelson. Both officers considered the stronghold a trap, and if not for Pillow they would be at Cumberland City. Pillow thought the purpose of the assault was to defeat Grant's army, after which the Confederates could decide at their leisure whether to withdraw from the fort and the Dover area.[82]

Either objective was plausible, but one had to be chosen. A plan to escape should have troops ready to retreat as soon as the escape route is opened. The withdrawing army should push the enemy back and hold them as far away as necessary. Eventually the rear guard would withdraw and follow the retreating column. A plan to crush Grant's army would have the Confederates launch as much force as possible against Grant's line.

Floyd was in command, and he should have ensured that his vision was carried out. Instead, Pillow's plan focused on defeating Grant's army, which led to disastrous confusion. The escape route was opened, but no Confederates were in position to use it. Pillow wanted to crush Grant's force, yet during the entire morning only about one-third of the Confederate army was actually heavily engaged. Floyd believed Fort Donelson could not be defended. Johnston told Floyd to get the army to Nashville if he could not hold the fort. He did not suggest that Floyd should try to drive Grant into the Cumberland River.[83]

The results of the Confederate breakout attack plan and the confusion it caused are discussed in regard to the next critical decision in this chapter, and in relation to the critical decisions made by Buckner, Pillow, and Floyd in the next chapter. Tellingly, each of the top three Confederate generals made a critical decision during the battle to the detriment of saving the Confederate army.

McClernand Sends McArthur's Brigade to the Far-Right Flank

Situation

On September 5 Grant led the Ninth and Twelfth Illinois regiments into the strategic town of Paducah ahead of the arrival of Confederate forces. Grant considered these two regiments the best in his army. On September 8 Brig. Gen. Charles Ferguson Smith was given command in Paducah. Over the next four months Union forces in the town grew, and by the end of January 1862 Smith commanded brigades under Brig. Gen. Lew Wallace and Col. John McArthur, along with cavalry and artillery. Other Union regiments not yet in brigades were encamped in Paducah and Smithland, Kentucky.[84]

On February 1 Grant ordered Smith to take all available forces that could be spared from Paducah and Smithland for the attack on Fort Henry. Wallace's and McArthur's brigades plus other regiments not yet in brigades would participate, leaving a minimum garrison behind. Leading the Seventh Iowa, Col. John Cook arrived at Paducah on February 3 and received orders from Smith to organize a third brigade from unassigned regiments. Cook was temporarily attached to McClernand's division, so his brigade landed on the east side of the river to assist in the storming of Fort Henry.[85]

McArthur's and Wallace's brigades waited at Paducah for steamers to come back and transport them upriver, where they would attack Fort Heiman on the west side of the Tennessee River. It was late on February 4 before Grant returned to load the men onto the transports. It took all day and late into the night of February 5 before McArthur's and Wallace's commands disembarked across from McClernand's landing spot.[86] Wallace's brigade then led the advance up the slopes to Fort Heiman and found it had been abandoned. That afternoon Smith returned to the east side of the river, leaving Wallace in command at the fort.[87]

John McClernand was born May 30, 1812, and by 1832 he practiced law in Shawneetown, Illinois. When the Black Hawk War broke out, McClernand served three months in the state militia. In 1836 he was elected to the Illinois legislature for the first of three two-year terms. In 1843 McClernand was elected to the US House of Representatives, holding his seat for eight years. He subsequently returned to practicing law in Illinois, then resumed his service in Congress in 1859. Lincoln and McClernand knew each other from Illinois politics and their law practices. The president recognized McClernand was a strong Unionist and influential in southern Illinois, which had secession sympathies. On July 30, 1861, Lincoln commissioned McClernand a brigadier general. By the end of August, McClernand was at Cairo, arriving just a couple of days before Grant. He led the Union advance at Belmont and assisted Grant in the move on Paducah.[88]

As McClernand's brigades marched toward Fort Donelson, Oglesby led the advance along the Ridge Road with Morrison following. William Wallace started on the Telegraph Road and then moved over to the Ridge Road, bringing up the rear of McClernand's column. Smith's brigades started from Fort Henry along the Ridge Road. Cook led followed by Lauman, while McArthur trailed behind because they spent the night of February 11 at Fort Heiman and had to cross the river.[89]

By nightfall of February 12, Smith took position to the left toward Hickman Creek. He encamped his division in the trees along the top of the ridges, facing rebel entrenchments across a deep ravine. Lauman's brigade took po-

Brig. Gen John McClernand.

sition farthest to the left toward Hickman Creek, with Cook's brigade on his right. McArthur's brigade trailed and set up camp for the night about one and a half miles to the rear of Lauman and Cook. Oglesby's and Morrison's brigades from McClernand's division encamped east of Indian Creek Valley, while William Wallace's brigade occupied the ridgeline on a hill west of Indian Creek. Wallace's men were situated to the right of Cook's brigade.[90]

The next morning, Lauman and Cook took up position on the ridge opposite Buckner's men on the Confederate right flank. McArthur brought up his brigade, but Smith kept him as a reserve since he had enough men to cover his line. As McClernand's regiments continued eastward along the Wynn's Ferry Road, William Wallace moved across the Indian Creek Valley. Oglesby's advance reached just beyond the Forge Road, but it was almost three-quarters of a mile to Lick Creek. Oglesby had no infantry to occupy the ridge beyond the end of his line.[91]

The gap between Smith's and McClernand's divisions grew, and the center of Grant's line was undefended. To narrow the gap McArthur marched at 4:00 p.m. across Indian Creek Valley, took position left of McClernand's division, and bivouacked for the freezing night of February 13. McArthur was now under McClernand's command.[92]

Grant had planned to keep the Confederates within their lines while Foote's gunboats destroyed the rebel batteries, but that did not happen. As Foote's damaged fleet floated downstream, Grant thought the Union army must prepare for a siege. The Third Division under Lew Wallace was now in position between Smith's and McClernand's divisions as night fell. During daylight on February 14 McClernand made no major adjustments to his line, but a potential siege made it essential that he extend his line farther toward Lick Creek. To do that McClernand needed more troops.[93]

Union cavalry patrolled the half-mile gap between Oglesby and Lick Creek, but infantrymen were needed. Oglesby urgently informed McClernand that he desperately needed a force to extend and strengthen the Federal right flank. As night fell, McClernand had to decide whether to do something immediately or wait until the next day.[94]

Options

McClernand had three options to close the gap between his right flank and Lick Creek. He could inform Grant he needed reinforcements and await their arrival. McClernand could also shift his entire line farther to the east, keeping the same order of brigades, or he could shift units within his lines to the area between Oglesby's right flank and Lick Creek.

Option 1

McClernand knew something had to be done immediately. There would be a significant delay if he requested reinforcements from Grant, as any additional troops sent could not arrive until at least the next day.

Option 2

McClernand recognized his right flank was much more vulnerable than his left flank, situated on the Wynn's Ferry Road east of Indian Creek Valley. He could close the gap to Lick Creek by putting his entire line in motion and shifting all his troops to the east. However, moving the whole line would be disruptive and cumbersome. Batteries were emplaced in key positions, and the men were familiar with the terrain and enemy forces to their front. If the troops moved to the east, they would be unfamiliar with their new positions.

Option 3

The most immediate and least disruptive option would be to move troops from the less threatened left flank of McClernand's line to the threatened right flank. This would leave most of the troops in position and minimize the number of men that would take new positions.

Decision

McClernand took the most expedient course. He ordered Col. John McArthur to move his brigade east from the left end of McClernand's line and become the right flank of the army.

Col. John McArthur.

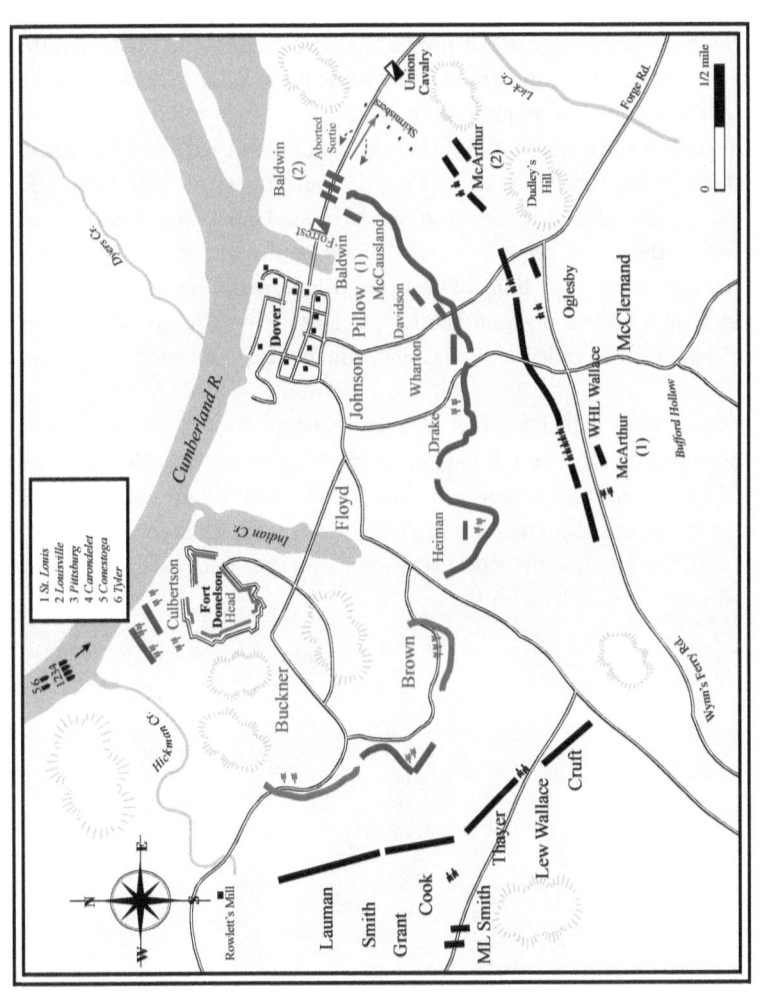

Valentine's Day

Results/Impact

McArthur's brigade stood fast on February 14 as the gunboat attack foundered. At 5:00 p.m. McArthur received an order from McClernand to move his brigade to the extreme right of the Union line. Col. Isaac Pugh's Forty-First Illinois led the column through the woods behind McClernand's line as the sun set. After arriving in the dark, McArthur bemoaned a lack of instructions and knowledge of the ground to his front and right. Pugh regretted it was too late to study the ground, and he sent out pickets as the regiment prepared to spend another night in the cold.[95]

McArthur's brigade took position on a prominent battlefield landmark known as Dudley's Hill. The Forty-First Illinois camped at the bottom of the hill and was the closest regiment to flooded Lick Creek. The Ninth Illinois gathered to the left of the Forty-First Illinois, and a gap of several hundred yards existed to the right flank of Oglesby's Eighteenth Illinois. The Twelfth Illinois took a reserve position behind the Forty-First Illinois. The soldiers looked out over the valley of Lick Creek, which was patrolled by Union cavalry units.[96]

Pillow's plan called for the advance to begin by 5:00 a.m., but Col. Davidson was ill. Col. John Simonton then took over the brigade, which delayed the time of attack to 6:00 a.m. Col. Baldwin led the advance in column because it was not expected to meet Union resistance for at least one and a half miles. But much to the rebels' bewilderment, they found a Union brigade around and atop Dudley's Hill.[97]

Col. William Baldwin.

No one expected resistance, and the column advanced in a narrow road with a single company serving as the advance guard. After not more than a third of a mile, the advance was fired on by presumed enemy pickets. Another company moved forward, but both units were driven back by a sustained fire. Less than thirty minutes into the grand breakout attempt, the lead Confederate brigade was brought to a standstill by heavy fire from the aroused Federals of the Forty-First Illinois.[98]

Baldwin sent word to Pillow that he had encountered a strong force. Pillow was surprised that in less than half an hour the armies were engaged in front of the enemy's encampment. The Confederate brigades did not advance in line of battle, and it took Pillow at least thirty minutes to bring brigades forward in a proper position to confront McArthur's force. From brigades in column Pillow sent soldiers to advance on the left and right of Baldwin's men.[99]

The Forty-First Illinois became an impediment to five Confederate brigades planning to form their lines at the base of Dudley's Hill before advancing toward McClernand's position. The pickets of the Forty-First Illinois looked down on the rebel lines toward Dover. At 5:45 a.m. the cold and drowsy pickets observed the rebel units start their advance, and soon the Union pickets fired on the astonished attackers. Several Federals ran back to camp to alert Pugh the enemy were approaching in large numbers. Pugh sent two companies out to reinforce the pickets and form a skirmish line.[100]

Union riflemen caught the rebel brigades in column and forced them to form a battle line under fire. To the right of Baldwin's column, rebels extended a battle line through the trees. To the left, in the open field covered by the Forty-First Illinois's guns, Pillow ordered the Twentieth Mississippi to form a line of battle in the woods, behind a fence and facing the open field. Pillow then sent the Mississippians into the field, but the movement failed when the Forty-First Illinois shot into their flank and Pugh ordered a bayonet charge. The Twentieth Mississippi retreated out of the field and over the fence, taking refuge in the woods. Pugh subsequently observed that no other Union troops had the temerity to charge the rebel lines. He halted in the field and watched with growing alarm as additional rebel troops appeared and marched toward his command to recommence the fight. Not only were fresh rebel soldiers advancing, but they were also extending their lines to Pugh's right with the intent of outflanking him.[101]

The Confederate timetable was disrupted by McArthur's brigade on Dudley's Hill. Pillow poised five brigades for a rapid surprise attack on Oglesby's brigade near the Forge Road, but McArthur's three regiments slowed Pillow's forward progress and provided Oglesby time to get ready. Pillow directed McCausland and Simonton to form their units to the right of

Col. Nathan Bedford Forrest. Courtesy of the State Archives of North Carolina.

Baldwin's line. To the left of Baldwin's line, Pillow ordered Wharton's and Drake's Brigades and Forrest's cavalry to flank the Union troops on Dudley's Hill and get behind them if possible.[102]

Oglesby took a ride to the east and found the Ninth Illinois a couple of hundred yards from his line, facing north toward Baldwin's Brigade. Pugh had moved the Forty-First Illinois to the right to challenge the rebel brigades attempting to outflank him. Oglesby found the two regiments heavily engaged, and he also noted a large force of Confederates swarming across the front of the Forty-First Illinois in an attempt to get around the Union right flank and behind the enemy line.[103]

As rebel brigades advanced, McArthur ordered the Twelfth Illinois from its reserve position to the right of the Forty-First Illinois. Even with the Twelfth Illinois extending the line, McArthur reported they were surrounded, with at least one regiment beyond the right flank of the Twelfth Illinois. In addition, Forrest probed through undergrowth that proved almost impossible to get a horse through.[104]

Oglesby rode back to his brigade with the foreboding that the Confederates were headed his way. Except for McArthur's interference, Oglesby would have been struck first. Now, rebel brigades moved through the icy ground and snow-covered shrubs and timber toward the Ninth Illinois and Oglesby's line near the Forge Road.[105]

After Oglesby's ride across McArthur's front, the heavy pressure finally caused McArthur to retreat south. The rebels caught the Forty-First in the right flank, and the regiment fell back, with a portion passing through the line of the Twelfth Illinois. This left the Twelfth no option but to retreat as well. McArthur lamented that with rebels punishing his troops with flanking fire and running short on ammunition, he had little choice but to order the withdrawal of his two right regiments.[106]

Under intense fire, the men of the Ninth Illinois stood their ground in line with the Eighteenth and Eighth Illinois regiments of Oglesby's brigade. Finally, with casualties mounting and ammunition getting scarce, the Ninth Illinois retreated to join the second line of McArthur's brigade. The combined units were located east of the Forge Road and perpendicular to the rest of McClernand's line in the Wynn's Ferry Road.[107]

Oglesby attempted to maintain contact with McArthur's brigade and ordered the Eighteenth Illinois to change front to the east and move toward McArthur's line. By 8:00 a.m. the Union line bent back at right angles just east of the Forge Road. McArthur's new line ran in a north–south direction, but the rebels had had enough of McArthur and did not heavily engage him at his line near the Forge Road.[108]

To the north, Oglesby continued to engage heavily with rebel brigades advancing through the shrubs and trees east of the Forge Road. Oglesby had to contend with this threat while, just three hundred yards away, Buckner's troops were available to join in the fray. Oglesby's men were bombarded by Confederate cannon as they fought to hold their line. The brigade suffered a large number of casualties, and ammunition ran perilously low. Finally, four of Oglesby's five regiments left the field, leaving just Col. John A. "Black Jack" Logan's Thirty-First Illinois fighting to the left of McArthur's brigade. But Logan's men ran out of ammunition and joined the retreat. When McArthur realized there was no support on his left, he withdrew farther to the rear into Bufford Hollow and was not engaged the rest of the day.[109]

The impact of the resistance by McArthur's brigade is shown in comments of frustrated Confederate commanders. Floyd, Forrest, and Wharton of the Fifty-First Virginia all used the word *obstinate* to describe the defense put up by the Union troops. Pillow noted that the Union troops fought most stubbornly, and it took two hours before rebel forces could make any headway. Baldwin desperately called for Pillow to send additional troops to the left to hit McArthur on his right flank. Baldwin believed at one point the attack was in extreme peril, and the rebels were in danger of being thrown back into their trenches.[110]

The unsuspected presence of Union troops on Dudley's Hill seriously impeded the rebel attack. McArthur's three regiments took on three rebel brigades and Forrest's cavalry. Getting warning the rebels were coming,

Oglesby held his position for a longer period because McArthur prevented the rebels from striking his right flank and rear.

As in most battles, time was of the essence. The longer the Union troops held back the rebel attack, the better the situation was for the Union army. McArthur's brigade bought time that allowed reinforcements to arrive from the Union center and join the fight.

Author's note: The critical decision to send McArthur's brigade to the far-right flank was made on the evening of February 14. However, the described results and impact occurred in the early morning on February 15 with the start of the battle.

CHAPTER 5

DAY OF BATTLE

SATURDAY, FEBRUARY 15, 1862

On the day of battle for Fort Donelson, seven critical decisions were made. First, Grant had to decide whether to leave the battlefield early in the morning, when Foote requested his presence on the flagship to discuss the conditions of the gunboats and future plans. Later, Grant had to determine what to do when he was informed a major battle was raging, and his right flank was one and a half miles west from whence it started the day. Wallace's first decision concerned what to do when McClernand appealed for help. Later, Wallace had another decision to make when he realized the rebels were headed his way.

For the Confederates, Buckner had to decide whether to keep his promise to strike Wynn's Ferry Road at the same time Pillow launched the attack on the Union right flank. Pillow had to decide what to do after the rebels forced back the Federal right flank and routes to Nashville were open. When Pillow countermanded Floyd's orders to Buckner, Floyd had to decide whether to adhere to his plan or acquiesce to Pillow's.

Grant Leaves the Battlefield to Visit Foote

Situation

Foote underestimated the amount of damage the Confederate batteries could inflict on the ironclads. At Fort Donelson the river was narrower than at Fort

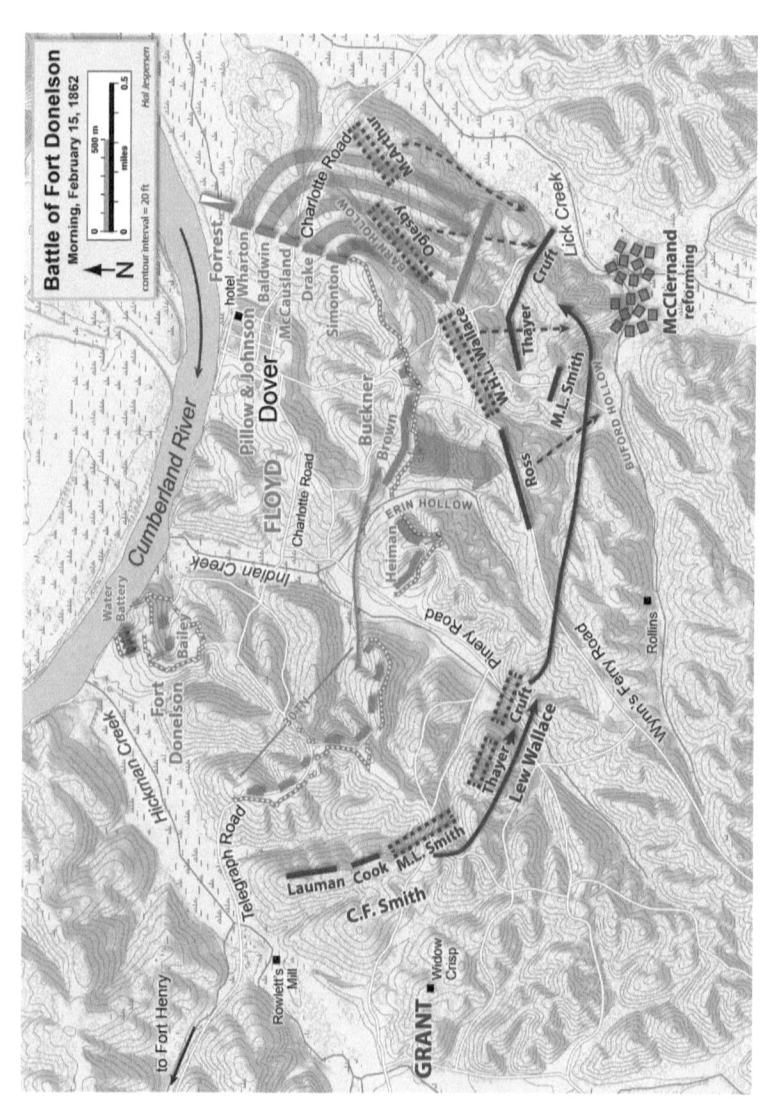

Morning of February 15
Map by Hal Jespersen, www.cwmaps.com.

Henry, and the rebel guns were perched higher and could deliver destructive plunging fire. The *St. Louis* and *Louisville* lost the ability to steer, while the *Pittsburg* was in danger of sinking. The *Carondelet* was shot to pieces, but the boat could still be steered.¹

Rebel gunners shot approximately 370 projectiles, and the Union gunboats reported being struck approximately 180 times, for an accuracy of almost 50 percent. The flagship *St. Louis* attracted the most hits with fifty-nine. The *Carondelet* came next with fifty-four strikes, followed by the *Louisville* with thirty-seven and the *Pittsburg* at about thirty. Already complaining of being short of men, Foote's fleet suffered eleven killed and forty-three wounded. Two men died on Foote's flagship (*St. Louis*), and eight were wounded. The *Carondelet* suffered five killed and twenty-eight wounded, while the *Louisville* lost four killed and five wounded. In addition, two men were wounded on the *Pittsburg*.²

Foote went into battle at Forts Henry and Donelson even though he did not feel fully prepared each time. He would not quit, but he would not attack Fort Donelson again until he had more gunboats, fixed the damaged gunboats, and brought up the mortar boats. The day after the defeat, Foote informed Gideon Welles there was nothing more he could do at Fort Donelson; Foote's services were needed more at Cairo to gather a large force to return and attack the fort.³

Crews worked throughout the night to repair damage. The *Pittsburg's* gaping holes were plugged to allow the gunboat to steam to Cairo. The steering mechanisms for the *St. Louis* and *Louisville* were fixed, making them available for limited use. The *Carondelet's* steering was functional, but the gunboat could barely move.⁴

Foote's wounded foot put him on crutches, but he thought he would recover in a week. Grant needed to know what condition the gunboat fleet was in and what Foote planned to do next. Foote could not travel, and he sent a message to Grant in the middle of the night that had unintended dire consequences for the events of February 15, 1862. Foote addressed Grant as follows: "Will you do me the favor to come on board at your earliest convenience, as I am disabled from walking by a contusion, and cannot possibly get to see you about the disposition of these vessels, all of which are more or less disabled."⁵

Options

Grant had several options for responding to Foote's request. He could decline to go and meet his fellow officer, or he could go and leave another officer in charge while he was gone. Alternatively, Grant could simply take off and leave no one to act in his stead.

Option 1

Despite his concern over how much damage the gunboats had incurred and what to do next, Grant could remain on the battlefield and communicate with Foote some other way.

Option 2

Grant could ride to the landing and leave an officer in charge to act in his absence, just in case the enemy did something that required command decisions. The highest-ranking brigadier general was John McClernand.

Option 3

Believing that he would commence any fighting that occurred, Grant could immediately ride to the landing without designating anyone to assume command in his absence. If the rebels initiated any fighting, the division commanders would be on their own.[6]

Decision

Grant thought the rebels did not have the audacity to launch an attack. He therefore instructed the division commanders to take no offensive measures, and he left to meet Foote without appointing someone to act on his behalf while he was gone.[7]

Results/Impact

A bitter winter grip of cold and snow froze the road from Grant's headquarters to the landing. Foote's message arrived at 2:00 a.m., and Grant departed headquarters at first light and rushed to see him. The timing of events remains shrouded in mystery. While the frozen road was more difficult to navigate than mud, how fast Grant could travel was not revealed.[8]

The Twentieth Ohio had arrived at the landing just in time to witness Foote's battered fleet drift downstream. The unit's soldiers spent the night on their transport and marched to join McClernand's division the next morning. Soon after dawn they passed Grant and staff officer Capt. Clark Lagow making haste through the bushes on the side of the road. The time of the meeting was given as a half hour after the rebels commenced their attack on McClernand's division, which would put it around 6:30 a.m.[9]

A small skiff took Grant to the *St. Louis* anchored away from shore. Foote broke the discouraging news that all the gunboats were seriously damaged and needed to return to Cairo for repairs. Grant's aspirations sank when Foote spoke of returning with more ironclads and mortar boats in ten days, when he would do the job right.¹⁰ Thus, Grant visualized the necessity for a siege, and Foote recommended the army entrench and wait for the navy to return. The army would need tents or newly constructed huts to shelter the men. Grant could use the entrenching tools Halleck sent, but the outlook was as gloomy as the weather.¹¹

When Foote revealed his angst to Gideon Welles, he explained that after consultation with Grant, the two agreed Foote would return to Cairo with two damaged gunboats. The other two ironclads would be left behind to protect the transports. Foote would return with mortar boats, the *Benton*, and other gunboats to make a successful attack on Fort Donelson.¹²

Lew Wallace and McClernand gave no indication they knew Grant was absent from the field until messengers gave them the startling news. Grant showed little concern for McClernand's right flank. He nonchalantly recommended that McClernand force his line to the river if possible; otherwise, McClernand should do nothing to bring on an engagement until receipt of further orders. Smith and Wallace received the same directive. Grant returned to his headquarters around 1:00 p.m., meaning that, with the attack starting around 5:45 a.m., the army had fought without a commander for over six hours. Subordinate generals with orders to stay put had to make decisions critical to the fate of the army.¹³

There is no record that Grant ever went over to Lick Creek to look at the situation. Had he done so, he would have crossed the avenue of rebel escape. Perhaps he would have deduced how vulnerable McClernand was to an attack against his right flank. Instead, Grant thought he knew Pillow and had a low opinion of his military skill. Moreover, Grant believed the rebels would just let him totally invest them with the thousands of reinforcements he received. But the plucky Confederates mounted a surprise attack while Grant was away visiting Foote. Grant's blunder put the army and his career at risk.¹⁴

Lew Wallace Orders Cruft's Brigade to Aid McClernand

Situation

The distance from Grant's headquarters to where Wallace deployed his division in the center of the line is around one mile. Wallace sent Thayer's brigade to the left, while Cruft's brigade went to the right overlooking Indian Creek Valley and took position closest to McClernand's division. Wallace sent pickets forward and set up his headquarters tent in the rear of his division, near the road that passed through the woods. He visited his freezing troops several times during the bitter night and wondered whether he "would [now] see a great battle."¹⁵

Lew Wallace was born on April 10, 1827, in Brookville, Indiana. His father served two terms as the state's lieutenant governor, one as its governor, and a term as US congressman. In 1846 Wallace served as lieutenant in the First Indiana in Mexico. His Mexican War experience was unsatisfactory, as the regiment fought in no battle, and after a year he returned to practicing law. As civil war loomed, Wallace trained a company of militia in Zouave tactics. He became known throughout Indiana as a military man despite having no professional military training. Governor Morton subsequently appointed Wallace adjutant general to raise the state's first regiments, and he took the position on the terms he would be sent into the field. In early June he led the Eleventh Indiana to Maryland, where the regiment aggressively pursued Confederates. After their three-month service, the regiment's men returned to Indiana in late July. During August, Wallace reorganized the regiment and added new recruits, and the unit mustered in for three years on August 31, 1861. On September 10 the troops were at Paducah, Kentucky, where they spent five months in garrison before the move to Fort Henry.[16]

Up early the next day, Wallace ventured outside to attend his horse and heard the perplexing sound of musketry far to the right. The sound grew, and Wallace alerted his staff to the growing crescendo of rifle fire. The Federals first thought the aggressive McClernand was pitching into the rebels, but they rapidly reached a different conclusion: "The Johnnies are out pitching into McClernand." When cannon opened fire, Wallace ordered the staff to get their horses ready, as it looked like they would have work to do. Men stirred, and Wallace lamented lacking cavalry that could have ridden to the far right and reported back what was happening.[17]

The suspense was torture as the sound of battle stretched into one hour and then two. McClernand surely expected Grant or someone from his staff to arrive and check out the continuous roar of muskets and cannon. It is not possible to reconcile the various accounts concerning the travels of the messengers sent from McClernand's command. There appears to be a logical sequence to these journeys, as indicated in McClernand's and Wallace's reports, but the times given conflict.[18]

Receiving word that McArthur had retreated, Oglesby was being flanked, ammunition was running low, and rebel pressure was increasing, McClernand sent for aid. He first sent Lieut. Carter of the artillery to Grant's headquarters around 8:00 a.m. to inform the general a battle was raging and McClernand needed reinforcements. Immediately on the heels of the first messenger, McClernand dispatched staff officer Lieut. Jones to headquarters with a more urgent plea for "prompt and efficient succor."[19]

Logically, McClernand sent an aid request to Grant before soliciting help from other division commanders. When McClernand learned the Union army was fighting without a commander on the field, he sent Maj. Mason Brayman to Lew Wallace for assistance. But Wallace wrote that Brayman arrived at 8:00 a.m. and told him McClernand needed immediate assistance. Brayman explained the whole rebel army had attacked; the right flank was being pushed back, and the men were running short of ammunition. Wallace recognized the emergency. But under Grant's order to hold his position, he reluctantly held his men in place while he sent Lieut. Addison Ware to Grant's headquarters seeking permission to aid McClernand. Brayman apparently returned to McClernand with the news Wallace wanted to help but needed word from Grant.[20]

Trying every avenue, McClernand sent Capt. G. P. Edgar to Charles Ferguson Smith. He returned with Smith's refusal to help. Wallace at least passed McClernand's request to Grant's headquarters, but there is no record of stodgy Smith contacting Grant's headquarters. Smith was content to stay put under the last orders he had.[21]

McClernand must have been in a foul mood. His division was being overrun. Grant was incommunicado somewhere off the battlefield, and his staff said McClernand would have to wait till he returned. Furthermore, McClernand's requests for aid from the other division commanders were refused, as both men replied they were to hold their positions and not go on the offensive. The situation rapidly changed for the worse, and McClernand sent Brayman back to Wallace. Brayman relayed the dire news to Wallace: "Our right flank is turned. The regiments are being crowded back on the center. We are using ammunition taken from the dead and wounded. The whole army is in danger."[22]

When Brayman returned a second time, Wallace had not yet heard from Grant's headquarters about his request to assist McClernand. Brayman's desperate plea placed a huge responsibility on a young, new brigadier general in division command. With no guidance forthcoming from the army commander, the responsibility of deciding whether to adhere to his latest orders or send aid to McClernand was Wallace's alone.[23]

Options

McClernand's messenger gave a dismal synopsis for the army if he did not receive aid. With no word from Grant, Wallace weighed his options of adhering to Grant's edict to hold his position or sending help to McClernand's sector.

Option 1

Wallace knew Grant left him to guard the center of the line and any major movement of troops. Thus, abandoning the position would be contrary to his orders. Wallace had sent for permission to assist McClernand, and he could remain in his assigned location until he received an answer.

Option 2

Wallace could conclude the situation was growing desperate and a divergence from orders was warranted. The sounds of battle were growing closer, and retreating, panicked soldiers were rushing past his position. He could send aid to McClernand.

Decision

Wallace realized the fight was coming to him, and he determined it would be better to engage the enemy distant from his position, as opposed to awaiting their arrival. To his everlasting credit, Wallace ordered Cruft to take his brigade and report to McClernand for instructions.[24]

Results/Impact

Wallace had surveyed his position, determining that he could order Cruft to the right to confront the Confederates coming from that direction while Thayer's brigade blocked any possible assault to Wallace's left flank. Wallace

Col. Charles Cruft.

feared his own division might panic should McClernand's division be rolled back on it. To forestall such a possibility, Wallace believed more than a single regiment should be sent. He split his command in two and bolstered McClernand's division with an entire brigade.[25]

Wallace directed Brayman to tell McClernand he would send Cruft's brigade. He then rode to Cruft at 8:30 a.m. and ordered him to rapidly march to reinforce McClernand's division. When Cruft's men started their movement, the rebel attack was approaching three hours old. Pillow had finally pushed McArthur off Dudley's Hill and set his sights on opening the Forge Road.[26]

Cruft's men marched south out of their lines, crossed Indian Creek Valley, and proceeded eastward on the Wynn's Ferry Road until they met the left flank of William Wallace's brigade. Then Cruft's troops veered into the woods and passed along the rear of Wallace's men toward Oglesby's line. The fighting in front of the left of Wallace's brigade was somewhat tranquil compared to the firestorm that had engulfed McArthur's and Oglesby's brigades and the right two regiments of Wallace's brigade. Cruft's regiments marched into battlefield mayhem.[27]

McArthur's second line formed east of the Forge Road at right angles to Oglesby's brigade. Oglesby gamely tried to keep contact with McArthur's brigade and ordered the Eighteenth Illinois to move to the right. Fortunately for McArthur, the rebels did not press the attack on his force, and the fighting to his front reduced to skirmishing. The Confederates concentrated on Oglesby's brigade because they held the key location across the Forge Road. The Eighteenth Illinois suffered heavy casualties, ran out of ammunition, and retreated, leaving a gap in the line.[28]

Cruft's brigade steadily marched on to the sound of the guns. McClernand envisioned a fresh brigade behind his faltering lines would serve as a reserve force his battle-weary troops could rally upon. Cruft expected to deploy in line of battle, but a messenger requested him to press forward and engage the enemy. Col. James Shackelford of the Twenty-Fifth Kentucky led the brigade as the column approached McClernand's headquarters. McClernand ordered Shackelford to proceed at double time, but the guide suddenly departed, and Shackelford later lamented he proceeded in ignorance of where he was needed and the position of the enemy.[29]

On Oglesby's line the soldiers of the Eighth Illinois had held their position on a ridge for over three hours, but they were running out of ammunition, and Lieut. Col. Frank Rhoads informed Oglesby the cartridge boxes were almost empty. Oglesby instructed Rhoads to hold his position because reinforcements were approaching. When the reinforcements arrived, the Eighth Illinois would swap out with one of the fresh regiments.[30]

Cruft's expectation he would form his brigade in line of battle evaporated with the deteriorating situation on McClernand's right flank. The Eighteenth Illinois had withdrawn, leaving a gap between McArthur's brigade and the end of McClernand's line. Cruft's brigade approached the gap with the intent of bolstering Oglesby's line and supporting McArthur's left flank.[31]

Oglesby led the Twenty-Fifth Kentucky forward with the intent they would replace the Eighth Illinois, but this was a difficult maneuver in the smoke and confusion for men under fire. Shackelford led the men against a horrific fire. Rhoads saw the Twenty-Fifth Kentucky approach with flags flying. He attempted to march the Eighth Illinois off the ridge and let the Twenty-Fifth Kentucky take its place, but the treacherous position swap never occurred. "From some unaccountable cause"—Oglesby and Rhoads used the same phrase in their reports—the Twenty-Fifth Kentucky fired into the ranks of the Eighth and Twenty-Ninth Illinois regiments from the rear. Troops in the Eighth Illinois were already retreating, but now the Twenty-Ninth Illinois joined them. The Thirtieth Illinois saw the two regiments heading to the rear and followed. Only the Thirty-First Illinois of Oglesby's brigade remained in the fight. Rather than bolster Oglesby's men, Cruft had to form a line under heavy fire between Union troops trying to hold the Wynn's Ferry Road and McArthur's brigade.[32]

McArthur saw the Union troops on his left had retreated and left him unsupported in that direction. His men were almost out of ammunition, and they had been pushed back a half mile from their starting location in the morning. In addition, McArthur's Federals were confronted by rebel brigades across their front and beyond their right flank, and they had already suffered over 430 casualties with seventy killed outright. Deciding to withdraw, McArthur calmly led the brigade back into Bufford Hollow.[33]

McArthur's men skirmished with the Confederates until their ammunition was exhausted. The colonel of Cruft's Thirty-First Indiana witnessed the withdrawal of McArthur's brigade, as a portion of the men retreated through the Indiana soldiers' line. This uncovered Cruft's right flank, but Cruft's brigade continued to keep the rebel attackers at bay and slow their advance.[34]

Troops in the beleaguered Thirty-First Illinois stood their ground, but ammunition ran low and the regiment retreated, leaving just William Wallace's brigade fighting for the Wynn's Ferry Road. Cruft's brigade had held the ground to Wallace's right and prevented the rebels from taking Wallace in flank and rear. But the gap opened by the retreat of the Thirty-First Illinois exposed Cruft's left flank to heavy fire, and enemy troops moved through the opening and attacked Wallace from behind. Rebel troops also moved past the brigade on the right since McArthur had withdrawn. Cruft recognized his line was now untenable and ordered the brigade to take a new position on a ridge to the rear. The position was better for defense and put the brigade between the rebels and a house serving as a Union hospital. Fighting died down to long-range sniping.[35]

The fierceness of the rebel attack and the stubbornness of McClernand's defense is found in the casualty count. Oglesby's brigade suffered over 850 casualties. McArthur's smaller brigade's total was more than 430. Cruft added over 230, putting the Union casualty count around 1,500 for the brigades that bore the brunt of the rebel breakout attack.[36]

The rebels drove the eight Union regiments of Oglesby's and McArthur's brigades from the field and left Cruft's brigade alone on the far right of the battle line. Cruft's brigade slowed the rebel advance and delayed Confederates from getting in the rear of William Wallace's line. This allowed Wallace to concentrate against Buckner while simultaneously aiding Oglesby's brigade. Once the last of the Union troops to his right retreated toward Bufford Hollow and the rebels were behind his line, Wallace ordered a withdrawal to the west along Wynn's Ferry Road to make another stand.

Buckner Breaks His Promise

Situation

Confederate leadership proposed an audacious plan on the night of February 14. Approximately one-third of the army under Pillow would assault McClernand's right flank at 5:00 a.m. Simultaneously, Buckner would attack and smash the Union line in the Wynn's Ferry Road. Pillow's assault was aimed at Oglesby's right flank, which stood just east of the Forge Road. Buckner would strike McClernand's line farther west. Concurrent attacks by Pillow and Buckner would limit McClernand's ability to move troops along his line.[37]

Gilmer witnessed the council of war and verified Pillow would lead the attack on the extreme right, while Buckner would lead the attack on the right center at the same time in the morning. Buckner stated, "The general plan was for General Pillow to attack his extreme right, and for that portion of my division remaining under my command, after being relieved in the rifle pits by Colonel Head's regiment, to make an attack upon the right of the enemy's center." Floyd wrote, "It was determined to move from the trenches at an early hour on the next morning and attack the enemy in his position. It was agreed that the attack should commence upon our extreme left, and this duty was assigned Brigadier-General Pillow. . . . To Brigadier-General Buckner was assigned the duty of making the attack from near the center of our lines upon the enemy's forces upon the Wynn's Ferry road." Buckner eyed the Union regiments on a ridge approximately four hundred yards away, having promised to attack those troops while Pillow rolled up the Union right flank.[38]

Simon Bolivar Buckner was born on April 1, 1823, in remote Kentucky nine miles east of Munfordville. His father admired the South American revolutionary—thus the name. The family held interests in a gristmill and ironworks, and Simon assisted in the business until he moved to Hopkinsville in 1838 to attend Christian County Seminary. He then applied to fill a West Point vacancy, entering the academy on July 1, 1840. He was one year behind Grant and graduated in 1844. During the Mexican War, Buckner served in Winfield Scott's army and participated in the battles that captured Mexico City. He resigned in March 1855 to pursue personal business and manage his father-in-law's valuable real-estate holdings in Chicago. Early 1858 found Buckner situated in Louisville, Kentucky. In March 1860 Kentucky passed an act authored by Buckner to organize the state's militia, and Buckner was appointed inspector general. The resultant Kentucky State Guard leaned toward secession, so the state's military board disarmed the unit, and Buckner resigned on July 20, 1861. Though Lincoln offered him a commission in the Union army around mid-August, Buckner rejected it and made himself available to the Confederacy on September 11. On September 14 General Johnston appointed Buckner a brigadier general pending government approval and put him in command of the forces sent to Bowling Green.[39]

The attack plan sent five brigades of Pillow's Division totaling 5,400 men to form for battle on the Charlotte Road beyond the end of the entrenchments. Forrest's cavalry of 600 men took position on the far left toward Lick Creek. The strength of Pillow's offensive force was approximately 6,000 soldiers. Heiman's sixth brigade of 2,200 men was left in the trenches. Buckner's Division had six regiments numbering about 3,900 men. Of note, Buckner's and Heiman's units combined equaled Pillow's force.[40]

Buckner's regiments arrived late at the position where he was to launch his attack as Pillow did the same. Buckner blamed Head for being tardy, but Head claimed he got the order to relieve Buckner at 2:00 a.m. and moved without delay. Buckner's regiment commanders stated they got orders to move starting from 3:00 a.m. to as late as 4:00 a.m.[41]

Col. Brown grew frustrated waiting for Head's regiment to arrive. He finally ordered his brigade to move to the left, leaving a small contingent of men in the trenches to follow once Head appeared. The three regiments from Baldwin's Brigade followed. The six units arrived at their destination in staggered intervals.[42]

Buckner reported that the Third Tennessee arrived before daylight and was ordered into the trenches. As the other regiments showed up, Buckner heard the sounds of Pillow's attack. The Fourteenth Mississippi and Eighteenth and Thirty-Second Tennessee regiments joined the Third Tennessee in the trenches. The Forty-First Tennessee and Second Kentucky went in reserve behind the fortifications. Buckner's regiments were late, but they arrived to the sound of Pillow's guns.[43]

Pillow's attack commenced at 5:45 a.m. By approximately 6:30 a.m., Buckner had his troops in position and knew Pillow's assault was underway. While Pillow struggled to make headway, Buckner understood his attack was already late. He had to decide whether to launch his offensive immediately.

Options

The sounds of battle to the east showed Pillow had engaged the enemy. Per Buckner's plan he would assault the Union troops to his front as Pillow attacked McClernand's right flank. Buckner could either strike the Federal center as promised straightaway, or he could delay this movement.

Option 1

Despite the staggered and tardy arrival of his troops, Buckner could form the regiments to attack the Wynn's Ferry Road as quickly as they arrived. This strategy would support Pillow's attack, which was even more crucial given the unexpected appearance of McArthur's brigade on Dudley's Hill. An attack by Buckner would put added pressure on the Union troops defending the crucial ground between the Wynn's Ferry and Forge Roads where the roads penetrated the rebel fortifications.[44]

Option 2

Rather than position his troops to attack, Buckner could keep the men in the trenches. This was not the plan, and it would let the Union troops concentrate on Pillow's force without concern of an attack by Buckner. Union forces that could have been engaged by Buckner would be free to fight Pillow.[45]

Decision

As his regiments arrived, Buckner placed four in the trenches and positioned two as reserves. He made no preparations for an infantry attack against the Wynn's Ferry Road. For the first three hours, the extent of his support for Pillow's assault was artillery fire into the Union lines.[46]

Present day photograph of the view from Buckner's trenches. William Wallace's regiments and artillery batteries held the Wynn's Ferry Road running atop the distant ridge. Photograph by the author.

Results/Impact

Pillow's work greatly increased with the surprise presence of McArthur's brigade. It took two hours of fighting to push McArthur's men off Dudley's Hill, and as Pillow's attack swept around the left flank of McArthur's line, the Confederates encountered resistance from the right two regiments of Oglesby's brigade. During the first three hours of the attack, the rest of Oglesby's brigade and William Wallace's entire brigade had a staring contest with Buckner's men in the rebel fortifications. The two sides exchanged artillery fire, but Buckner made no attempt to carry the Wynn's Ferry Road as promised.[47]

By 8:00 a.m. Pillow's brigades swept around McArthur's left flank and extended their lines to the west. These forces targeted Oglesby's brigade, crossing over the Forge Road in front of Buckner's regiments hunkered down in the trenches. Pillow's line was approximately two hundred yards ahead of the rebel earthworks.[48]

Rebel brigades concentrated their efforts in a fierce fight against Oglesby's brigade. The Confederate line kept extending to the west, and the right two regiments of William Wallace's brigade were brought into the fray. All this action occurred east of where the Wynn's Ferry Road curved down through the rebel works. Up to this point, Buckner's contribution in lessening Pillow's labors was solely through artillery fire into the Union positions. Heiman's Brigade remained in place to protect Buckner's right flank during Buckner's assault. Buckner described the Union position as a vital point, and he was supposed to make a vigorous strike against it in conjunction with Pillow's offensive. Buckner did not attack at the start of Pillow's movement, and he also launched a feeble assault when he finally made one. The simultaneous attack by Pillow and Buckner against the Union line was a mirage. Pillow fought for three hours and traversed over a mile and a half of ground, pushing Federals while Buckner stayed in his trenches.[49]

Surprisingly, Buckner admitted it was only at Pillow's urging via a messenger at 9:00 a.m. that he finally moved against William Wallace's brigade. Buckner ordered Maj. W. L. Doss to send out two companies of the Fourteenth Mississippi as skirmishers. Buckner claimed Doss requested an officer to direct the movements of the regiment, and Maj. Alexander Casseday of Buckner's staff advanced with the force. Shortly after the skirmishers went out, Doss was ordered to attack a battery located four hundred yards away. His men marched partly up the hill and traded shots with the Federals for upward of an hour. Buckner ordered Maj. Nathaniel Cheairs of the Third Tennessee to support the Fourteenth Mississippi and attack the same battery. The Third Tennessee advanced to the left of the Fourteenth Mississippi and engaged the Federals for about forty-five minutes.[50]

Until around 10:00 a.m., the extent of Buckner's effort was sending two of his six regiments into battle and engaging Wallace's troops for approximately an hour. Buckner took heavy casualties in the fighting, and he was unable to reach the road. The Eighteenth Tennessee was moving forward to support the attack when Casseday, Buckner's appointed proxy, ordered the Fourteenth Mississippi and Third Tennessee to retreat. Doss wanted to rally his men on the Tennesseans and continue the fight, but Casseday insisted all three regiments return to the trenches.[51]

Buckner's men reentered the earthworks just as Pillow's Division drove the Union forces out of the crucial area of the Forge and Wynn's Ferry Roads. William Wallace watched in dismay as the support on his right disappeared. McClernand told him to hold as long as he could and gave him the authority to retreat when his position became untenable. Wallace saw that time was now, and he ordered his six regiments to withdraw west on the Wynn's Ferry Road with the intent of forming a new line of battle.[52]

When the men of the Thirty-First Illinois, the last of Oglesby's brigade, retreated, the intrepid Eleventh Illinois from Wallace's brigade moved to take their place. Forrest moved from the rebel left flank to the area of Buckner's Division near the Forge Road and set his sights on the beleaguered Eleventh Illinois. Forrest charged twice but was repulsed each time.[53]

The right regiments of Pillow's attack line stretched across the Forge Road and interposed themselves between William Wallace's defenders and Buckner's regiments still in the trenches. Col. Roger Hanson of the Second Kentucky observed the rebel assaults on the stubborn Eleventh Illinois from the trenches. Baldwin and McCausland approached Hanson with the disturbing news that unless they got ammunition and reinforcements, the Union troops might drive the rebels from the ground won. Ammunition was provided, and around noon Hanson sent for Buckner to get authorization to join in the fight.[54]

Pillow had requested the Second Kentucky for the breakout attack, and Buckner refused. It was now noon, and Pillow fought for six hours while the Second Kentucky never left the trenches. No word came from Buckner, so Hanson took it upon himself to advance against the Eleventh Illinois.[55] Unfortunately, the Eleventh did not receive the order to withdraw. As Wallace's other regiments retreated along the Wynn's Ferry Road, the left flank of the Eleventh Illinois was exposed, and Forrest saw it. Pillow's troops hit the Federals in the front and flank. With Oglesby and Cruft gone, rebels moved around and hit the Illinois troops from behind. Forrest's cavalry rushed around the left flank and also attacked from the rear, while the Second Kentucky hit from the front.[56]

But the Eleventh Illinois consisted of hard-dying men. Led by seriously wounded Col. Thomas Ransom, they fought their way through rebel infantry and cavalry and followed the retreat of Oglesby's brigade into Bufford Hollow. Pillow's Division swept the Union forces to the west and held the Forge Road. Wallace proceeded west with the infantry toward the position defended by the Illinois batteries of Capts. Edward McAllister, Jaspar Dresser, and Erza Taylor.[57]

Pillow reached the Forge Road area, where the plan called for Buckner to attack. The silence from Buckner's area was deafening. Pillow feared there had been a misapprehension of orders, and joined by Gilmer he rode to see why there was no activity in this portion of the field. Pillow did not find Buckner, but he found Buckner's Division in rear of the entrenchments behind a ridge, taking shelter from the fire of Wallace's batteries.[58]

Pillow's men started fighting just before 6:00 a.m., drove three Union brigades from the field, and pushed the Union right flank approximately a mile and a half west. Now, around noon, Pillow found Buckner's entire division still behind the entrenchments. Meanwhile, Pillow's own men cleared the enemy from the road in front of Buckner's troops. A furious and perplexed Pillow immediately ordered Col. Edward Cook to lead the Thirty-Second Tennessee regiment of Brown's Brigade across the entrenchments and attack the battery on the road.[59]

As Cook led his regiment across the entrenchments, Buckner and Brown appeared and inquired what he was doing. When Cook responded that Pillow had ordered him to attack the battery, Buckner instructed him to proceed and ordered the Eighteenth Tennessee to support the attack. Buckner explained to Pillow that he had made an attack with his two best regiments, but the units had retreated back to the trenches in the face of heavy musket fire and cannon shot. The men needed a little time to recover from their demoralization, and the officers were attempting to rally them.[60]

Buckner claimed he first opened up with artillery in order to silence the Union guns and soften up the support infantry. Since he was to serve as the rear guard, he thought it best not to attack until his artillery fire took effect. Of course, it never took effect. Southern guns were mostly short-range smoothbores, while the Union batteries had long-range rifled guns. Only furious infantry and cavalry attacks (by Pillow) silenced Union batteries.[61]

There are just two reports of Floyd being seen by anyone during the breakout attempt. A hospital steward claimed he saw Floyd with the brigade surgeon around 11:00 a.m. near the Wynn's Ferry Road egress through the trenches. Another witness saw an enthusiastic Floyd jump on the ramparts when the Second Kentucky moved out to attack McAllister's battery. "Now, Charge them boys," Floyd yelled, and he waved until someone pointed out he was exposed to fire, making him climb down. These two sightings place the commander behind the trenches with Buckner around five hours after Pillow launched his attack.[62]

Floyd approved the plan of attack, yet no evidence indicates he did anything to carry it out. He did nothing to get Buckner moving in conjunction with Pillow's attack per the strategy Buckner proposed. When Floyd jumped on the earthworks, he did so after Pillow's brigades had cleared the Yankees from the road in front of Buckner. At this point, the Forge Road was open, the Union soldiers were in retreat, and it was time for Floyd to show leadership and put the escape plan in effect. Instead, the army commander rode away from the critical point of the breakout operation. What could possibly go wrong?[63]

When Buckner got the 9:00 a.m. message from Pillow to attack the Union troops and batteries on the Wynn's Ferry Road, he sent forth the Fourteenth Mississippi and Third Tennessee. He left four other regiments in the trenches. Buckner did not lead the offensive or even monitor it. Instead, he assigned a staff officer to take charge of the assault. The two regiments fought about an hour, and then the staff officer (Casseday) ordered the entire attack force back to the trenches.[64]

The rebel attack plan is described as a massing of troops on the Confederate left to attack the Union right flank. Pillow's force totaled approximately 6,000 men. McClernand's division numbered 8,400 troops, a force augmented during the night with McArthur's brigade of 1,600 soldiers and Cruft's brigade of 2,000 men. Pillow's 6,000 combatants faced twice their number during the morning attack, and Buckner had 3,900 men under his command. Buckner's lack of aggression, along with Floyd's negligence, put the onus on Pillow to clear the Wynn's Ferry Road of Union regiments.[65]

Pillow did it. To his credit and that of the officers and men of his division, they pushed the Union right flank into Bufford Hollow and cleared the Wynn's Ferry Road for a distance of half a mile west of Forge Road. The rebels succeeded by constantly outflanking the Union regiments, causing them to use up all their ammunition and retreat.

William Wallace's batteries were clustered on the Wynn's Ferry Road, approximately three hundred yards west of where the road turned north to pass through the rebel entrenchments. As Wallace's regiments retreated westerly, the Union batteries became the next objective of the rebel attack.[66] While Pillow dispatched Forrest along the Wynn's Ferry Road, he ordered Buckner to send his troops into Erin Hollow and take the batteries on the ridge from the rear. Forrest charged the Union batteries and captured two of McAllister's guns as Buckner's men approached from Erin Hollow. Wallace then ordered a retreat, and the Union troops left before Buckner's men could engage them.[67]

Now the pursuit of the Union army became Buckner's focus. Forrest and his horsemen were still in the mix, but the rest of Pillow's Division was played out. Six hours of combat had disorganized and mixed up the regiments. Pillow's front grew to a mile in length and stretched from the Wynn's Ferry Road into Bufford Hollow.[68]

There was a lull in the fighting as Buckner directed Brown to pursue the fleeing Federals. The escape routes were opened, but a retreating foe is always a tempting target. In addition, the Wynn's Ferry Road rose in elevation to the west, and there was a natural tendency to want to occupy the high ground. Despite Buckner's lackadaisical effort that cost the rebels crucial time, their confidence was high as Brown, joined by Forrest and his cavalry, advanced to finish the rout of the Union right flank and center.

But Brig. Gen. Lew Wallace had a surprise waiting for them.

Alternate Decision and Scenario

The rebel attack plan lasted approximately thirty minutes. McArthur's brigade saw to that. The Confederates massed their forces on the left and eventually overwhelmed McClernand's division, but at the start McArthur's men stalled Pillow's advance for two hours. The fact that Pillow's attack bogged down at the beginning made it even more important that Buckner keep his promise and attack the center of the Union line. Three hours into the fight, it was Pillow's men that were fighting in the critical area just in front of Buckner's position.

The rebel army was in peril and needed an all-out attack on the Union army. Pillow fought with about one-third of the rebel force, while the other two-thirds stayed behind in the trenches. If Buckner had kept his promise, he could have sent three thousand attackers against McClernand's line in the critical area. Oglesby would have been hard pressed to shift any of his brigade to the right to confront Pillow's brigades that were flanking him. William Wallace's right regiments might have been occupied by Buckner's attack and unable to assist Oglesby's brigade.

McClernand's line might have been shattered by 9:00 a.m., before Lew Wallace could send reinforcements and Grant was even on the field. With the Forge Road open and Grant's right flank in disarray, the rebels could have commenced a retreat since it was early in the day. Smith would not have attacked the rebel right flank without orders, so troops west of Indian Creek could have headed to the escape routes.

If Buckner had kept his promise, the Confederate army might have made it to Nashville.

Lew Wallace Orders Thayer's Brigade to Stem the Rebel Tide

Situation

Lew Wallace stood near his tent and listened to battle sounds creep closer. He had no contact with Cruft's brigade and could only wonder what was happening. No guidance came from Grant, but his aide, Capt. John Rawlins, joined Wallace to discuss the situation. The road behind them showed an army in retreat. Yelling men rushed up the hill from Indian Creek Valley, followed by the sounds of wagon wheels and hoofbeats of horses. Worried that the stream of fugitives would cause Thayer's brigade to join in the exodus, Wallace sent an orderly to ride fast and bring back a report. The orderly recounted that the road was jammed with men, horses, and wagons, all headed in the direction of Wallace's command. It was obvious McClernand's division was in full retreat.[69]

Rawlins asked Wallace, "What are you going to do?"[70]

Options

Wallace had little time to weigh possible responses to Rawlins's question. He could hold his position and await developments, or he could retreat and join Smith's division to concentrate their forces. But rather than wait or withdraw, Wallace might advance his last brigade in the direction of the battle and engage the enemy.

Option 1

There had been no contact with Cruft's brigade, and Wallace was ignorant of the situation east of Indian Creek. He could hold Thayer's brigade in their position and wait for more information about the condition of McClernand's division, but the rabble of panicked soldiers could spread their panic to Wallace's men.

Option 2

The strength of the Confederate attack headed toward Wallace was unknown to him. He had just one brigade left, and he could retreat from his present position toward Smith's division to concentrate forces with it.

Option 3

Wallace could follow the military axiom of "move to the sound of the guns." Thayer's brigade was fresh, and it would be bad for morale to retreat from the enemy without a fight. It was obvious McClernand's division was in distress and needed additional assistance. Wallace could order his last brigade to march toward the enemy.

Decision

With little time to waste, Wallace ordered Thayer to march his brigade across Indian Creek Valley and advance against the rebels. Three additional regiments of reinforcements for Wallace's division had arrived and were attached to Thayer's command, giving the reinforcement column a total of seven regiments. The size of this force increased Wallace's confidence in the decision.

Col. John Thayer.

Results/Impact

Thayer put the First Nebraska in the lead, followed by the three Ohio regiments from Buell's department. Three Illinois regiments landed the morning of February 14 and spent the day marching toward and into the Union lines. On February 15 the early morning sounds of fighting hastened the units' efforts to report to Wallace. They arrived at an opportune time to join Thayer's brigade, which grew to seven regiments totaling approximately five thousand men.[71]

Wallace and his staff rushed ahead to get clear of the demoralized mob, soon passing through the walking wounded, wagons, and horses. It was a trying experience to advance toward a victorious foe while not knowing what lay ahead. After Lew Wallace crossed over the ridge east of Indian Creek, he started downhill and met William Wallace leading soldiers with no panic or undue haste in their walk.[72]

As Thayer's brigade crested the ridge and came into view, Lew Wallace asked William Wallace whether the rebels were coming. Told he just had time to form a battle line where he stood, Lew Wallace scanned the terrain and gratefully noticed he was on the crest of a small ridge that gave him the high-ground advantage. The decision to bring his artillery from Fort Henry was fortunate, and he sent an aide to Lieut. Peter Wood's First Illinois Light Artillery, Battery A with an order to come quick.[73]

Thayer quickly formed a line across the Wynn's Ferry Road stretching from Erin Hollow across the road, then extending toward Bufford Hollow. Wallace wrote that one of the most stirring sights of his life was the arrival of Pete Wood's battery under full gallop as its soldiers took position in the gap left for them across the road. To the left of Wood's battery were two guns from Taylor's battery. Taylor borrowed ammunition from Wood, and eight Union muzzles were ready to greet Brown's Brigade coming up the hill.[74]

Forrest ventured forth and sent out scouts to see what the Federals were doing. Reports came back that Union regiments and a battery were moving up the road from Fort Henry. The battle entered a crucial phase at this point. Union forces had retreated, and the rebel front was half a mile west of the Forge Road. Escape routes to Nashville were open, but flaws in the escape plan surfaced, as each Confederate general had a different vision of what should happen next.[75]

Forrest informed Pillow of the position of the Union force. Pillow and Buckner ordered the attack to continue. Brown directed his brigade to assault the next line of Union defense, and the soldiers straddled the road and advanced fervently toward Thayer's line.[76]

Floyd had watched with satisfaction as the rebels cleared the Union troops from the Wynn's Ferry Road. He ordered Buckner to hold the road to prevent the Federals from reoccupying the ground now held by the Confederates. Floyd did not expect to retreat toward Nashville until the next day. Any delay to the rebel army's withdrawal played into Grant's hands.[77] Then Floyd

Wynn's Ferry Road. Looking east from Bomba Lane, Thayer's brigade blocked the road in the vicinity where the view of the road ends.

committed another blunder, leaving the crucial area of the battlefield to see whether things were secure on the right. He intended to move the whole army southward into the country past the Randolph Forge on the Forge Road. If the whole army was to retreat, it made no sense to defend areas farthest from the escape routes. However, no orders to prepare for departure were given to the men at the water batteries and inside the fort, and the right-side earthworks, because Floyd overlooked a Union counterattack.[78]

Buckner ordered his three remaining regiments and artillery forward to consolidate his division to hold the Wynn's Ferry Road. Heiman realized there was no enemy to his front, and he ordered two of his regiments to support Buckner's advance. Nearly five thousand Confederates moved westward toward Thayer's line.[79]

Brown's skirmishers could not ascertain the position and number of Union defenders due to trees and thick undergrowth. The rebels moved by column until they were near enough to engage the enemy and were then ordered to deploy and storm the battery.[80] But it was not to be. When the rebels came into view, Wood's battery and the First Nebraska opened fire. But the terrific barrage of grape and musketry launched against the Confederates mostly passed over their heads. Col. Joseph Palmer lamented that he and his comrades of the Eighteenth Tennessee were met by heavy fire as they started to deploy. A member of the regiment shuddered "at the awful condition" the unit found itself in that day.[81]

A newspaperman reported that the rebels came screaming up the road under the belief the Union troops were in retreat. The rebel attack centered on the battery and the First Nebraska, as Wallace marveled how the Nebraskans loaded and fired their muskets as if they were on the parade ground.[82]

The two combatants faced off for approximately three-quarters of an hour. The rebels kept trying to form their lines but fell back a couple of times. On the third attempt, Lieut. Col. Thomas M. Gordon of the Third Tennessee was wounded, and the regiment's men retreated 150 yards in confusion until Col. Brown rallied them. However, the other two regiments also withdrew to seek the protection of a hill, where the soldiers worked to put their old, wet flintlocks back into working order.[83]

Brown's Brigade prepared to renew the assault, and Buckner waited for the rest of his infantry and artillery to arrive. Then the Confederates had to decide whether to pursue the Federals or defend the position as ordered by Floyd.[84]

Wallace concluded the enemy had been repelled because the fighting ceased and the rebels did not return. He marveled at the small damage done to his division owing to its advantageous uphill position and the rebels' lack

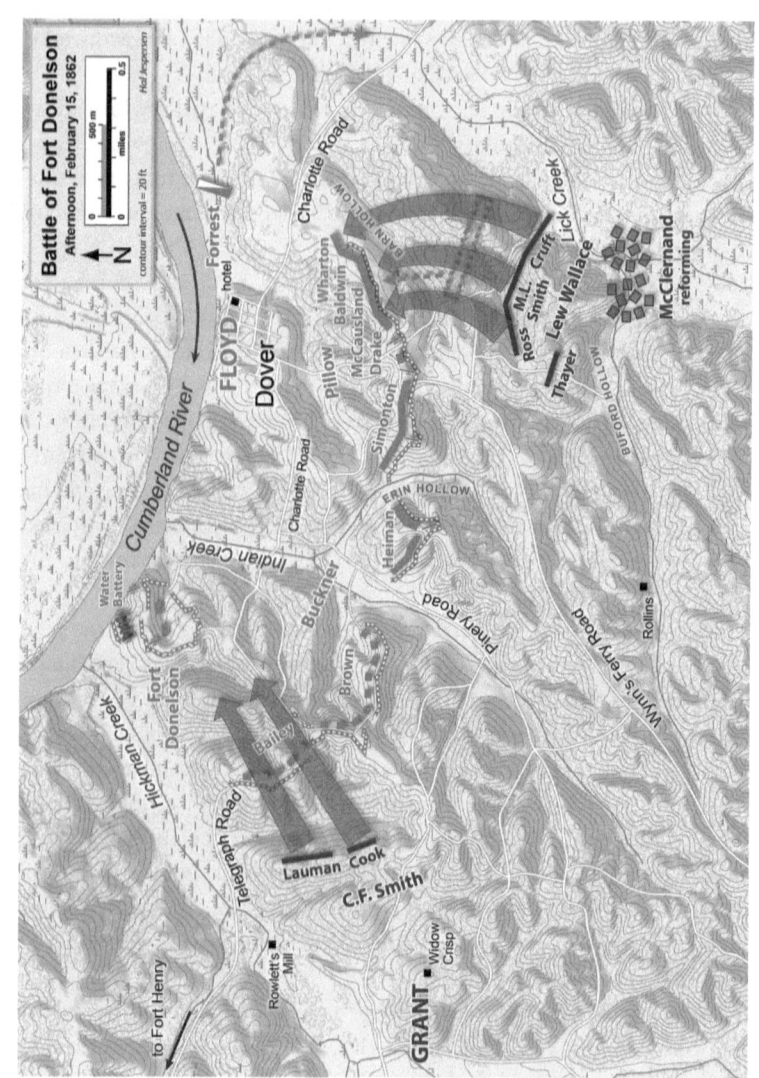

Afternoon, February 15
Map by Hal Jespersen, www.cwmaps.com.

of enthusiasm. The battery had just three men wounded, while the First Nebraska had three killed and seven wounded.[85]

The rebel offensive ended when Brown's Brigade retreated from its position in front of Thayer's. The breakout attack successively drove back regiments in the Union right flank for about a mile and a half, and the escape routes were opened. But time was not on the Confederates' side. Up to this moment they had the initiative, and Grant's army was bruised but not destroyed.[86]

Grant was not on the field to give orders in response to the disastrous rebel attack. Floyd and Buckner understood the ground gained should be defended, but Floyd did not appreciate the urgency to escape before the Yankees regrouped. Floyd visualized holding on to the fort for the night and leaving in the morning.

The fortunes of the day turned with the arrival of Thayer's brigade across the path of the victorious Confederate assault. Wallace first sent Cruft's brigade, which slowed the rebel attack, and then Thayer's brigade stopped it. McClernand's division was scattered and needed time to re-form and obtain ammunition. The two sides fought for over seven hours, and both armies were spent, but the roads to Nashville were clear of Union troops.

Seeing that Buckner's failure to take the battery had ended the quest to destroy Grant's army, Pillow called off any further pursuit. The armies still faced each other, and a decision had to be made on what to do next. With severe consequences, Floyd was not around to make that decision, and Pillow ranked Buckner.

Pillow Orders the Rebels to Return to the Entrenchments

Situation

Pillow rode to the hill where Maney's battery stood and Heiman's Brigade manned the trenches. He had a good view of the attack on McAllister's battery, and he watched as William Wallace's brigade withdrew west on the Wynn's Ferry Road. In a telegram to Johnston at Nashville, Pillow claimed victory on his honor as a soldier.[87] But Pillow's Division was out of steam. The rebel regiments were scattered, mixed up, short of ammunition, tired, and cold. The line south of the Wynn's Ferry Road stretched for approximately one mile into Bufford Hollow, where Cruft's brigade stood in front of a Union hospital. McClernand's brigades were re-forming their ranks and getting cartridges.[88]

Bushrod Johnson wanted to keep the attack going but needed reinforcements. The rebels' line was stretched so thin they could not make a massed attack, and there were no reserves to throw against what was left of the Union defenders. Sporadic skirmishing continued, but the rebels could advance no farther. Johnson did not get any additional troops.[89]

Wynn's Ferry Road became the center of attention. Pillow claimed his and Buckner's forces united in pursuit of the Federals and fought for nearly an hour against large numbers of fresh troops. Brown's Brigade attacked Thayer, while Pillow's men advanced adjacent to Brown's left flank but did not become heavily engaged.[90]

In their official reports, Pillow, Buckner, Brown, Cheairs, Palmer, and Cook all claimed the soldiers of Thayer's brigade retreated after the rebels attacked them. But these officers also stated that the Confederates retreated and took refuge behind a ridge while they cleaned and dried their old flintlock muskets in preparation for continuing the fight. Brown claimed he was getting ready to resume the pursuit, while Thayer boasted he would have put the bayonet to the rebels except that the thick underbrush prevented it.[91]

At approximately 1:00 p.m. Buckner's forward progress ended. The Confederates had to decide whether the attack on Lew Wallace should continue. Buckner called for the rest of his infantry and artillery to move forward, but Floyd was absent while Pillow was present. Floyd had ordered Buckner to hold the Wynn's Ferry Road, but he apparently did not tell Pillow about his instructions to Buckner. The three generals' ineptness with communication defies description. Pillow led the breakout attack and took the prerogative to decide the next move once the offensive sputtered to a stop.[92]

Options

Assuming authority to decide what to do next, Pillow assessed the options. He might allow Buckner to try again to attack Thayer on the Wynn's Ferry Road. With the Forge Road open, Pillow could confirm Floyd's order for Buckner to hold the Wynn's Ferry Road. Or, based on his understanding of the plan, Pillow could stop the fighting and have all the rebel forces return to the entrenchments from which they started in the morning.

Option 1

Buckner's men were relatively fresh compared with Pillow's. Pillow could let Buckner continue the assault on Grant's army in an attempt to further damage the Union forces.

Option 2

Pillow could order Buckner to hold the Wynn's Ferry Road while the rest of the army prepared to evacuate Fort Donelson and Dover to join Johnston in Nashville.

Option 3

Once Pillow realized Grant's army could not be pushed any farther, he believed the Southern troops would return to the trenches to prepare to evacuate Fort Donelson and Dover. After Thayer's brigade stopped the rebels' progress, Pillow could order Buckner and all the other troops back to the entrenchments, even though that meant the Federals could reoccupy the ground they lost in the morning.

Decision

To the disbelief of Buckner, the consternation of Floyd, and the bewilderment of military authorities and historians over the last 160 years, Pillow ordered the rebels to give up all their hard-fought gains. The Confederates returned to their original positions in the earthworks, the positions from which they had moved in the early morning hours.

Results/Impact

In his first battle report, Pillow did not acknowledge the attack had been stopped by a large number of fresh troops. He only noted that further pursuit was called off after seven and a half hours of bloody fighting. Orders then went to all the commands to immediately retire from the battlefield. Soldiers went back to their original early morning positions in the trenches. Pillow later admitted that Buckner did not carry the battery, and that Thayer's brigade stopped the pursuit.[93]

Buckner was preparing to defend his position when he received reiterative orders from Pillow to return to the entrenchments he had held the day before. Buckner had called for his infantry and artillery, over a half mile in the rear, to join him and defend the road. However, Pillow intercepted these units and ordered them to reoccupy the trenches on the right. Maj. Cheairs, now commanding the Third Tennessee, felt Pillow's wrath when he contended that Buckner told him to hold his position. Pillow rose from the saddle and told Cheairs to obey the order because he was the general in command at Donelson.[94]

Pillow's Division had pushed the Union regiments into Bufford Hollow, and the antagonists faced off in a line stretching approximately three-quarters of a mile from a point south of the Wynn's Ferry Road to across the road that ran through Bufford Hollow. The brigades of Simonton, McCausland,

Baldwin, and Wharton were in line starting south of the Wynn's Ferry Road. They had fought their way for one and a half miles through hilly terrain, trees, and thick underbrush. The brigades were low on ammunition, and the Union troops disappeared in front of them. The Confederate advance came to a halt because the enemy fled and there were no orders to keep up the pursuit.[95]

Battered but still organized, Cruft's brigade formed a line across the road in Bufford Hollow. Opposed to Cruft were Drake's Brigade and the Twentieth Mississippi regiment. Johnson still had fight left and eyed Cruft's brigade as a target.[96]

When Pillow issued his order to return to the trenches, just one-half of the attack force was unprepared to retreat from the field. Excluding Forrest's cavalry, Pillow started with approximately 5,400 infantry, 800 of which came from Baldwin's two regiments. These 800 attacked carrying blankets and knapsacks in preparation to retreat from the field. That left 4,600 men that needed to return to the trenches. Buckner had 3,900 men in his division. The rebels had 4,700 men ready to leave from the battlefield. Some of Buckner's men left their knapsacks and blankets behind the fortifications when they attacked, intending to retrieve their equipment later.[97]

Buckner and his men were not demoralized by the unsuccessful attack on Thayer's brigade, as evidenced by Brown rallying the brigade to try again. Pillow later blamed the Confederates' failure to rout the Union army on their failure to take Thayer's battery. Had Buckner been successful, the rebels would have gained the high ridge overlooking the Indian Creek Valley. In this event, the rebels would have had a good defensive line, but the Union army still had Smith's division, and the other units were reorganizing. However, the Confederates could have started a retreat, and the Union army would have been hard pressed to prevent it.[98]

Despite his disagreement with the order and previous personal conflicts with Pillow, Buckner reluctantly started his command to the trenches. He did not seek out either Floyd or Pillow before moving his troops. As Buckner directed his men toward their destination, Floyd rode up and inquired why the soldiers were moving away from the Wynn's Ferry Road. Floyd expressed surprise when Buckner explained the order from Pillow.[99]

Alternate Decision and Scenario

Pillow observed Buckner's attack on Thayer's line from the prominent point where Maney's battery was located. From there, Pillow could see Smith's position and the view back along the rebel trench line to Forge Road, approximately one mile away. Grant was not on the field. Smith was ensconced in his trenches waiting for an order, while McClernand's division was shattered and reorganizing. Lew Wallace was content to have stopped the rebel breakout attack, and taking the offensive had to wait for orders from Grant.

It is one thing to retreat as a defeated army and another to retreat as a victorious one. If Pillow had recognized the importance of holding the ground won while commencing an immediate withdrawal, he would have allowed Buckner to consolidate his division. Buckner's men could then have served as a rear guard while the soldiers in Pillow's Division withdrew to the trenches and retrieved their blankets and knapsacks. Heiman's Brigade and Forrest's cavalry were in position to also serve as rear guards. The artillerymen and troops west of Indian Creek could have commenced a retrograde movement to join the army east of Indian Creek.

When he finally arrived, Grant would have found a victorious Confederate army on the move with an established rear guard. The terrain and lack of roads in the forest would have prevented him from striking at the enemy's flanks. A frontal assault would push the rebels in the direction they wanted to go. On the ridges and in the forest, a Union advance would have been slow for fear of ambush from soldiers whose uniforms blended in with the trees.

As long as the Confederates were outside the trenches, Grant had to respond to them. One can envision numerous scenarios of the result had Pillow not ordered Buckner back to the trenches, but the capture of eleven thousand five hundred rebel soldiers is not one of them. The two steamboats were available to transport men across the river or beyond Lick Creek. Rebel doctors and assistants could have remained to treat the wounded. Grant probably would have picked up some prisoners, but the rebel soldier was resilient and could have found a way to avoid capture if given the opportunity.

Floyd Sustains Pillow's Order to Buckner

Situation

Floyd asked Buckner his opinion about Pillow's order to return to the trenches. Buckner responded that the necessity of evacuating the fort was still paramount. The mission of the day was accomplished, as the road was open; the army should immediately take the opportunity to escape. Floyd seemed in agreement. Forty-seven years later, an aged Buckner added that he told Floyd the order meant the surrender of the army.[100]

Telling Buckner to halt his troops, Floyd in the meantime found Pillow to discuss the order with him. He thought Pillow must have misapprehended previous orders given. When Floyd caught up with Pillow, he bellowed, "In the name of God, General Pillow, what have we been fighting all day for?

Certainly not to show our powers, but solely to secure the Wynn's Ferry Road, and now after securing it, you order it to be given up."[101]

Floyd put the emphasis on securing the Wynn's Ferry Road, not on starting a retreat from the battlefield. His wishful thinking was that Buckner would hold the Wynn's Ferry Road through the night, and then the whole army would march out to the south on the Forge Road in the morning. Floyd felt no urgency to get the army moving immediately, and no troops in the fort proper, the water batteries, or west of Indian Creek needed to be sacrificed.[102]

The rebel commanders sold their soldiers short. First, Buckner claimed his men were demoralized after their attack against William Wallace's infantry and batteries in midmorning. They needed time to recuperate. Now, Pillow gave Floyd the lame explanation that fresh Union reinforcements were on the way, and that Buckner's men were not fit to fight them because Brown's Brigade had been repulsed and disheartened by Thayer's force. Buckner awaited word on what to do, as Floyd listened to Pillow explain why he ordered Buckner to return to the trenches.[103]

Options

Floyd could countermand Pillow's order and stay with the plan to have Buckner hold the Wynn's Ferry Road, or he could accede to Pillow's argument that all the troops should return to the trenches.

Option 1

Pillow's order contradicted Floyd's instructions to Buckner. Floyd listened to Pillow's arguments for sending Buckner back to the trenches, but he could instead order Buckner to remain on, and hold, the Wynn's Ferry Road.

Option 2

According to Floyd, possession of the Wynn's Ferry Road was the objective of the breakout attack, and he had ordered Buckner to hold it. Floyd chose to get Pillow's explanation for the movement rather than immediately countermanding the order. After hearing the explanation, Floyd could accede to Pillow's directive and have Buckner complete the withdrawal from the Wynn's Ferry Road back to the trenches.

Decision

Floyd listened to Pillow and then directed Buckner to return to the trenches. Floyd's weak justification for this decision was that Buckner had already almost completed the movement, and it was too late to reverse Pillow's order.

Results/Impact

Pillow crowed over persuading Floyd that his decision was best and convincing him to approve the order. However, Floyd explained that he sent Buckner back to the trenches not because he thought Pillow was right, but because Buckner had almost finished the movement. Moreover, the enemy was seen making preparations to attack the fortifications on the right.[104]

An anxious Buckner finally received a response from Floyd; he was to return to the trenches as quickly as possible because the position on the right was under threat of attack. Buckner's Division would end the day in the same position in which it had started approximately twelve hours earlier. This disastrous result was caused by incomplete planning that failed to account for how the army would retreat to Nashville once the escape route via the Forge Road was opened. The objective was to save the army, not hold the fort. When the breakout attack was planned, any thoughts on how to extricate the men at the water batteries and the fort proper were ignored. Pillow used the lack of orders to Heiman's Brigade and the troops west of flooded Indian Creek as one of the justifications for recalling the whole army to the trenches.[105]

The stalled brigades waited for orders whether to continue the pursuit. Simonton waited a considerable time until he received word to return to the rifle pits. Wharton got the same order, and McCausland noted that Pillow sent him back to the trenches. Baldwin did not receive an order, but when he noticed the other brigades were withdrawn, he led his regiments back to the lines.[106]

Johnson received no orders but saw that there was no longer support on his right. He wanted to continue the fight with Drake's Brigade against Cruft, so he sent a request back to the trenches for reinforcements. Rather than more troops, Johnson was ordered to report to Floyd for instructions.[107]

The rebel high command determined all ground won by the Confederates since early morning should be abandoned. It was Floyd who informed Johnson that all the brigades except Drake's should immediately take positions back in the fortifications. Drake's men should be displayed before the enemy for a time before returning to the trenches. These mindless orders did nothing to further the escape of the army.[108]

Each of the three generals had a different notion of what the rebel attack was to accomplish. Pillow assumed the Union army would be so decimated that the Confederates would have time to return to the trenches, gather equipment and supplies, and retreat at their leisure. Floyd figured they would hold the Wynn's Ferry Road open till next morning, when the whole army would just march out. Buckner thought he would drive the enemy back along the Wynn's Ferry Road, open the escape routes, and then serve as the rear guard while the army retreated to Nashville. Between the three of them, they ended up losing the army. The catalyst for the loss was Pillow being in the position to order all the attack force to return to the trenches per his own conception of the plan. But subsequent decisions by Floyd and Buckner led to the surrender.

Floyd later argued that Pillow put him in an impossible situation, because Buckner had nearly completed his return to the trenches before Floyd became aware of the withdrawal from the Wynn's Ferry Road. But Floyd stopped Buckner and told him to await further orders. Lew Wallace and McClernand were satisfied with blocking the breakout attempt and wondered what to do next. Wallace did not immediately advance down the Wynn's Ferry Road. Buckner could have set up a defensive line farther toward the Forge Road, but Floyd ordered Buckner to comply with Pillow's order because the rifle pits on the rebel right were threatened.[109]

The need to hold the fort and the water batteries late in the afternoon should have vanished with the escape plan. The trenches could have been defended with only the men available west of Indian Creek, including the two regiments left in the fort that served no purpose. All the forces west of Indian Creek could have been given orders to withdraw toward Dover if they could not hold their positions. Floyd and Buckner were remiss instructing Heiman and Head to retreat to the fort if overrun.[110]

The water battery artillery crews spent the night preparing for another attack. To save the gun crews, it was necessary for the whole army to retreat quickly to get out of range of the gunboats' cannon. Once the bluecoats were aware the water batteries were abandoned, gunboats would sail up the river. The gun crews could only be saved if the army started retreating as soon as escape routes were opened.[111]

Floyd's idea he could hold all the entrenchments, the water batteries, and the fort and then retreat in the morning was overly optimistic. Floyd and Pillow commanded with no sense of urgency in starting the retreat of the army. Pillow ordered Forrest to collect weapons from the battlefield while the wounded were gathered and put on the steamers. Tending to the wounded was a moral obligation, but it should not have taken precedence over the escape of the army.[112]

Buckner's men were ready to escape, but they fought with the understanding they would be the rear guard. Pillow's Division needed to return to the trenches so troops could retrieve their equipment and supplies; but Buckner's did not. For soldiers who went into battle unencumbered with equipment, the lack of preparation for them to return to the trenches for filled knapsacks and blankets and immediately commence retreat defies analysis. The rebels spent blood winning the ground. Instead of just giving that ground up, they should have made the Federals spend blood to retake it.

When their entire attack force returned to the entrenchments, the rebels gave up the initiative. Most of the Confederate success was due to the bravery and pluck of their soldiers. They drove an obstinate foe from the field, but once they got behind the entrenchments again, the advantage transferred to the Union army. The Union commanders watched the rebels retreat back to their lines instead of escaping. Now the Federals could decide how to capture them.

Grant Orders Counterattacks

Situation

When Grant returned to shore after meeting Foote, he had no intimation of the battle raging in the hills and snow south of Dover. He was in a pensive mood, focusing on the siege of Fort Donelson he would have to initiate. But that soon changed.[113]

The exact time when Grant's headquarters staff realized someone should probably ride to the landing and inform the general the right flank of his army was being destroyed is not known. The time at which McClernand and Wallace sent messengers to headquarters looking for Grant is also unknown. When he reached shore, Capt. Hillyer brought news the rebels had attacked McClernand's division, scattering it and putting the right flank into full retreat.[114]

No participant left an account that explained why Grant spent hours on the flagship with Foote. This blunder threatened Grant's command. Early accounts written by newspapermen and supporters like Albert Richardson and Adam Badeau shielded Grant's reputation by claiming falsely that he was at his headquarters by 9:00 a.m. A time between 1:00 p.m. and 2:00 p.m. is closer to the truth. In his memoirs, Grant made no mention of how long he was gone or when he reached headquarters.[115]

Grant rode to the battlefield as rapidly as possible over the frozen road. He stopped by headquarters and then hurried to see Smith, who showed little concern over what was happening on the right. Messengers from McClernand requesting assistance were dismissed as outside his standing orders.[116]

Smith's division spent the day skirmishing and firing artillery at the Confederates, but the troops otherwise remained quiet under Grant's orders. Men in the division heard the raging contest and were befuddled by their hours of inactivity. The Twelfth Iowa's regimental historian summarized their frustration: "The men of this division had heard the terrible roar of the conflict as it approached from the right; had listened with bated breath and clasped

Brig. Gen. Charles Ferguson Smith.

musket waiting orders which would send them to the help of their comrades but as yet had been unable to take any active part in the fray."[117]

Morgan Smith's small brigade had joined Charles Ferguson Smith's division the previous day and remained in reserve. Now Grant arrived with warnings of the collapse on the right and ordered Charles Ferguson Smith to send Morgan Smith to McClernand. Grant then set off for McClernand's sector.[118]

McClernand had searched out Wallace to decide what to do next. The tardy army commander finally arrived and joined the other officers. McClernand saw Grant and voiced frustration in his greeting: "This army wants a head." "It appears so," Grant replied. Wallace noticed Grant carried dispatches in his hand and was accompanied by Col. Joesph D. Webster.[119]

Grant fought to keep his composure and spoke of the necessity to withdraw beyond the range of the fort's guns, dig in, and wait for reinforcements that were on the way. When he arrived on the right, the fighting was over and the rebels had withdrawn to their trenches. Grant did not yet grasp that McClernand's retreat left the escape routes in the hands of the Confederates. Wallace pointed out that the Federals no longer had any men on the right, adding that the escape road to Clarksville was open. Moving the Union line farther back would increase the chance the rebels could get away during the night.[120]

Wallace saw Grant's face redden. Grant had a decision to make, and quickly.[121]

Options

Grant quickly analyzed his options. He might settle in for a siege of Fort Donelson until Foote returned with new and repaired gunboats and mortar boats. With the escape routes open and the enemy retreating back to their trenches, he could also counterattack the rebels' weakened right flank and attempt to retake the Wynn's Ferry Road.

Option 1

Lacking confidence he could carry the fortifications with his green troops, Grant wanted the support of the gunboats. He could order the Union forces to take position out of range of the batteries in the fort and wait for Foote's return and more reinforcements.

Option 2

Prior to meeting Wallace and McClernand, Grant focused on the necessity of a siege. To conduct a siege and block the escape routes, Union forces had to retake the ground lost on the right. Grant could order counterattacks on the left to seize Fort Donelson and on the right to reclaim the lost terrain.

Decision

Grant's choice showed the necessity for an army to have one general in command. Watching the victorious Confederates retreat to their fortifications, Grant seized the opportunity to strike back. McClernand's division was disorganized, but Lew Wallace's and Charles Ferguson Smith's were ready to fight. Grant ordered McClernand and Wallace to take back the Wynn's Ferry Road, and he then rode to Smith and ordered him to attack Fort Donelson.

Results/Impact

In a flash Grant's focus switched from defensive mode to aggressive mode: the Union army would strike back at each flank of the rebel earthworks. Grant and Webster quickly rode to give Smith orders to attack. With no time to reorganize his men into an attacking force, McClernand turned to Wallace to counterattack with his division. Grant made no reference in his memoirs to the conversation with Wallace and McClernand where he changed his mind about a siege and ordered McClernand to take back the road he lost.[122]

Wallace connected with the wayward Cruft and swiftly formed an assault force. Morgan Smith's brigade appeared, and Wallace made that unit the spearpoint for the attack. Col. Leonard F. Ross reported with McClernand's Third Brigade to augment the available force. Thayer's brigade stayed blocking

Grant Arrives

the Wynn's Ferry Road, except the Fifty-Eighth Illinois joined Wallace's assault team for a total of nine regiments.[123]

Wallace was ignorant of the terrain he had to conquer. The Wynn's Ferry Road turned north into Dover approximately five hundred yards west of the Forge Road, so taking it back did not block the Confederate exits of Forge Road and Charlotte Road. Rebels from Drake's Brigade were visible on the ridge opposite Cruft's brigade. Wallace scouted the ground to determine where to launch the attack. Morgan Smith's brigade would lead the assault out of Bufford Hollow, with Cruft providing support with a portion of his brigade. The balance of Cruft's brigade would attack to the right of Smith's brigade. On Cruft's right, Col. T. Lyle Dickey, leading the Fourth Illinois cavalry, dismounted his men and had them fight as infantry. Ross gave support to the left of Smith's brigade.[124]

Wallace ordered the advance with two hours of daylight left, and Morgan Smith sent his men forward while Wallace rode with Ross to put that brigade in position. Morgan Smith gave the honor of leading the column to the Eighth Missouri, followed by the Eleventh Indiana. Wallace rode to a clearing with a good view of the battlefield.[125]

Over a thousand men climbed the slippery slope in bursts of movement. They could see Morgan Smith, who remained exposed on horseback, cheering them on and giving them confidence. Cruft and Ross put their brigades in motion when they saw Smith start up the rocky hill. Wallace observed the progress of all three units as they inched upward and approached the crest of the hill from which Drake's Brigade fired down on them. Then he became aware of the sounds of musketry and artillery from the Union left—Charles Ferguson Smith's attack was underway. As they neared the top of the hill, the rebels unleashed a furious fire, but it was answered by the first volley from Morgan Smith's brigade. With their goal within reach, the men scrambled forward on hands and knees as Cruft's and Ross's brigades also neared the summit. Wallace left his observation point and hastened to join his command at the top of the hill.[126]

Bushrod Johnson observed the attack against Drake from the trenches and ordered Forrest to go forward with the cavalry and offer support. But with ammunition running low, Drake's Brigade could not stand a prolonged fight once the Union men crested the hill. The rebels gave way rapidly toward the entrenchments with the Yankees in pursuit.[127]

Meanwhile, Grant had rushed to headquarters and sent a message to Foote informing him a terrible battle had ensued that demoralized a portion of Grant's command. If Foote would send some gunboats and shell the fort, it might help gain a victory. If not, all might be defeated. To raise the spirits

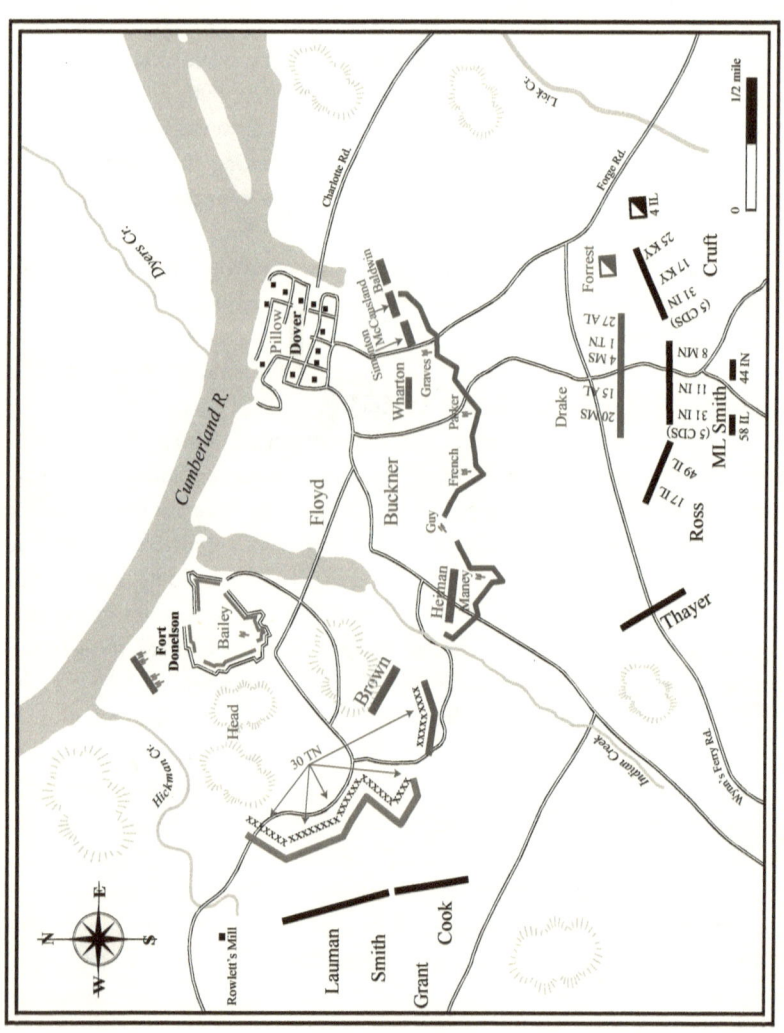

Lew Wallace's Counterattack

Col. James Tuttle.

of his demoralized army, Grant explained, "I must order a charge to save appearances." Foote had already left for Cairo, so Commander Benjamin M. Dove acted on the message. Grant then hurried to give orders to Charles Ferguson Smith.[128]

Smith was sitting under a tree when Grant rode up and exclaimed everything had failed on the right. When Grant said Smith must save the day and take the fort, Smith exclaimed, "I will do it." As Smith determined the best chance for success was on the far-left flank, the Second Iowa got the honor because it was in that position. The artillery opened a barrage, and Smith rode up to the troops' colonel, James Madison Tuttle, and laid out what he wanted them to do. Smith ordered the soldiers to remove the caps from their guns and make the charge at the point of the bayonet. The men were not to slow down to fire their weapons during the charge. Not until they broke through the rebels' lines were they to shoot. All along the line regiments prepared to advance and sent out skirmishers in support of the Second Iowa.[129]

The regiment was divided into two wings of five companies each. Col. Tuttle commanded the left wing leading the assault on foot, while the right wing, commanded by Lieut. Col. James Baker, followed in support 150 yards behind. Smith took a position in front of Baker's battalion to join the ascent. He made a conspicuous target on horseback and shouted encouragement and blasphemies as the battalion climbed toward the rebel trenches. Cook's brigade made a feint attack to Lauman's right to freeze rebel defenders in place. Tuttle advanced his battalion across the ravine, tore down a rail fence, and started up the slope, which for two hundred yards consisted of open woods.

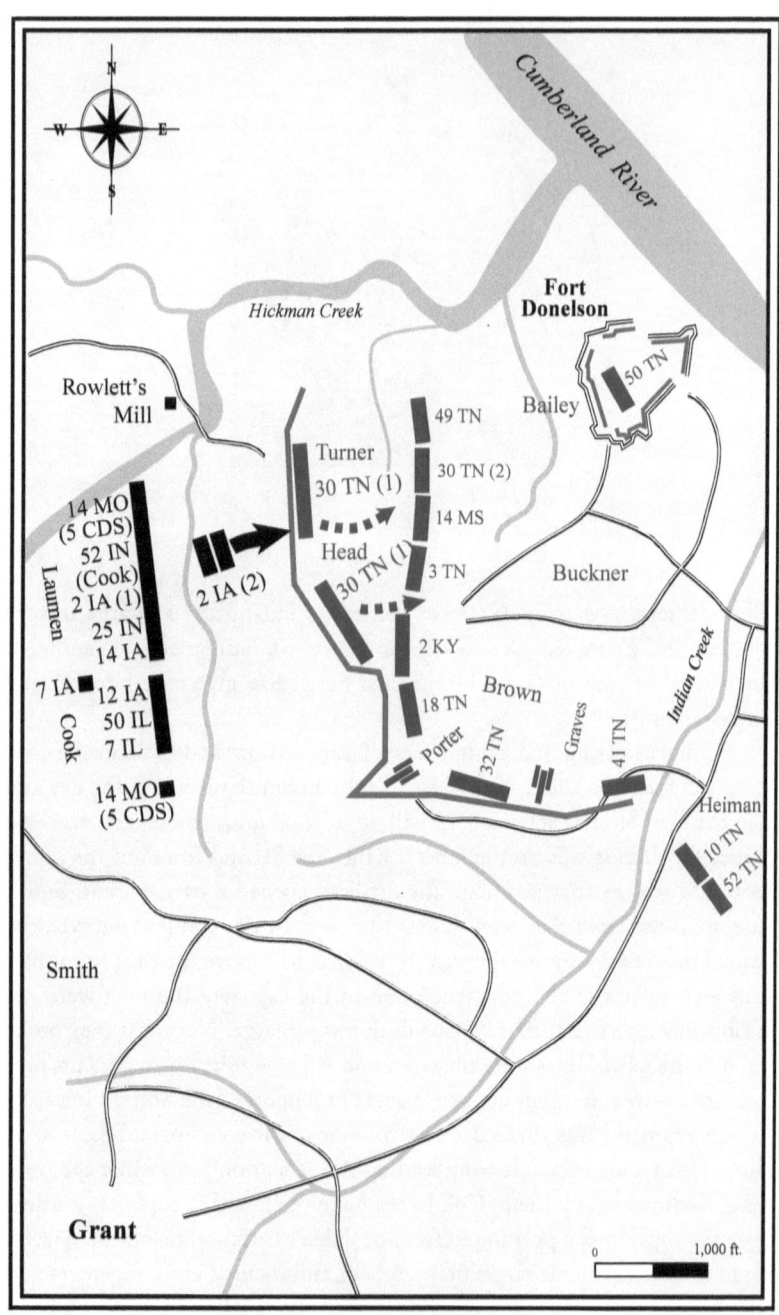

Smith's Attack

Then the troops encountered the abatis, and the rebel works came into view. The Iowa soldiers saw the entrenchments extended far to the left and right of their column. The distance to the earthworks was down to 150 yards of fallen trees when the waiting rebels opened fire, their bullets flying through the trees and dropping twigs and leaves on the men.[130]

Tuttle encouraged the men through the fallen trees at great cost. The attackers reached the open space in front of the breastworks, and he yelled for them to go right over the top. Six color-bearers bore the Iowa colors up the slope; five of them did not make it. The sixth, Volare Twombly, planted the flag on the top of the breastworks and received the Medal of Honor in 1897 for doing so. Smith described the charge as gallantly performed in an awesome display of soldierly conduct. The Confederates saw they could not hold the line, so they turned to retreat through a ravine and up the slope to form another line five hundred yards to the rear. Finally, the Iowans could fire their muskets and aimed at the fleeing Confederates. The two Iowan battalions joined in an immediate charge toward the second rebel line.[131]

The rebels should have ordered more men to hold the trenches. Fortunately for the Union cause, only three companies manned the trenches in front of Tuttle's charge. Confederate command left two regiments in the fort that were sorely needed on the front lines.

Lauman's other regiments quickly reached the rebel entrenchments, and half of Cook's brigade passed through the abatis into the rebel earthworks. Setting their sights on the new rebel line, the soldiers of the Second Iowa crossed the ravine and moved up the slope but found a stronger enemy defense. Buckner's regiments returned to join Head's meager numbers. Troops in the Second Kentucky tried to reclaim their spot in the trenches they had held in the morning, but they were too late. The Kentuckians were pushed back, and they formed a line with other Buckner regiments that rushed to contain the Union breakthrough. In addition, Head ordered the Forty-Ninth Tennessee and half of the Fiftieth from the fort to confront the Union attack.[132]

Fighting raged for over an hour, but the Second Iowa could make no additional headway. Rebel artillery bombarded the Union lines while the Federals brought artillery into position in the captured trenches. Night ended the fighting, and the Union troops retired to the captured earthworks. Although Buckner could not retake the lost entrenchments, he managed to form a line consisting of four regiments and two half-regiment battalions plus artillery. Col. Hanson of the Second Kentucky stated the line was stronger than the one the Confederates had lost.[133]

The charge of the Second Iowa at Fort Donelson is one of the most iconic events of the Civil War. According to Halleck, the men in the Second proved to be "the bravest of the brave." Historians heaped accolades on Smith while ignoring Tuttle, but Smith made it clear the unit's soldiers charged up the slope, led by their colonel. In a letter to his wife, Smith assured her he was not the first man to enter the entrenchments, but instead followed the storming party closely into the works.[134]

Although Smith's division did not capture the fort, its men seized the last six hundred yards of earthworks on the Confederate right flank. The Second Iowa suffered nearly two hundred casualties attacking three companies armed mostly with shotguns in the rebel trenches and the assault across the ravine against the stronger second line. Buckner had positioned the equivalent of five regiments plus artillery on top of the ridge. Grant concluded the rebels were demoralized, since they made a breakout attempt and returned to their works instead of heading for Nashville. One can only surmise how many casualties Union forces would have suffered with an assault across the deep ravine, for the Confederate soldiers would have offered a stout defense.[135]

As Smith's men consolidated their position, Wallace completed retaking Wynn's Ferry Road. Drake's men put up a spirited defense, but Union troops flanked them on both ends. Then the bluecoats pursued the retreating rebels, and Wallace feared the men might follow them into the trenches. He therefore slowed the advance with skirmishers thrown out in front. Wallace's men passed by the dead and wounded of the morning's battle, and the enemy's earthworks came into view, stretching far to the left and right.[136]

Once Drake's men got inside the trenches, rebel artillery shelled the Federals. Approximately three hundred yards from the earthworks, Wallace thought briefly of continuing the attack but doubted he had authority to keep going. He left a screen of skirmishers and ordered his men to fall back behind the ridge and bivouac for the night in anticipation of attacking the earthworks in the morning. A note from Hillyer on February 16 credited Wallace with saving the day on the right.[137]

Wallace stated the Confederates surrendered the next day because he had secured the Wynn's Ferry Road. However, the situation was not that simple. A combination of factors ended with that result. Interestingly, Grant made no mention in his memoirs of Wallace ending the day astride the Wynn's Ferry Road. Instead, Grant gave sole credit to Charles Ferguson Smith for the fort's capitulation.[138]

Grant did not think the rebels would attack his army to open the escape routes, and he had over 2,600 casualties to show he was wrong. Nevertheless, the Union army went to sleep again believing the only fighting on the morning of February 16 would occur when Grant ordered the Federals to storm the rebel fortifications.[139]

Present day photograph of Forge Road, the infamous road that the Confederate Army would have escaped on. Photograph by the author.

The evidence conflicts as to how securely Wallace blocked the Forge Road. He was sitting on his horse in a road behind Cruft's brigade—probably the Forge Road—when he halted the attack. During the night, soldiers gathered wounded from the Eighth, Eleventh, and Twentieth Illinois regiments and took them to hospitals. These regiments fought astride and near the Forge Road. Cruft encamped for the night and made no mention of improving his position for defense or extending his line to the east. Cruft was the right flank of the army and made no mention of the Forge Road.[140]

Grant was not familiar with the escape routes, and neither he nor his staff monitored the effort to retake the road. Wallace moved up with his brigades and stopped to water his horse when Webster arrived to state there was a change of plans. The colonel subsequently issued Grant's order for Wallace to withdraw beyond cannon range and construct earthworks. A bewildered Wallace asked whether Grant knew the Federals had retaken the hill and possessed the Wynn's Ferry Road. Webster replied that Grant did not know that. If Wallace followed Grant's order, he would give up the Wynn's Ferry Road, which he was directed to retake. With a wink and a nod, Wallace told Webster he had received the order, and Webster rode off. Once again, Lew Wallace determined the actual situation necessitated ignoring another Grant order.[141]

Grant wrongly thought the rebels went back to their trenches because they were demoralized. The rebel soldiers were victims of their vacillating commanders, and Grant seized the initiative from the enemy. He ended the day with a force on the left flank in possession of outer rebel trenches. As for Grant's force on the right flank, Floyd and Buckner would believe it had reoccupied the ground the rebels had won during the breakout attempt.

At this point, the rebel commanders assumed the Union army would attack in the morning, and they held a conference to decide what to do.

CHAPTER 6

DAY OF SHAME

SUNDAY, FEBRUARY 16, 1862

Floyd, Pillow, and Buckner assumed the army could just walk out of Fort Donelson to Nashville unmolested the morning of February 16. Floyd issued orders to commence a withdrawal starting at 4:00 a.m. Then reports came in that the escape routes were blocked again by Union troops. The three commanders dithered as to what to do now.[1]

Floyd Surrenders Fort Donelson

Situation

Darkness on February 15 found Smith's men in the outer entrenchments on the Confederate right flank, threatening the fort proper and water batteries. Wallace took position along the Wynn's Ferry Road and covered the Forge Road similar to Oglesby's brigade the night of February 14. Wallace made no preparations against another rebel assault. McArthur's brigade rejoined Smith's division and did not return that night to search for missing comrades. The Confederates removed their dead and wounded, so Dudley's Hill had mostly Union casualties on it who were trying to keep warm.[2]

The Confederates spent the afternoon and evening gathering up the dead, the wounded, and discarded Union arms. Not until the two available steamers went upriver to Clarksville around midnight loaded with sick and wounded

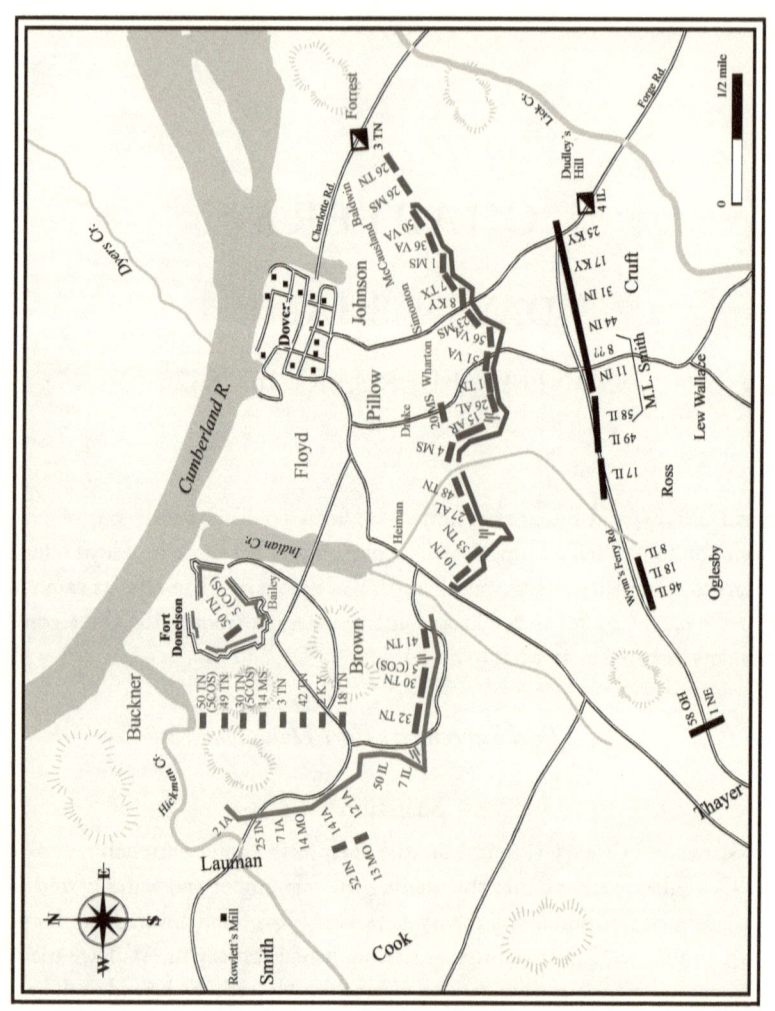

End of Day, February 15

rebels and Union prisoners did Floyd finally get around to saving the army. Policing and cleanup of the battlefield was important but the priority should have been to save the army.[3]

Randal McGavock knew Floyd and Pillow well and rode to Pillow's headquarters in the Rice House for the latest information. Maj. J. E. Rice served as an aide-de-camp for Pillow and had offered his house to use for headquarters. Just Floyd and Pillow were there, with Floyd writing a telegram for Johnston describing the day's battle and sending it at 11:00 p.m. The message declared the enemy driven from the field with heavy losses. There was no hint of coming disaster or a planned evacuation. Buckner arrived, and McGavock left believing the fight would be renewed in the morning.[4]

Despite the fact that Union troops held rebel entrenchments on the right, and Lew Wallace's men occupied a significant portion of the morning's battlefield, the rebel commanders continued to discuss their options and waste valuable time. The Confederate response was to talk instead of act. The victory message went out, but no one had issued orders to move the army toward Nashville.[5]

Once the steamers were gone, Floyd called the brigade and regimental commanders to Pillow's headquarters. Scouts reported that Union transports were landing reinforcements, and Floyd declared the fort could not stand against additional enemy reinforcements and must be evacuated. Around 1:00 a.m., nearly twelve hours after Pillow ordered Buckner back to the trenches, the rebels received instructions to march out on the road leading to Charlotte at 4:00 a.m. Floyd's shortsightedness was exposed when he dispatched the only two steamers that could have ferried men across the river; he was unaware the Charlotte Road was submerged to a depth of approximately three feet at the Lick Creek Ford.[6]

Buckner claimed retreat would occur only if the Federals had not reoccupied the ground in front of Pillow. Two couriers arrived to report that large forces of Yankees were congregating in front of Buckner's line and moving in the direction of the rebel left. Increased forces in Buckner's front should not affect the retreat order since the entrenchments would be abandoned. The brigade and regimental commanders left to prepare their troops for departure, and the three generals waited for 4:00 a.m.[7]

A report came in that barking dogs had convinced the troops in the trenches the enemy was reinvesting the Confederates' position on the left. Floyd subsequently ordered Pillow to send out scouts to verify the account. Only a report of barking dogs goaded Floyd to take measures he should have taken much earlier, rather than just a couple of hours before the army was to evacuate.[8]

Pillow sent out two scouts who returned and reported that campfires were seen in the same locations enemy troops had occupied on Friday night. In addition, a large force was closing up the routes to the interior. Pillow correctly had doubts about the report. There were two routes to the interior: the Charlotte Road and Forge Road. Union troops were not blocking the Charlotte Road, but they were in the vicinity of Forge Road.[9]

Before attending the council Floyd summoned a civilian, Dr. James W. Smith, to his quarters and showed him a map of the battleground indicating roads and creeks. Dr. Smith was forty-three years old and a practicing physician in Dover. He understood the map because the Charlotte Road crossed Lick Creek on property that had been his home since he was a boy. Floyd requested Dr. Smith to ride out, investigate the condition of the ford, and determine whether it could be crossed on horseback. Dr. Smith went alone to survey the area.[10]

Pillow doubted the reports from the trenches and the two scouts he had sent out. He requested Maj. Rice and Col. Forrest join the council. Rice was first to join the meeting, and responded to Pillow's questions about the potentially unfavorable condition of the road to Charlotte. About that time, Dr. Smith arrived and declared the water across the ford was deep enough to reach the saddle skirts. The physician saw no signs of the enemy and declared the crossing easily fordable.[11]

Due to the evacuation decision, Pillow instructed his aides-de-camp to gather all papers and books and told the quartermaster to burn all the stores at 5:30 a.m. However, by the time Forrest arrived at the council, the three generals were discussing surrendering because the reports of enemy reoccupation meant they had to fight their way out. Buckner accepted this situation as defeat rather than a challenge. Forrest could not believe what he heard, arguing that he had ridden down the Forge Road for two miles late in the evening while his men were on the field collecting weapons and wounded men. No Union soldiers had been in sight as late as 9:00 p.m. Pillow ordered Forrest to ascertain the condition of the Lick Creek Ford and locate the position of the enemy. Forrest rushed to his camp and sent out his two most trusted scouts, Adam Rankin Johnson and Bob Martin. By war's end Johnson would be a brigadier general and Martin a lieutenant colonel.[12]

Johnson and Martin had spent four days infiltrating the Union lines and had obtained valuable information. Now Forrest ordered them to search out an escape route for his command and locate the extent of the Union position. The two men waded the Lick Creek backwater and found a ford (probably Lick Creek Ford) that could be crossed on horseback. They estimated the nearest Union forces were half a mile off.[13]

Like Dr. Smith, Johnson and Martin reported water at the ford up to a horse's saddle skirts and mud about half a leg deep in the overflow bottom. The bottom width was about a quarter mile and the water width approximately one hundred yards. Most important, the scouts saw no enemy. There were fires in the area that had likely been set by wounded soldiers. Forrest vouched for the veracity of his men, but his assurance fell on deaf ears.[14]

The consequences of reports of Union reoccupation and approximately three-foot-deep water at the Lick Creek Ford loomed large over the surrender conference. The medical director of Floyd's Virginia brigade stated that half the soldiers who walked through the water would die of pneumonia. Johnson's and Martin's information was recorded only in Forrest's report. Floyd, Pillow, and Buckner asserted the Union army reoccupied the ground. Pillow, Maj. Gus Henry, and Lieut. Hunter Nicholson claimed the reconnaissance of the earlier scouts was confirmed by a second set of scouts who described the woods as alive with the enemy. They could only mean Forrest's scouts, who had reported they saw no enemy.[15]

Floyd did not adapt to changing circumstances and commanded without urgency concerning the predicament. His original plan assumed the army would head for Nashville in the morning. But when Buckner returned to the trenches instead of holding the Wynn's Ferry Road, Floyd made no modification in strategy. The retreat should have commenced immediately and proceeded during the night. Instead of saving Albert Sidney Johnston's army, Floyd wrote him a telegram.[16]

After the 1:00 a.m. evacuation order, Bushrod Johnson led his command out to the Charlotte Road as he had done the morning before. Head moved his brigade from the fort to Dover. While the men waited in the cold, the generals pondered the facts before them. A frustrated Floyd opened discussions about what best should be done now. Pillow responded that it was difficult to decide what was best in the situation, but he favored continuing with the orders already given. If necessary, he believed the army should cut their way out.[17]

Buckner indicated that his command was in no condition for further fighting; the position of the army was desperate, and it was hopeless to wage another battle. The troops were worn out, cold, hungry, and low on ammunition. The Union army was four times the size of the Confederate forces. Even if they did manage to escape, the rebel troops were too exhausted to make an extended march. The water batteries would fall, and the gunboats would assail the Confederate position. The result would be a massacre and the loss of three-fourths of the men. Floyd chimed in, saying that the army was demoralized and he agreed with Buckner's pessimistic prognosis.[18]

Pillow suggested staying in the trenches another day and shuffling Confederate troops across the river when the steamers returned. But Buckner retorted that he could not hold his line for thirty minutes, adding that when he tried to evacuate from the earthworks, the Union troops would spot the withdrawal and tear his men to pieces. Forrest joined in and stated he would screen Buckner's retreat with his cavalry, but he spoke to no avail. The cavalry leader offered to break through the Union line at any point designated to allow the infantry to evacuate while his cavalry held off the Union cavalry. The response to this idea was that the enemy would bring their artillery to bear on the retreating Confederates. Forrest then stormed from the meeting in disgust. Buckner was fixated on surrender, and no suggested alternatives could change his defeatist mind.[19]

The 4:00 a.m. time set for evacuation was fast approaching, and Brig. Gen. John Buchanan Floyd had a decision to make.

Options

Floyd heard the aggressive Pillow and Forrest advocate fighting their way out. He also listened to Buckner's forlorn outlook on every suggestion to fight on. Floyd struggled with the options: He could stick with his order to commence the evacuation at 4:00 a.m. On the other hand, he could cancel the order and hold the fort for another day while waiting for the transports to return. Finally, Floyd could give up and surrender.

Option 1

Most of the men had either moved into position to evacuate or were doing so. They waited in anticipation for the order to move. The position and strength of the Union forces were uncertain. Floyd could stick to the plan, commencing the evacuation at 4:00 a.m. and reacting to the situation as it developed.

Option 2

If Floyd concluded the troops could not fight their way out but could hold the fort for another day, he could cancel the evacuation and wait for the steamers to return and transport men to the other side of the river. This would result in a definite battle because Grant intended to storm the fortifications at daylight. Buckner warned the others he could not hold his line, but that was another uncertainty. The rebels had repulsed Union attacks when the trenches were amply manned, and if the lines held, Grant might decide a strike was too costly and settle into a siege instead.

Option 3

If Floyd decided the rebels could not fight their way out or hold the trenches, then there was nothing to do but give up and surrender. This course of action meant the loss of over half the Confederate army's forces in Tennessee, and it was contrary to Johnston's instructions and expectations.

Decision

Floyd admitted he was strongly influenced by Buckner and decided to surrender the army, but not himself. At a time that called for audacity, Floyd showed timidity, and approximately 11,500 Confederate prisoners were sent off to Northern prisons.

Results/Impact

Buckner argued the whole army had to surrender because he could not hold his trenches. But Col. Brown had already left with his three regiments and marched toward Dover, leaving just three of Buckner's regiments in the earthworks. Over three-fourths of the rebel army was east of Indian Creek, poised to move out at 4:00 a.m. on a road more than two miles from Buckner's position. The trenches did not need to be held. Buckner could have applied rearguard tactics starting at the fortifications as the army headed toward Nashville.[20]

Floyd agreed with Buckner: all had been done that could be done, and it would be needless sacrifice to attempt to cut through the lines. Pillow's idea to hold out for another day died with Buckner's lament that he could not maintain his trenches for thirty minutes. Pillow considered the issue settled with Buckner's negative response, declaring the only thing left was to capitulate. But, like Floyd, Pillow also declared he would not surrender himself or the army either. He would die first.[21]

A perplexed Buckner responded that such actions were for personal considerations and should not affect the military decisions of a general. Floyd understood, but command nevertheless passed from Floyd to Buckner through Pillow. Buckner sent a message to Grant proposing a six-hour armistice to discuss terms of surrender. Forrest remonstrated, contending there was more fight left in the men than Floyd and Buckner gave them credit for. Angry and frustrated, Forrest let it be known he had not come to Fort Donelson to surrender his command, and he would lead his men out if he saved but one.[22]

Floyd did not hesitate to abandon the men he had commanded for the past three days. He asked Buckner whether he could take his own brigade and cut their way out through the Union lines. Buckner had no problem if the withdrawal was done before Grant accepted the surrender. Maj. Rice secured

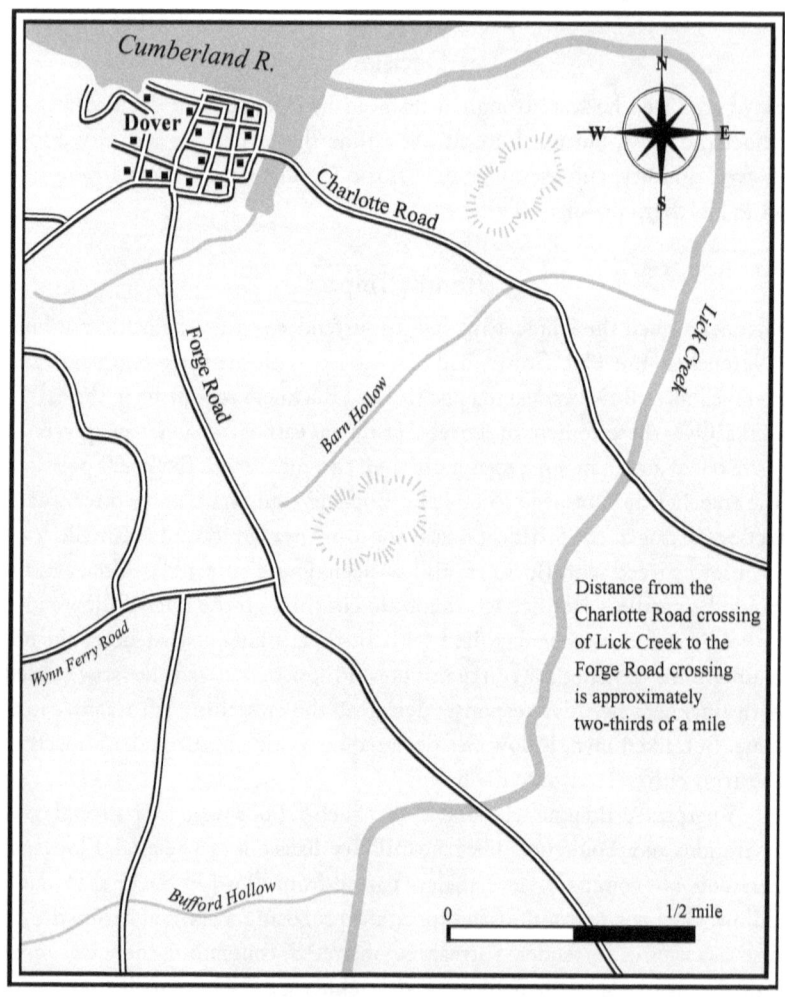

Lick Creek Crossings of Charlotte and Forge Roads

a small raft, and he, Pillow, and Gilmer braved crossing the Cumberland River.[23]

Four o'clock came and went as soldiers stood waiting for orders to move out. Heiman's and Head's Brigades waited in Dover, while Brown's Brigade was en route from Buckner's sector toward Dover. Rather than orders to escape, Head and Brown received word to return to their starting positions. Bushrod Johnson was ordered to report to Buckner. At the same time, rumors of pending surrender raced through the army, and hundreds of soldiers gravitated toward Dover to seek a way out.[24]

Floyd believed his actions were fully justified and beyond reproach. He claimed all the principals agreed that a considerable portion of the army could have been saved, but a larger proportion would have been slaughtered in a battle against vastly superior numbers. *Slaughtered* means *killed*. According to Floyd, it was probable that over half the army would end up dead if the rebels attempted another breakout. Approximately three hundred Confederates were killed during the breakout attack. It was a gross exaggeration that another such attempt would result in over seven thousand dead men.[25]

When Forrest led his command and those who joined the procession out of Dover toward Lick Creek, he solicited Dr. Smith to show the way. Forrest and his brother, Lieut. Jeffery Forrest, were in front when the advance scouts reported the presence of a battle line of soldiers moving along and across the road. The Forrest brothers approached the location where the enemy battle line was supposedly posted, but they were met with silence and no evidence of Federals. They found themselves staring at a line of picket fencing that resembled a line of infantry in the dim light. On Dudley's Hill the brothers found only wounded soldiers, which satisfied them there were no Union forces in the area. Forrest was convinced the picket fence that fooled his scouts had also fooled the earlier scouts who reported the picket fence as a line of infantry when addressing the surrender conference. Had there been time, Forrest would have gone back to report to Buckner, but it was too late.[26]

Forrest approached Lick Creek and plunged his horse into the water, which came up to the saddle skirts. He had no difficulty getting to the other side, and five hundred men from his command and two hundred from other commands traversed the creek with no signs of Union soldiers. Forrest estimated that two-thirds of the army could have marched out without loss. He based his assessment on the fact that his command spent two hours crossing at Lick Creek, during which time nobody shot at them. Nor did Forrest and his men encounter a single Union soldier.[27]

It was obvious the water would get shallower and narrower upstream of the ford. There is no indication the commanding generals ever gave thought to crossing the army above flooded Lick Creek Ford. The Confederates hoped to march out on the Forge Road, which intersected the creek just 3,500 feet farther upstream. Dudley's Hill offered a defensible position to protect the army while crossing Lick Creek above the ford. The soldiers were ingenious men. Given the opportunity to cross Lick Creek or go north to Union prisons they would have found ways to get across the water.[28]

Dr. Smith went upstream approximately three hundred yards from Lick Creek Ford and crossed at Hay Ford, where the water was only eighteen inches deep. James Chandler of the Twenty-Seventh Alabama joined two other members of his regiment and walked to Lick Creek, where they crossed on a footlog. They did not see or hear any Federal soldiers. Four members of the Fourteenth Mississippi trekked along the west bank of the creek until the water was shallow enough to wade through. James Woodard of Tennessee procured a horse and rode along the bank of Lick Creek until he crossed where the water was not deep. He passed other Confederate soldiers on foot and saw no sign of Union men. With two other officers, the son of Col. Daniel Russell of the Twentieth Mississippi waded through breast-deep water approximately fifty yards wide and made it to Columbia, Tennessee. Men could brave the icy water and live to tell about it.[29]

Dr. Smith stated there were no Federal soldiers closer than Bufford's place, which was about one mile from where Forrest crossed. Local citizen G. W. Bufford confirmed this observation. He spent Saturday night at his mother's house and saw no Federal soldiers then or early the next morning between the Bufford place and the Lick Creek Ford. M. L. Vesey of the Fourteenth Mississippi met a member of his company who decided to walk out on the Forge Road. A year later, Vesey learned the man walked away without difficulty. These accounts substantiate the fact that Forrest and over seven hundred men escaped without seeing a Federal soldier.[30]

Floyd explained to Jefferson Davis that he thought it important to save as much of the command as possible. When the two steamers returned, Floyd ordered Maj. William Brown of the Twentieth Mississippi to station his regiment to prevent stragglers from getting on the boats. The Virginia regiments would board first, and the Twentieth Mississippi would be last. The first boatload included Pillow's staff and horses, but time ran out. To protect Southern honor Buckner sent word to Floyd that the surrender was finalized, and he added that the steamers must leave immediately or he would shell them. Floyd sailed from the landing, leaving an irate Maj. Brown staring in disbelief as the boat steamed away. Davis had commanded the First Mississippi Rifles in the Mexican War, and Brown had fought alongside Davis in the Battle of Buena Vista. The Confederate president took a keen interest in the fate of the Mississippi regiment, wondering why Floyd and his Virginia regiments escaped but the Twentieth Mississippi did not.[31]

On the rebel left flank Buckner instructed Bushrod Johnson to approach the Union lines and arrange a cease-fire. Johnson met a suspicious Lew Wallace and requested a halt in hostilities while surrender terms were negotiated. Wallace knew Buckner and asked Johnson to lead him to rebel headquarters. There, Buckner greeted Wallace and served him a sparse breakfast as they awaited the arrival of Grant. Grant and Buckner were acquainted from West Point and the Mexican War. In 1854, after resigning from the army in California, Grant was destitute in New York on his way home. He could not afford his hotel bill, and Buckner assisted him by vouching for payment of his costs.[32]

If Buckner thought his friendship with Grant warranted lenient treatment for the rebel defenders, including parole, he miscalculated. Grant's famous assertion that "no terms except an unconditional and immediate surrender can be accepted" shook Buckner, but he was in no position to refuse. Buckner accepted the "ungenerous and unchivalrous" terms.[33]

Union divisions moved forward to take possession of the fort. Grant arrived at the Dover Hotel, and despite the harsh terms he offered, his meeting with Buckner was cordial and polite. Grant wanted the prisoners shipped up north as soon as possible. Rations were issued, and the prisoners boarded steamers for the trip to Cairo and beyond.[34]

Dover Hotel. Courtesy of the National Park Service.

Halleck moved quickly to locate destinations for the prisoners. Camp Douglas in Chicago received 4,459 captives. Camp Butler, five miles east of Springfield, Illinois, took 2,000. In Indiana, Camp Morton received 3,700, Terre Haute 500, and Lafayette 800. Lower-ranking officers went to Camp Chase near Columbus, Ohio, and subsequently to Johnson's Island, while higher-ranking officers, including Buckner and Tilghman, were shipped out to Fort Warren in Boston Harbor.[35]

The United States and Confederate governments were close to an agreement to make prisoner exchanges. Soldiers not traded would be paroled to their own government and await a future exchange. The capture of over 11,500 rebels at Fort Donelson caused the Federal government to change its position to one of equal exchanges of prisoners. Inmates would no longer be paroled. Fort Donelson prisoners suffered a long incarceration because an exchange agreement did not occur until July 22, 1862, when the Dix-Hill Cartel was signed.[36]

It took three days to process the prisoners and send them north. Kentucky sent a sheriff with a writ charging Buckner with treason. Feelings ran hard against Buckner, but he was a Federal prisoner, and the Lincoln administration would not turn him over to Kentucky. Halleck issued instructions Buckner was not allowed to communicate with anyone, and he was not to be paroled. The Confederacy had no description of the fight from Buckner until he was released in August.[37]

Casualty estimates placed the number of Confederate dead at around 300 and the number of wounded at 1,100. Floyd and Buckner justified the surrender on the estimate of high casualties with another breakout attack. Johnston left Bowling Green with 14,000 men, yet 5,600 fell out of ranks, leaving him but 8,400 bedraggled troops. There were more prisoners from Fort Donelson than there were troops in Johnston's army at Nashville. Forrest refused to surrender his men to the rigors of Northern prisons, but Floyd had the effrontery to justify his actions with the explanation his Virginians faced greater threats by escaping than surrendered prisoners experienced in captivity. According to Floyd, prisoners of war no longer faced any personal risk and were free from all personal danger.[38]

Prison records show more Fort Donelson prisoners died in captivity than on the battlefield. Of the 4,500 men sent to Camp Douglas, 518 (11.5 percent) succumbed to camp illnesses. In March, Camp Douglas recorded 125 deaths and Camp Morton 144 deaths, and Camp Butler reported 148 deaths by the end of March.[39] The number of Fort Donelson prisoners who died in captivity surpassed 1,500, or at least five times the number who died in combat. If given the chance, a lot of the soldiers would have found a way out. Instead of leading the men to freedom, the generals banished them to months of captivity, sickness, and death.

Johnston went to bed the night of February 15 with the news the Confederates had beaten back Grant's invading army. When word got out that Fort Donelson had surrendered, Nashville devolved into a state of panic, as the crowds expected gunboats and Union soldiers to appear at any moment. Floyd and Pillow arrived in Nashville early Monday morning, February 17. The disturbing details of the surrender were unknown, and the two generals were credited with having escaped with a small portion of the army.[40]

When Johnston learned most of the garrison was lost, his immediate reaction was to save the army he had left. Had the Fort Donelson army arrived at Nashville, there would have been opportunity to make an orderly exit from Nashville. Instead, Johnston hurriedly withdrew the army to Murfreesboro and left Floyd to keep order and ship army stores south.[41]

Pillow boarded a train to take him home to Columbia, Tennessee. Help came to Floyd on February 18 in the presence of Forrest and his cavalry. Floyd left on February 20 and marched to Murfreesboro, then to Chattanooga and later to Knoxville. Forrest took over command of the city and did not leave until the evening of February 23 upon the appearance of Union troops.[42]

Neither Floyd nor Pillow realized a storm was brewing over their actions at Fort Donelson. Men who were now prisoners condemned the officers vehemently, but Johnston did not second-guess the surrender. Any review of the disaster of Fort Donelson had to wait until more information was known. Johnston sent a letter to Richmond on February 27, giving no facts on the surrender and stating he had just eleven thousand effective men in his command. President Davis needed facts to defend his friend. If Johnston was not at fault, who was? Davis was baffled as to why the army surrendered without a final effort to cut through Grant's lines and retreat to Nashville.[43]

The reports of Pillow and Floyd describe their views on the decision to surrender without an attempt to fight through the Union lines. The War Department dismissed their accounts as unsatisfactory. Johnston's army was in Decatur, Alabama, on March 11 when Davis ordered Johnston to suspend Floyd and Pillow from command. He also chastised Johnston for not providing a chronicle of the Fort Donelson affair.[44]

Pillow was in Decatur when the suspension order arrived. He prepared a supplemental report including affidavits from four staff members and Forrest. In his account, Pillow explained he had wanted the rebels to cut their way out, but Floyd and Buckner insisted on surrender. A weakness of Pillow's defense was his acceptance of the unrealistic casualty rate of three-fourths of the army if the troops attempted to break out again. He made no forceful argument against this figure. But he conceded that, if Buckner and Floyd thought such a high number of casualties would be incurred, the effort to withdraw would be wrong.[45]

Floyd was in Knoxville when news of his suspension reached him. Thunderstruck at the dishonorable charges the War Department hurled against him, he postured that he never dreamed he had done anything for which he needed to present a defense. Nor had he neglected his duty. The aggressive tone of Floyd's answers could not have sat well with Davis. He was defending Johnston against his many attackers and did not need Floyd to cast aspersion Johnston's way.[46]

Floyd lectured Davis, telling him that Johnston and the War Department surely knew Fort Donelson could not withstand the might of the Federal forces. There were only two roads the army could use to escape, Floyd explained. The upper Forge Road was believed to be strongly held by the enemy, while the lower Charlotte Road required the men to wade through water three feet deep. Floyd blamed the medical director for the opinion that half the men who waded the cold water would die of pneumonia. He also gave a glowing tribute to Buckner's superior military ability, his judgment, his courage, and his patriotism. Thus, the commanding officer passed over the judgments of the second-in-command because he was strongly influenced by the third-in-command.[47]

Johnston thought remaining silent was the best approach, rather than commenting and taking action before the facts were known. Davis recognized Johnston's reluctance to blame subordinate generals, but the country clamored for someone to blame, and Davis wanted it to be someone other than Johnston. When Johnston finally submitted his report, he admitted he had scarcely read Pillow's and Floyd's reports before he transmitted them. He had to concentrate on saving what was left of his army, so a review of the generals' conduct had to wait.[48]

Johnston recognized Buckner as the officer who advised surrender and Floyd as the officer who agreed to it. In his account, he made no mention of Pillow's attempts to convince the other two generals the army should cut its way out. However, Johnston alluded to the generals' agreement that they could not hold the fort, and that extricating the command through the Union lines would involve a great sacrifice of life. Forrest's escape made Johnston note that the investment was not as strong as the scouts convinced the generals it was.[49]

Pillow chafed under the suspension from command. On May 15 he expressed impatience in a letter to George Randolph, Confederate secretary of war, that a decision concerning his service had not come. The frustrated general identified his actions at Fort Donelson as the most meritorious of his career, and the facts showed he opposed the surrender of the army. So why the delay? Like Floyd; Pillow believed his actions at Fort Donelson did not deserve censure.[50]

On June 21, Pillow wrote Randolph to say that if no action was forthcoming, he should retire from the military since the government no longer wanted his service. Randolph replied that his suspension was not an act of censure, further observing that the investigation could not be completed until the Fort Donelson prisoners were exchanged and had given their reports and testimonies. Pillow remarked that this information was the first he had received about an investigation, and he added that the only missing actor was Buckner. Pillow noted he had been suspended for four months already, and it might be four more before Buckner returned. He questioned why a decision was withheld, since there was ample evidence Pillow opposed the surrender.[51]

Buckner and the other officers left Fort Donelson on February 20 destined for Fort Warren. Buckner was placed in solitary confinement for a period of almost five months. The prisoners were released in late July and by August 6 most had arrived in Richmond where the officers submitted their reports. They had obtained copies of Floyd's and Pillow's accounts and thought Pillow's varied with the facts, but Floyd could not escape responsibility for the surrender. Randal McGavock noted in his diary the soldiers' bitter feelings against the two generals for their execrable conduct at Fort Donelson.[52]

By the time Buckner arrived in Richmond, Johnston had died at Shiloh, and John Floyd was back in Virginia serving as a major general in the state militia. Floyd did not pursue reinstatement to command in the Confederate army. The remaining question was what to do with Pillow.

At Fort Warren the prisoners read Pillow's report and knew his defense: he could not be blamed because he wanted the rebels to cut their way out. Floyd and Buckner were the ones who quit. But Buckner and his officers blamed Pillow more than Floyd, and they had almost five months at Fort Warren to decide what they would put in their reports. One common theme focused on Pillow's orders that sent Buckner's regiments back to the entrenchments. A second theme was the troops' exhaustion, which meant they could not cut their way out. Thus, the rebels had no option but surrender, and it was all Pillow's fault.[53]

The official Union reports of Brig. Gen. Lew Wallace and Col. John Thayer state that Col. John Brown's brigade attacked but failed to drive Thayer's brigade from the position on the Wynn's Ferry Road. That ended the rebel offensive, and Thayer's force remained in place until the next morning. Yet the official reports of Confederates Buckner and Brown and the three regimental commanders all claim Thayer retreated. In addition, these accounts note that while the Wynn's Ferry Road was completely opened, Pillow ordered the rebels back to the trenches, giving the road up. Bucker stressed the idea that Pillow's order to return to the trenches was the reason the army was lost.

Pillow wanted to fight, but Floyd agreed with Buckner, so Pillow gave up and Buckner surrendered the army.[54]

Davis and Randolph agreed that Pillow was the main culprit for the surrender and the Confederacy had its scapegoat. An August 22 message informed Pillow he was judged guilty of "grave errors of judgment" that resulted in the surrender at Fort Donelson. However, there being no reasons to doubt Pillow's courage and loyalty, his suspension was removed.[55]

A stunned Pillow ventured to Richmond for an interview with Davis and Randolph in early September and followed up on this meeting with a letter on September 18. He was charged with two errors of judgment. The first was that Pillow should have accepted the command from Floyd and then either led the army in an attack to cut its way out or surrendered it. The second error was Pillow's order to Buckner to return to the trenches from the Wynn's Ferry Road. Pillow disagreed but accepted Davis's decision he should not have passed on the command but did not accept he erred when he ordered Buckner back to the trenches because no preparations were made to leave from the battlefield since that was never the plan so the order to Buckner did not cause the surrender of the army.[56]

Pillow considered the censure decision unwarranted. He did not know Buckner's opinion until he read Buckner's report and saw the damage to his own reputation and career. Pillow struck back and took an aggressive tone in an October 10 letter demanding the government correct its unjust action. Otherwise, he would retire from the service. Pillow also touted his troops' success in driving back McClernand's division. He asserted that if Buckner's men had produced the same success, Grant's army would have been destroyed. Instead, Buckner failed to capture the battery on the Wynn's Ferry Road. Furthermore, Buckner allowed the enemy to seize a portion of his rifle pits after Pillow had won the battle, thereby rendering the fort untenable. Pillow fumed that the officer who caused the surrender was held blameless and uncensored by the government, while he was left to bear the Confederacy's odium and hostility resulting from the surrender of Fort Donelson. Unless the War Department reversed this injustice, Pillow would promptly resign.[57]

Randolph responded quickly (on October 21), contending that Pillow provided nothing new in his arguments except the idea that Buckner should be the one blamed for the surrender. Randolph confirmed his opinion was not swayed; the order would not be rescinded. Since Pillow made that repeal a condition for remaining in the service, Randolph noted that the government accepted his resignation.[58] A shocked Pillow then prepared another lengthy letter to dispute that he had resigned. He presented the same arguments and got the same result. There would be no withdrawal of the censure, but the

War Department accepted Pillow did not intend to retire and revoked its acceptance of his resignation.[59]

The surrender fiasco was caused by incomplete instructions at the war council. Pillow had the responsibility to make the instructions clear and complete. But Floyd was in command, and he should have recognized the deficiencies in the plan. The escape strategy required that orders be given to the entire garrison, and those should have included when the retreat would begin. Believing the Confederates would open up the escape routes and then retreat at their leisure was fatal. The instructions should have reflected the need to commence the escape as soon as the Forge Road was opened.

Alternate Decision and Scenario

Floyd issued evacuation orders at 1:00 a.m., and the army went into motion to leave at 4:00 a.m. Soldiers were assembled, and if Floyd had adhered to the evacuation order, a large portion of the army could have escaped. Union troops held the Forge Road, but the Charlotte Road was wide open, as proved by Forrest's exit over the span of several hours.

Grant's army was not positioned between the rebels and Nashville. The rugged terrain was not conducive to moving batteries and cavalry. Grant was preparing to attack the trenches, the fort, and the water batteries, not to block the Charlotte Road. Many men might have escaped before he was aware they were leaving. The Confederate army could have easily crossed Lick Creek, with cavalrymen shuttling infantry across the slough. The Forge Road crossed the creek just two-thirds of a mile south of where the water was three feet deep. Merely by walking south along the creek, the soldiers could have crossed in shallow water. Once the rebels moved south into the broken terrain, Grant's army might have captured stragglers, but the Federals were in no position to block their way to Nashville.

CHAPTER 7

AFTERMATH AND CONCLUSIONS

Johnston held a meeting with Beauregard and Hardee on February 7. The officers decided to abandon Bowling Green; withdraw the main body of troops from Columbus, leaving just a garrison force; and, if necessary, leave Nashville and retreat to Stevenson, Alabama. Johnston alerted Richmond of this plan on February 8, 1862; the fall of Fort Henry meant Fort Donelson would soon be attacked. The abandonment of Bowling Green was therefore necessary, and the army would retreat to Nashville. The fall of Fort Donelson and loss of most of the army there made any Confederate defense of Nashville impossible. When asked after the war why Johnston could not defend his chosen line, the general's aide-de-camp, Col. Edward Munford, replied that Johnston had no army. Johnston had a manpower shortage, and he took the military risk of splitting his inferior numbers in the face of advancing Union forces.[1]

When Halleck ordered Grant to make a demonstration, he did not do so in response to a strategic plan devised by high-level command. Halleck responded to what he believed would be a movement by Buell against Bowling Green, based on communications from Buell and President Lincoln. Halleck decided to order a military operation conducted by Grant. The Confederates were put in the position of responding to the movements of Union forces. They were not operating under a specific strategic plan, but reacting to Union actions with military operations of their own.[2]

The twenty-one critical decisions identified during the campaign are split between the combatants, with thirteen made by the Union side and eight by the Confederates. The Union made ten operational decisions and three tactical decisions. The Confederates made two personnel decisions, three operational decisions, and three tactical decisions. This emphasis on operational decisions stemmed from the campaign being dominated by troop movements versus combat. Federals started their advance with a limited objective of taking Fort Henry, but their goal expanded to an assault on Fort Donelson. Each side made operational decisions in response to what the other side did.

There were no national-level critical decisions because Halleck, a departmental commander, initiated the campaign that resulted in the taking of Forts Henry and Donelson. He made three critical operational decisions at the departmental level, and Buell made one. Johnston was responsible for two personnel decisions at the department level for the Confederacy. It is significant that the department head for the Confederacy made no operational or tactical critical decisions.

The Union made nine critical decisions at the army and division level, while the Confederacy made six. At the army level, Grant made four operational decisions, while McClernand and Foote each made one, for a total of six. At the army level, Tilghman made one operational decision at Fort Henry, and Floyd made two, including the surrender, at Fort Donelson, for a total of three.

All six tactical decisions were reached during the breakout attempt on February 15. For the Union, Lew Wallace made the division-level choice to send reinforcements to the right on two occasions, and Grant issued the army-level order for counterattacks. These decisions benefited the Union effort to stop the rebel breakout. Floyd, at the army level, and Pillow and Buckner, at the division level, each made one for the Confederacy. Buckner's decision to not aggressively attack William Wallace's brigade was detrimental to the rebel cause. Then Pillow's decision to order the Southern troops back to their entrenchments and Floyd's approval of that choice were disastrous.

Grant was absent from the field during the breakout attack, and he made his critical decision after the Confederates were returning to the trenches. Floyd was around, but he never seemed to be in the right place at the right time to ensure the subordinate generals carried out the plan instead of sabotaging it.

William Swinton covered the Civil War as a correspondent for the *New York Times*. In 1867 he published *Twelve Decisive Battles of the War*, crediting the Fort Donelson capture with securing the western border states for the Union. Swinton discussed Union success at Fort Henry in conjunction with the battle for Fort Donelson. He weighed Fort Donelson heavier due to the dynamic surrender of a rebel army, but modern analysis gives an increased value to the capture of Fort Henry, as that success opened the Tennessee River for exploitation.[3]

Johnston had no good options. Historians with hindsight claim he should have massed his forces and struck at Grant and destroyed him. But Johnston understood that moving all his army to attack Grant would leave Buell's army in his rear unopposed. Even if he stopped Grant's advance, the idea that he would have destroyed the Federal general is unrealistic. Grant's army was better armed and better equipped. He was supported by gunboats and transports and received a constant flow of reinforcements and supplies. Johnston's ability to move men from Bowling Green to Fort Donelson was hampered by a scarcity of locomotives and rolling stock.[4]

When Johnston ordered Floyd and Buckner to Clarksville in the first week of February, he intended for the troops defending the Cumberland River to delay the Union advance as long as possible while they fell back toward Nashville. The first line of defense was at Fort Donelson. Once the bastion could no longer be held, the garrison would fall back to Nashville. No other place than Fort Donelson could engage the gunboats, as Clarksville's fortifications were incomplete.[5]

The capture of the twin forts brought panic to the South. For months the Confederate citadels of Bowling Green and Columbus were believed impregnable to Yankee attack. It was unfathomable that the rebels would give up both strongholds, along with Nashville, without a fight. Overseas, the news blunted efforts to gain foreign nations' recognition of the Confederacy. Commissioner John Slidell reported that the losses had an unfavorable influence, and unless a military Confederate success was forthcoming, any hopes for recognition were lost. From Madrid, the Spanish secretary of foreign affairs, Mr. Calderon Collantes, expressed surprise the Confederates did not offer more resistance before surrendering, behavior that indicated the Confederacy could not defend itself. The Southern people wanted answers to hold someone accountable.[6]

The public chose Johnston to be that someone. Rather than go to the site where Union forces threatened the weak center of his line, Johnston left the crucial decisions in the hands of a bickering trio of brigadier generals. Meanwhile, the Federals had just one determined commander with a clear objective making the decisions. Grant intended to take Fort Donelson, and his subordinate generals knew that was what was to be done. Confederate command chaos proved the truth of Machiavelli's warning "Let only one command in war; several minds weaken an army."[7]

Johnston fell under the sway of Pillow's optimistic messages he could defend and hold Fort Donelson. Johnston then ordered all available troops to Fort Donelson. Pillow determined the army should defend the stronghold and believed he was the man to do it. Floyd had no clear directives from Johnston and informed Johnston the best place to concentrate was at Cumberland City. While Floyd took measures to mass troops there, Johnston ordered him to Fort Donelson, a place neither of them had ever been. Buckner was at the fort against his better judgment.[8]

It is inconceivable that Johnston would consider abandoning Fort Donelson without an attempt to defend it. He later claimed he chose to defend Nashville at the fort and gave the greater part of his army to do it. However, Johnston also asserted that Nashville could not be defended just at Fort Donelson because the main threat was from Buell's large army advancing from Kentucky. Johnston split his army and had only eleven thousand effective men left at Nashville to confront Buell. Pillow stated Fort Donelson was to be defended to protect Johnston's flank and rear. Floyd and Buckner both claimed the mission was to hold the fort until Johnston's army completed the retreat from Bowling Green to Nashville.[9]

The fall of Forts Henry and Donelson ended Johnston's dreams of holding a defensive line through Tennessee and Kentucky. The general did not intend to lose his army trying to defend Nashville, and he would play for time in order to join the two branches of his army west of the Tennessee River. On February 8 Johnston received word that the government had ordered large reinforcements to join his men so he could build up the army and strike a blow at the Union invader.[10]

The careers of Pillow, Floyd, and Buckner have warranted just a single biography each, all presenting a sympathetic view of their subjects. There is a lot more to the story of these men's military service than what can be learned from just studying the Battle of Fort Donelson.

So who was to blame for the loss of Fort Donelson? There are two aspects to this question. First is the loss of the fort, but of more importance is the loss of the army. Floyd and his defenders condemn Johnston for sending Floyd to Fort Donelson without sufficient forces to hold it against the burgeoning Union army. Johnston made decisions on a strategic level, but the loss of the army occurred on the local level, where Floyd was commander. Johnston clearly told Floyd to bring the army to Nashville if he could no longer hold the fort.[11]

Pillow cast aspersions on Buckner for not keeping his promise to attack the Union forces on the Wynn's Ferry Road in conjunction with his own attack on the right flank. In addition, Pillow criticized Buckner for his defeatist proclamations that he could not hold his line against a Union assault the morning of February 16, and for arguing the army was in no condition to fight their way out. Buckner infected Floyd's resolve, and Pillow gave up the fight.[12]

Pillow later claimed that Buckner's obstinate opposition was based on their personal conflicts from the Mexican War. But Buckner believed personal considerations should not influence the decisions of a general, and he maintained that he should share the fate of his men. When Pillow ordered him not to take his men out of Fort Donelson under Floyd's order, Buckner obeyed. When Pillow ordered him back to the trenches, Buckner obeyed. Buckner took his honor seriously and would not have made decisions that adversely affected men under his command based on his dislike of Pillow.[13]

Buckner pinned the loss of the army solely on Pillow and convinced Jefferson Davis to concur. In his official reports, Buckner gave his opinions as to what caused the surrender. After the war, he told those who asked him about what had happened that he would not disrespect his superior officers because it was an unsoldierly thing to do.[14]

Floyd remained popular in his home territory in western Virginia, but his supporters' entreaties that Davis restore him to duty in the Confederate army were ignored. The Commonwealth of Virginia commissioned Floyd a major general to defend southwestern Virginia. He took the field in October 1862, but his recruitment plans conflicted with the Confederacy, and by April 1863 he was without a command. On April 26, 1863, Floyd died in Abingdon, Virginia, and he is now remembered as a general who foolishly surrendered his army and then fled.[15]

Even though Buckner spurred the surrender of the army, he escaped censure because he did the honorable thing and suffered the surrender with the men. Davis promoted Buckner, and by the end of the war he was a lieutenant general in the Department of the Mississippi, where he surrendered another Confederate army on June 2, 1865. After the fighting ended, Buckner rebuilt his life and served as governor of Kentucky from 1887 to 1891. He benefited from the disdain of Pillow and Floyd, which shielded him from scrutiny for his contributions to the surrender.[16]

Buckner never spoke of Fort Donelson, claiming the memory was too painful and he did not wish to criticize the commanding officers. In 1909 he gave an interview for the *Nashville Banner* in which he remained steadfast to his belief the Confederate army was in no condition to fight another battle. In his opinion, the decision to surrender was the correct one because the Union army blocked the escape route. Buckner was the last surviving Confederate lieutenant general when he passed away on January 8, 1914, at the age of ninety.[17]

Unlike Grant, Gideon Pillow had no defenders high in the government. Thus, Davis chose a bishop over Pillow for command of the Department of the West. Pillow looked on Secretary of War George Randolph as an enemy because Randolph's brother-in-law had been a chief witness during Pillow's controversy with Gen. Scott during the Mexican War. Soldiers and newspapers excoriated Pillow for deserting the troops at Fort Donelson, and no Confederate general wanted to serve with him except for Nathan Bedford Forrest. Forrest witnessed the surrender conference and fought with Pillow during the breakout attempt, so when Pillow searched for a respectable command, Forrest requested him but to no avail. Pillow's arrogant and argumentative personality gathered no sympathy.[18]

Rightfully so, Pillow questioned how he could be censured for the surrender when he wanted to continue the fight. It was with the understanding that he would eventually receive justice from the government that he remained in service without a command. Pillow was instead assigned to recruitment duties, which he diligently pursued.

In October 1863 Pillow wrote a personal letter to Davis in which he assumed the president had not seen all the testimony concerning events at Fort Donelson. Pillow noted he had submitted sworn statements from four witnesses that the enemy had not reinvested the army as believed, and that the surrender was made because of the delusion. The army could have escaped but for the actions of Floyd and Buckner. Pillow appealed to Davis's sense of justice directly, as the War Office had never responded to him. Davis apparently made no reply.[19]

Pillow and Davis exchanged pleasantries in 1870, when Davis got wind that Pillow had given a speech implying he had accusations to make against Davis but was holding them back for the occasion. The former Confederate president invited Pillow to set forth whatever allegations he wanted to make. In a quick reply, Pillow declined to enter into the past and said Davis misunderstood the remarks. Even so, the former officer noted that Davis should recognize the injustice done to him. If Davis would only acknowledge that fact, their friendship could be restored. The two men periodically appeared together in public, but it is unlikely their relationship was restored.[20]

After the war ended, Pillow quickly took the oath of allegiance in order to fight for the restoration of his plantation near Columbia. He spent the postbellum years attempting to rebuild the wealth he lost during the war. Pillow's first wife died in 1869, and he married a younger woman in 1872. He later had some success but eventually lost his properties, and in the last year of his life, he ended up broke. Pillow passed away on October 8, 1878, at age seventy-two.[21]

There is no shortage of decisions made by the three rebel generals that led to the unnecessary surrender of most of the army. Each one prepared his reports with the purpose of deflecting blame from himself. Not one of them regretted any of the decisions they made.

Despite the commanding officers' bad choices, including Pillow's order to

Buckner to return to the trenches, most of the army was poised to evacuate starting at 4:00 a.m. on February 16. None of the generals went to see with their own eyes whether the Union forces had reoccupied the ground blocking the escape routes. Instead, they decided to surrender based on reports from scouts unknown to history. Rather than devise ways to overcome the obstacles, the generals accepted defeat and shamed the soldiers by surrendering them.

The reports, diaries, letters, and prison autograph books of the rebel troops bluntly reveal the outrage they felt at the surrender. Capt. B. G. Bidwell led his company from the Thirtieth Tennessee as artillerists in the lower battery. He judged the capitulation wrong and unnecessary. McGavock and his men reacted with shock, sorrow, humiliation, and anger. The captives raged at the traitors Pillow and Floyd and hoped for the chance to shoot them as they would a dog.[22]

After the fall of Fort Henry, Halleck petitioned McClellan to combine the departments in the West into a new Western Division under Halleck's command, giving him control of Buell's army. With the evacuation of Bowling Green, Halleck no longer considered Nashville as important and pressed for Buell to assist in the attack on Fort Donelson and Clarksville. But McClellan ordered Halleck to move on Nashville via the quickest route should Fort Donelson fall.[23]

Upon receipt of Grant's telegram on February 16 that Fort Donelson had fallen, Halleck reiterated his demand for overall command in the West. Halleck's strategy conflicted with McClellan's and Buell's, which blunted the Union's ability to exploit the destruction of Johnston's defensive line. As McClelland and Buell contemplated the occupation of Nashville, Halleck was not satisfied and wanted to prepare for another important movement. However, he did not want to head toward Nashville. Rather, Halleck envisioned an advance up the Tennessee River. He predicted to Buell there would be no battle at Nashville.[24]

A frustrated Halleck solicited the aid of Thomas Scott, assistant secretary of war, to bypass McClellan and present the plan for a Department of the West to Stanton. McClellan rejected Halleck's plan, deeming it unnecessary because Buell knew more of what was going on from his position in Bowling Green than Halleck did from his post in St. Louis. Stanton thought Halleck's plan was praiseworthy. But when it was presented to Lincoln, the president chose not to make any changes to military departments. Halleck accepted defeat, but he let Scott know that if Buell would not come to the Cumberland, he would attempt his plans without him.[25]

Foote was at Cairo on February 17 when the *Carondelet* steamed up with news of the surrender of Fort Donelson. Leaving quickly with gunboats,

Foote proceeded to Clarksville. He picked up some army troops at Fort Donelson and had possession of the town by end of the day on February 19. Foote planned to bring up more gunboats and join the army in an attack on Nashville. Grant, too, was ready to move toward Nashville. On February 21, Smith's division occupied Clarksville. Grant then let Halleck know he could capture Nashville by March 1 if given the go-ahead.[26]

But a telegram from Halleck dated February 18 ordered Grant not to send gunboats past Clarksville. McClellan telegraphed Halleck on February 20, notifying him that efforts should now be directed at Nashville. Buell and McClellan concluded the Confederates would send reinforcements and defend Nashville, so McClellan ordered Halleck to aid Buell in taking the city. In response, Halleck ordered on February 23 a concentration of gunboats and twenty thousand men at Clarksville. Grant wondered what the next move would be.[27]

The same day, Grant received information that Johnston had evacuated Nashville and Buell's army had advanced to Edgefield just across the river. On February 24, Brig. Gen. William "Bull" Nelson's brigade from Buell's department arrived at Fort Donelson, and Grant ordered him on to Nashville. Buell was at Edgefield with his advance cavalry and Brig. Gen. Ormsby Mitchel's division of nine thousand men. Estimating that Johnston had a force of thirty thousand, Buell did not intend to cross the Cumberland into Nashville until he had sufficient numbers to run no risk.[28]

Nelson landed the first Union troops in Nashville the morning of February 25. Buell reluctantly crossed over to the city, giving him a force of approximately sixteen thousand men. Brig. Gen. Alexander McCook's division was still two days away, so Buell sent steamers to Clarksville with an order for Smith to come to Nashville immediately.[29]

Halleck learned of Buell's possession of Nashville, so with a message on February 25 he promptly countermanded his orders to concentrate men and gunboats at Clarksville. With Buell in Nashville, Halleck considered it unnecessary to keep forces on the Cumberland River. He wanted Grant, including Smith's division, and Foote, with gunboats, back on the Tennessee River at Fort Henry.[30]

Unaware of Halleck's plans to concentrate at Fort Henry, Grant decided to visit Nashville to learn what Buell knew of Johnston's movements. He left Fort Donelson on February 26. When Grant reached Clarksville, he was much surprised to find Smith's regiments boarding steamers to comply with Buell's order to go to Nashville because Buell needed men.[31]

Grant arrived at Nashville early on the morning of February 27 expecting to meet with Buell, but he was across the river. Grant then wrote a message

Aftermath and Conclusions

to Buell, saying that he would be glad to provide more troops if necessary, but that he saw no need to do so, as the enemy was near the Tennessee line. He also informed Buell that Smith would arrive by evening with two thousand men. Grant requested that these soldiers be sent back if they were not needed, as he expected orders at any time that would require his entire force. Toward evening, as Grant prepared to depart, he ran into Buell, and the two men held a frosty meeting. Buell insisted he knew the enemy was nearby in superior numbers and Nashville was in danger. A dubious Grant returned to Fort Donelson.[32]

Communications between Halleck and Grant fractured because messages from St. Louis went to Cullum at Cairo, and he would forward them to Sherman at Paducah. Sherman would then send the messages by steamer to Grant at Fort Donelson. On March 1, Halleck ordered an expedition up the Tennessee River to destroy the Bear Creek Bridge at Eastport, Mississippi, and other connections at Corinth, Jackson, and Humboldt. Halleck instructed Grant to send Smith and his division to Fort Henry.[33]

On February 28, Grant informed Cullum in Cairo that he had just gotten back to Fort Donelson from Nashville, and that Buell had ordered Smith to Nashville. Cullum realized Grant had not received Halleck's orders directing Smith to Fort Henry and requiring all forces to be made ready for the field after assigning garrisons to Forts Donelson and Henry. Warning Grant that Halleck thought he was at Fort Henry, Cullum rushed copies of the aforementioned orders to Grant, who received them the evening of March 3.[34]

Without understanding Grant belatedly received his messages and was anxiously awaiting instructions for the next move Halleck received a message dated March 2 from Cullum that Grant wrote from Fort Donelson he had just returned from Nashville and Smith's division went from Clarksville to Nashville per orders from Buell. A vengeful Halleck sent a scathing message to McClellan on March 2, arguing that Grant deserved censure for leaving his command without permission and not communicating with headquarters for over a week. McClellan answered by saying such actions as Grant's threatened future success. He declared that Halleck should not hesitate to arrest Grant and put Smith in command for the good of the service.[35]

While Halleck did not arrest Grant and remove him from command, he directed that the expedition up the Tennessee River be turned over to Smith. On March 4 Halleck sent a terse three-line message to Grant ordering him to put Smith in charge of the mission and demanding of him, "Why do you not obey my orders to report strength and positions of your command?"[36]

A bewildered Grant replied on March 5 that he was not aware of ever having disobeyed an order. He also included an estimate of the strength of his command. But Grant's response to Halleck did not reach St. Louis until March 9. Another message from Halleck on March 6 castigated Grant for not reporting the strength and location of his command; in addition, his visit to Nashville was not authorized. Grant angrily countered that he reported daily to Halleck's chief of staff, and he maintained it wasn't his fault if Halleck did not receive his letters. The Nashville trip was for the good of the service. Grant told Halleck to remove him at once if his performance was not satisfactory.[37]

Copies of the nasty exchange quickly found their way to Elihu Washburne, Grant's supporter in Washington. Washburne promptly alerted President Lincoln and Adjutant General Lorenzo Thomas that the victor of Fort Donelson was in danger of being shelved.[38]

On March 6, Halleck sent a second blistering message to Grant and enclosed an anonymous letter outlining frauds committed in his command. Halleck warned Grant the irregularities had been noticed in Washington and he was to remove Grant from command if they were not immediately corrected.[39]

Just two days later on March 8, an impatient Halleck sent a short message to Grant demanding an immediate answer by telegraph as to his location and forces. Grant sent the requested details, along with a statement that the information had been mailed to Halleck from Paducah on March 6. He renewed his request to be relieved of duty.[40]

Halleck softened toward Grant on March 9 upon receipt of Grant's March 5 response with a message containing a caution to not let it happen again. Halleck instructed Grant to leave small garrisons at Forts Henry and Donelson and send all other troops up the Tennessee River as fast as possible. Once that was done, Grant was to be ready to resume direct command of the expedition. In addition, Halleck alerted McClellan, based on the information from Grant, that he was too weak for operations on the Tennessee River without help from Buell.[41]

The day after Halleck decided to reinstate Grant to command the advance, he received a message from Lorenzo Thomas. Thomas directed Halleck to report details about Grant leaving his command without authority, and to address the issue of whether Grant had made proper reports. If he had committed any acts of military insubordination, the president and secretary of war wanted to know what they were.[42]

Halleck had already let Grant out of the doghouse, and he delayed a response to Washington. But he sent another message to Grant on March 10 alerting him that more troops from Missouri would be sent to Fort Henry. Grant was to ready himself to take general command and forward arriving soldiers up the river. Halleck let McClellan know he was making his move without help from another department, and he designated Savannah, Tennessee, as the point of rendezvous for the expedition.⁴³

On March 6, Grant started transports up the river accompanied by gunboats. Smith was put in command on March 7, and the first troops landed at Savannah on March 8. But Halleck restored Grant to command of the expedition on March 11. However, the same day, Grant opened Halleck's delayed letter of March 6 and read the accusatory letter of frauds against the government. Off went his third request to be relieved of duty until the matter could be set right.⁴⁴

Fortunately for the war effort in the West, President Lincoln finally issued an order on March 11 giving Halleck sole command of a new Department of the Mississippi. Halleck's authority covered his own department along with Buell's area west of Knoxville. Even better, Lincoln removed McClellan from leadership of military departments other than the Department of the Potomac. Halleck was now supreme commander in the West, and he reported to Lincoln.⁴⁵

Halleck assuaged Grant's hurt feelings on March 13 with a brief, inspiring message—there was no reason for Grant to be relieved from command, and Halleck wanted him to lead the army to new victories. In his March 14 reply, Grant said he would assume command and make every effort for success.⁴⁶

Halleck now had one loose end to tidy up. With Grant restored to command, Halleck answered Lorenzo Thomas's March 10 inquiry on March 15, reporting that an investigation showed Grant had gone to Nashville with good intentions. However, poor telegraph access delayed submittal of returns. Grant had made proper explanations, and he had been directed to resume command in the field. According to Halleck, no further notice of the situation should be taken. Grant arrived at Savannah on March 17 and resumed full command of the army.⁴⁷

Johnston determined to combine the two parts of his army to build up a force capable of confronting the Union army. He moved southeast to Murfreesboro to indicate he was headed toward Chattanooga. But then Johnston started his army across the Tennessee River at Decatur and moved west into Mississippi to rendezvous with Beauregard at Corinth. When Maj. Gen. George Crittenden joined the remnants of his army to Johnston's, the total force numbered seventeen thousand men. Beauregard got reinforcements from Louisiana, Florida, Alabama, and Kentucky, and on March 6 he had approximately thirty thousand men available for the field.⁴⁸

Johnston and Beauregard believed they could join their two segments and bring in reinforcements if only they were given enough time. By March 17 Johnston was in Decatur, but the lead troops stretched to Corinth. On

March 25 Johnston informed Davis he was in Corinth; the army was united, and troops were stationed in Mississippi at Burnsville, Iuka, and Tuscumbia.[49]

Halleck started the expedition up the Tennessee River assuming he would get no help from Buell. He limited the mission to cavalry raids against rebel railroads and warned subordinates not to bring on a battle. In the end, Halleck's plans to cut the railroads were ineffective. Corinth was designated a target to hit, but Smith discovered a large rebel presence there and reported that it could not be struck under the restriction of not bringing on a battle.[50]

The rebels got the time they needed. Not until March 16 did Halleck order Buell to move by land to the Tennessee River and join forces with Grant at Savannah as quickly as possible. Buell's infantry started the 130-mile trip, but by March 19 the column was delayed at the Duck River at Columbia. Not until March 30 did Buell let Halleck know they would reach Savannah on April 6 and 7. Grant anxiously awaited Buell's arrival, but even with the delays and knowledge of Confederate reinforcements, Grant confidently told Halleck that the rebels were demoralized and Corinth would fall easier than Fort Donelson.[51]

Grant blamed the split departments for wasting the opportunity for an aggressive campaign in which the Union army could have occupied key locations such as Chattanooga, Corinth, Memphis, and Vicksburg. By March 17 rebel reinforcements occupied Corinth, and Grant received intelligence that the Confederates were strong in Mississippi from Chickasaw to Corinth. Johnston's men were among the troops, and Grant noted that the presence of Johnston was much against his expectations. Rebel commanders understood the necessity of striking Grant before Buell arrived. Yet the Union commanders believed no major engagement would occur until Buell joined Grant, at which point Halleck would lead the attack against Corinth. Meanwhile, Johnston reached Corinth with his seventeen thousand men and united with Beauregard's thirty thousand, putting Johnston's army near par with Grant's while Buell's army was still en route.[52]

Despite the military axiom that Johnston should strike Grant's army before Buell arrived, Grant ignored the possibility of such an attack. So once again, this time on April 6, a large force of determined rebels struck a Grant army while Grant was away from the field. However, as at Fort Donelson, Union divisions under command of volunteer brigadier generals put up stout resistance to a rebel surprise attack, giving Grant time to arrive on the battlefield and strike back. Whatever Grant's shortcomings in underestimating rebel commanders' determination and ability to strike his army, he did not panic. He gave his men the chance to emerge victorious at both Fort Donelson and Shiloh.

Grant's future proved the accuracy of Machiavelli's observation "A battle that you win cancels all your mistakes."[53]

Grant's mistakes at Shiloh on April 6 would have ended his career except that he had no quit in him. Buell added thousands of reinforcements during the night, and Grant ordered a counterattack that drove the Confederates back to Corinth. Union spirits were raised on April 7 when seven thousand Confederate defenders of Island No. 10 surrendered to Brig. Gen. John Pope's Army of the Mississippi, opening the Mississippi River to Memphis.[54]

Amid cries throughout the country and army for Grant's ouster for his failings at Shiloh, Halleck arrived at Pittsburg Landing on April 11 to lead the attack on Corinth, for which he had amassed a force of one hundred thousand men. Maj. Gen. Buell led the west wing with the Army of the Ohio. Maj. Gen. John Pope arrived with the Army of the Mississippi and commanded the east wing. The Army of the Tennessee was the center wing, but command was given to Maj. Gen. George Thomas, while Halleck made Grant second in overall command of the army.[55]

With the addition of Maj. Gen. Earl Van Dorn's Army of the West, Beauregard had approximately sixty thousand troops at Corinth. Halleck took almost three weeks to prepare for the advance. When he finally did start on April 29, he proceeded at a slow pace with delays to build fortifications. The distance to travel was just twenty miles, but not until May 29 was the army outside Corinth. As Halleck planned an assault, Beauregard planned an exit. During the night of May 29, trains surreptitiously transported rebel troops out of Corinth south to Baldwyn, Mississippi. Union forces entered Corinth on May 30 to find the town abandoned. Halleck gained the crossroads, but the rebel army was still a threat.[56]

After Corinth the Union focus became control of the ground won. The Confederates harassed Union troops with cavalry raids led by bands of partisan rangers and cavalry columns under the command of Nathan Bedford Forrest, John Hunt Morgan, and others. The Confederacy planned to slow Union advances by attacking Federal supply and communication lines, with emphasis on the railroads.[57]

In consideration of the Mississippi summer, Halleck dispersed the armies and planned no campaigns. Union troops occupied Memphis on June 7; Grant was restored to command of the Army of the Tennessee and tasked with guarding railroads to Memphis and Columbus and driving guerrillas out of West Tennessee. Pope was assigned to northern Mississippi, including Corinth, and guarding the railroad to Decatur. Pope was called to Washington in late June, and Maj. Gen. William Rosecrans replaced him at the head of the Army of the Mississippi. Buell and the Army of the Ohio were ordered

Aftermath and Conclusions

on June 10 to move east toward Chattanooga and East Tennessee. The officer's movements were hampered by his responsibility to protect Nashville. Andrew Johnson had arrived in Nashville as military governor in March, and he constantly pressured Buell to assign more troops to the city and send Union support into East Tennessee. Confederate cavalry attacks against his supply system and the need to rebuild the Memphis and Charleston Railroad stalled Buell's progress at Huntsville, Alabama, in mid-July, although Mitchel's brigade was in Bridgeport and Stevenson in anticipation of crossing the Tennessee River.[58]

Gen. Braxton Bragg had replaced Beauregard on June 17 as commander of the rebel army, which still remained in Tupelo. The success of Confederate cavalry raids convinced Bragg to make a thrust into Middle Tennessee, which would require Buell to react to Bragg's invasion. Bragg decided to lead thirty-four thousand men to Chattanooga while leaving thirty-two thousand men under command of Van Dorn and Price to defend Vicksburg and central Mississippi.[59]

On July 11 Halleck was ordered to Washington by Lincoln and promoted to commander of the armies. The Department of the West was divided between Grant and Buell, each answerable to Halleck. Grant took control of an expanded district that included the area of Mississippi that Rosecrans covered.[60]

Bragg started moving troops to Chattanooga by railroad in mid-July via Mobile and Atlanta. To Buell's surprise, he got reports of rebel troops arriving in Chattanooga in late July. This torpedoed his plans for the city, and Buell instead prepared to move north to protect Nashville, Middle Tennessee, and Kentucky from Bragg.[61]

Maj. Gen. Edmund Kirby Smith commanded twenty-one thousand men in East Tennessee from Knoxville. On July 29, he and Bragg met in Chattanooga and agreed to mount a joint invasion of Tennessee and Kentucky. Smith left Knoxville on August 14 and moved fast toward Lexington. He obliterated a Union force at Richmond, Kentucky, on August 30 and entered Lexington on September 2. Bragg left Chattanooga on August 28 and headed for Kentucky to join forces with Smith. Buell was uncertain as to Bragg's destination and moved north parallel to him. The invasion climaxed at the confused Battle of Perryville on October 8. Bragg and Smith finally joined forces at Harrodsburg, but the fight had gone out of Bragg. Kentuckians had failed to rally to the Confederate army, and Bragg headed back toward Tennessee, where he went into camp at Murfreesboro near the end of October. Smith retreated east to his department in East Tennessee.[62]

In northern Mississippi, Price and Van Dorn attacked Rosecrans and

Grant in order to regain Corinth. By threatening Grant, they could prevent the movement of troops from West Tennessee to reinforce Buell against Bragg. Price moved first and destroyed Grant's supply depot at Iuka on September 14. Grant and Rosecrans subsequently attempted to trap Price in Iuka, but what was supposed to be a joint attack by Rosecrans and Maj. Gen. Edward Ord turned into an attack by Rosecrans alone on September 17. Rosecrans's force was too small for the intended task, and after a short, fierce fight, Price withdrew and joined up with Van Dorn.[63]

Van Dorn took aim at Corinth and on October 3 launched an assault against the crossroads. The night fell with rebels inside the outer defenses, and the next morning they renewed the attack. The Confederates entered the town and there was fighting in the streets, but by early afternoon Van Dorn and Price were in retreat to Holly Springs, which ended any major threat to Union forces in West Tennessee and northern Mississippi.[64]

By mid-October the two Confederate offensive campaigns in the West had failed. Northern eyes turned toward opening the Mississippi River. Grant initiated the intriguing and complicated Vicksburg Campaign by planning a land invasion along the Mississippi Central Railroad. Pressure from Washington forced an accompanying river movement out of Memphis, with the intent that Grant's forces and those from Memphis would join up north of Vicksburg and take the city. Disasters struck in the forms of Nathan Bedford Forrest and Earl Van Dorn. Forrest went on a cavalry raid cutting Grant's communications, and on December 20 Van Dorn torched Grant's supply depot at Holly Springs, ending Grant's ability to move forward. Sherman was given command of the river force. Ignorant of Grant's withdrawal, he landed at Chickasaw Bayou on December 29 and attempted to move east. Waiting Confederates slaughtered the Union attackers, and Sherman moved back to Milliken's Bend to await developments. The development was that Maj. Gen. John Alexander McClernand arrived and took command from him.[65]

Lincoln's patience finally ended after Perryville, when the president thought Buell did not pursue Bragg aggressively enough. On October 24, Rosecrans replaced Buell with the expectation he would move against Bragg at Murfreesboro. Rosecrans also tried the administration's patience but finally advanced on December 26. Fighting commenced at Stones River on December 31, 1862, and ended on January 2, 1863. The next day, Bragg retreated south across the Duck River and took up headquarters at Tullahoma.[66]

With West Tennessee secure, Grant resumed the advance on Vicksburg. He tried several approaches through the waterways west of the town, but those were unsuccessful. On April 30 he landed troops south of Vicksburg at

Bruinsburg and headed for Vicksburg via Jackson, Mississippi. Battles were fought at Port Gibson, Raymond, Jackson, Champion Hill, and Big Black, and then Lieut. Gen. John C. Pemberton withdrew into Vicksburg. Grant followed and launched a couple of failed attacks and then laid siege. On July 4, 1863, he received his second surrender of a Confederate army.[67]

Ignoring pleas from the administration to move against Bragg, Rosecrans waited at Murfreesboro for six months until he felt ready. Finally, on June 24, 1863, Rosecrans commenced a movement against Bragg known as the Tullahoma Campaign. Through a series of flanking maneuvers and feints, Rosecrans convinced Bragg to start a retreat from Tullahoma to Chattanooga on July 2. Again, Rosecrans frustrated Lincoln and his staff by not immediately pursuing Bragg, but the Union general wanted to fix railroads, build bridges, and accumulate supplies. On August 16, Rosecrans at last moved toward Chattanooga.[68]

As Rosecrans approached Chattanooga, an army under command of Maj. Gen. Ambrose Burnside left Cincinnati to conduct the long-awaited Union invasion of East Tennessee. The Confederate Army of East Tennessee under command of Maj. Gen. Simon Bolivar Buckner was in Knoxville. Bragg ordered Buckner to evacuate Knoxville and move south toward his own army at Chattanooga. On September 3, Burnside entered Knoxville, causing the rebel troops at the Cumberland Gap to surrender on September 10.[69]

As Rosecrans approached Chattanooga, Bragg retreated into Georgia on September 8 before he could be trapped in the city. Rosecrans pursued, but Bragg struck back, and the large Battle of Chickamauga was fought September 19 and 20. The Confederates scored an astounding victory that forced Rosecrans back into Chattanooga. The Federals feared they would have to retreat farther, but Bragg did not pursue. Instead, he laid siege to the city with the intent to starve the Federals out. Despite the fact that Maj. Gen. Joe Hooker arrived with twenty thousand reinforcements in the first week of October, Rosecrans took ineffectual measures to relieve the siege.[70]

After Vicksburg Grant looked for another operation, but he had not started one when President Lincoln created the Military Division of the Mississippi and put Grant in command of it. The general immediately headed for Chattanooga, replacing Rosecrans with Thomas along the way. Grant arrived at Chattanooga on October 23. Sherman joined Grant with his division around mid-November. Supply lines were reestablished, and on November 23 Union troops moved to dislodge Bragg's surrounding army. On November 24 the iconic Union charge up Missionary Ridge penetrated the rebel line, leading Bragg's army to make a chaotic retreat into Georgia. Grant pursued for a couple of days but then sent troops to Knoxville to relieve a besieged Burnside.

On November 29 Lieut. Gen. James Longstreet made a last attempt to take Knoxville but failed, and he retreated to the northeast. Longstreet lingered in East Tennessee through the winter before returning to Virginia. With his departure, the state was free of any sizable Confederate military force. The last rebel army was out of Tennessee.[71]

The South never recovered from the loss of the twin forts, along with 11,500 men as prisoners. Rebel efforts to retake the lost ground in Kentucky and hold on to what they had left in Tennessee completely failed with the loss of Chattanooga in November 1863. At this point the Army of the Tennessee set their sights on Atlanta.

The battles for Forts Henry and Donelson are often overlooked despite their importance to the success of Union military operations in the West, and their role as the first major stepping-stones in Ulysses S. Grant's meteoric rise through the Union ranks until he reached the highest level as lieutenant general of the army. In 1912 the General Service Schools in Fort Leavenworth, Kansas, compiled a volume containing source material for the study of the Fort Henry–Fort Donelson Campaign. Fifty years after the forts fell, no adequate work existed for students to study the campaign.[72]

President Abraham Lincoln elevated Grant to commander of the army on March 2, 1864. The general's national acclaim commenced when he received the request from Buckner to form a commission to discuss the surrender of Fort Donelson. Grant's response that nothing but unconditional surrender would be accepted was instrumental in his journey from being a lowly mustering officer in Springfield, Illinois, to becoming commander of the US Army and accepting the surrender of Gen. Robert E. Lee at Appomattox Court House.[73]

Then it was on to the White House, with Grant serving two terms as president from 1868 to 1876. And it all began in earnest on the snow-covered hills above Fort Donelson in February 1862.

APPENDIX I

BATTLEFIELD GUIDE TO THE CRITICAL DECISIONS AT FORTS HENRY AND DONELSON

The starting point for this tour is the Fort Donelson Visitor Center, located approximately one mile west of Dover, Tennessee. Up-to-date information can be found on the battlefield's website, accessible through the National Park Service's website. The major fighting for the breakout attack on February 15, 1862, took place in the hills and hollows to the south of the visitor center.

You will travel close to locations where critical decisions were made and carried out. More than one critical decision was made at some stops on this journey. Unfortunately, the terrain, trees, and vegetation block long-range views. The tour is designed to give you a feel for the distances involved and the nature of the broken terrain of ridges and valleys over which the soldiers marched and fought.

Turn right as you exit the park. Travel west about 1.4 miles on US 79, and turn right onto State Route (SR) 461. Proceed north about 3.7 miles, and turn left to go west on Fort Henry Road. After about 1.7 miles, the old Telegraph Road joins Fort Henry Road. From this point you are on the original Telegraph Road.

From the intersection with old Telegraph Road, proceed about 2.4 miles and stay right, traveling onto Forest Service Road (FSR) 206 at the road fork. This is the vicinity of Boyd's place, where McClernand blocked the Telegraph

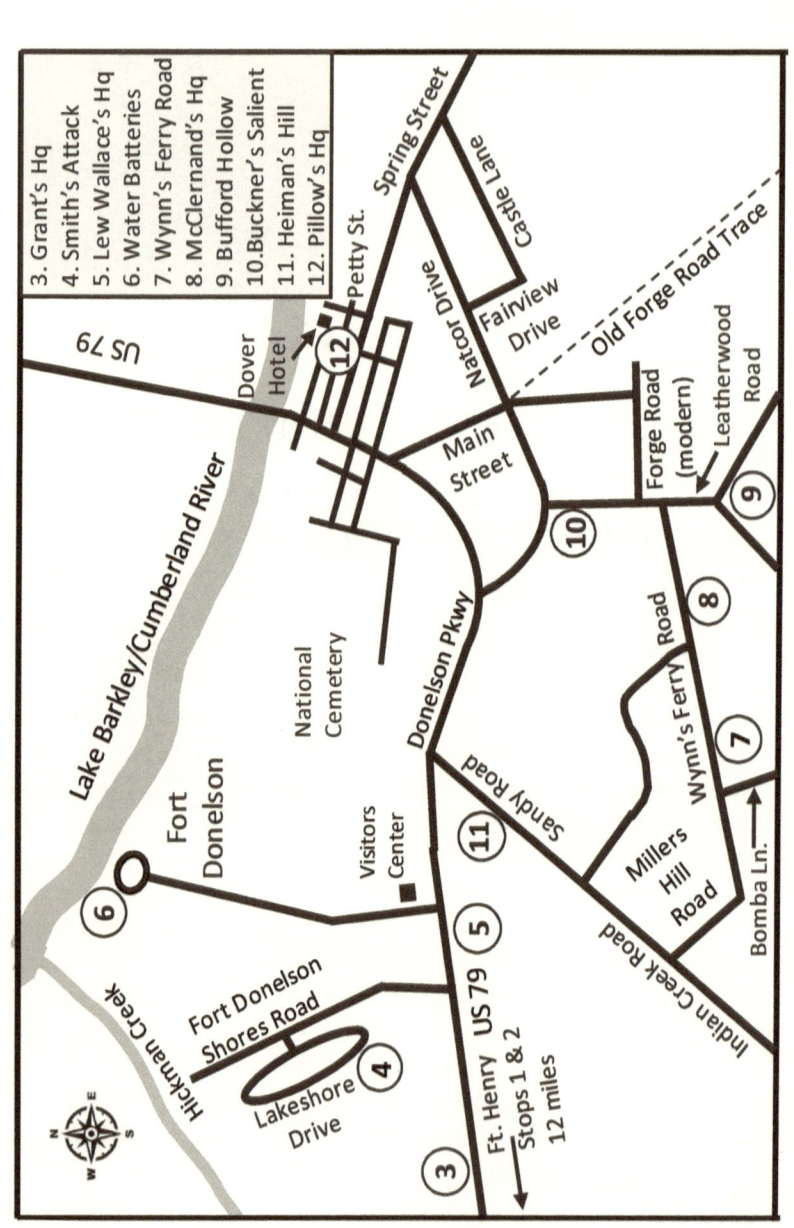

Road. Head north on paved FSR 206 for about 6.4 miles, and pull over at the intersection with FSR 225, Hughes Bay Road.

Stop 1: Camp Halleck

Brig. Gen. Grant arrived at Camp Halleck as a result of Halleck's first two critical decisions made in St. Louis: ordering demonstrations in early January, and commanding Grant to take Fort Henry in late January. Grant made critical decision three to attack Fort Henry immediately despite not having cut off the Confederate escape routes because rebel reinforcements could arrive at any time.

Camp Halleck was located on the ground to the west between Hughes Bay and Byrd Bay. Kentucky Lake is approximately one mile west of the intersection. You are approximately 6.4 miles from Boyd's place via the road, and you crossed approximately twelve drainage courses of varying sizes along the way here. In a straight line it was approximately four miles from Camp Halleck just to the Telegraph Road. This stop indicates how far the Union troops had to march to reach Fort Henry. Heavy rain the night of February 5 flooded the drainage courses between here and Boyd's place, significantly slowing the progress of the troops.

The following statements by Lew Wallace and Philip Smith describe the arrival of the Federal troops on February 5, which put them into position to attack Fort Henry the next morning.

Lew Wallace: An Autobiography

The going was mostly at night. Stopping in good time the day following, about five miles below Fort Henry, McClernand's division landed on the right bank; ours drew to the left bank; and, under cover of the gunboats, the debarking of both took place, after which they went into bivouac.[1]

Diary of Philip Smith, Eighth Missouri Infantry, USA, February 5, 1862

The anxiously awaited for Order to move came today. By One o'clock we were on board the Steam Boat ___ and by Two were on our way up the River. At Nine Oclock arrived at the locality where troops that had proceeded us were camped on both sides of the River. . . . Our Boat has tied up on the West side, but we are to remain on

> board and disembark early tomorrow Morning, both sides of the River are lined with Boats and the shores present a beautiful appearance being dotted with campfires.[2]

Head back south to the intersection with Fort Henry Road, and turn right to go west on FSR 230. Travel about 1.9 miles, and turn right onto the paved road for Boswell Landing. After about 500 yards, continue straight ahead for another 500 yards on the unpaved road for Fort Henry Trailhead, then park in the parking area. It is about a 400-yard walk to the edge of the lake. Walk southwesterly out of the parking area until you come to a dirt road, then turn right and continue to the water's edge. Fort Henry is underwater about 0.4 mile out in the lake. Fort Heiman is approximately 1.5 miles away on the opposite shore.

Stop 2: Fort Henry

Tilghman made critical decision four to defend Fort Henry, which damaged the gunboat fleet so that three of the four gunboats returned to Cairo. The Confederate garrison escaped to Fort Donelson, and Grant informed Halleck he would immediately attack the stronghold. Halleck then made critical decision five in St. Louis to support Grant's campaign with reinforcements. Buell made critical decision six in Louisville to send reinforcements to Halleck. Johnston made critical decision seven from Bowling Green to order Pillow to take command at Fort Donelson. After several days of delays, Grant made critical decision eight and ordered the attack on Fort Donelson.

The arrival of the Union force was described by two Confederate officers.

Journal of Maj. Randal McGavock, Tenth Tennessee Infantry, CSA, February 4, 1862

> Our pickets this afternoon report that eight gun-boats and nine large transports are three miles below at Marburry and that they were landing forces. This evening we could hear plainly music from their brass band. They regaled us with Yankee Doodle, Hail Columbia, The Star-Spangled Banner, and St. Patrick's Day in the Morning.[3]

Report of Col. Adolphus Heiman, Tenth Tennessee Infantry, CSA, Commanding First Brigade

On the morning of the 4th instant, at 4:30 o'clock, the sentinel at our 3-gun battery announced a rocket signal from the picket at Bailey's Landing, when three more rockets went up from the picket, announcing the approach of three of the enemy's gunboats.[4]

Lloyd Tilghman watched the ominous gunboats and growing numbers of Yankees land and knew Fort Henry could not be held. The fall of Fort Henry would open the Tennessee River to Union invasion into Alabama.

Report of Brig. Gen. Lloyd Tilghman, CSA, Commanding Fort Henry

I argued thus: Fort Donelson might possibly be held, if properly re-enforced, even though Fort Henry should fall; but the reverse of this proposition was not true. The force at Fort Henry was necessary to aid Fort Donelson. . . . I retained only the heavy artillery company to fight the guns, and gave the order to commence the movement at once.[5]

Lieut. Col. Milton Haynes, chief of artillery, arrived at Fort Henry at daylight on February 5. He was not optimistic about the Confederates' prospects.

Report of Lieut. Col. Milton A. Haynes, CSA, Chief of Tennessee Corps of Artillery

After hastily examining the works . . . I gave it as my opinion that Fort Henry was untenable, and ought to be forthwith abandoned.[6]

After the surrender, Grant prepared to attack Fort Donelson by sending out reconnaissance patrols and moving forces and supplies beyond the flooded lowlands. As weather conditions improved and reinforcements arrived, Grant felt ready to advance on Fort Donelson. He called for a conference with high-ranking officers at 3:00 p.m. on February 10, 1862, to discuss the impending movement.

Lew Wallace: An Autobiography

Grant stepped to the table and said, ever so quietly: "The question for consideration, gentlemen, is whether we shall march against Fort Donelson or wait for reinforcements. I should like to have your views." Smith and McClernand answered to move immediately without delay. Grant turned to Wallace: "Grant turned to me, nodding, and I said, 'Let us go, by all means; the sooner the better.'". . . Finally, General Grant wound the meeting up by saying: "Very well, gentlemen, we will set out immediately. Orders will be sent you. Get your commands ready."[7]

Grant's General Field Order No. 7, February 10, 1862

The troops from Forts Henry and Heiman will hold themselves in readiness to move on Wednesday, the 12th instant, at as early an hour as practicable. Neither tents nor baggage will be taken, except such as the troops can carry.[8]

Drive back east on FSR 230 and Fort Henry Road to the intersection with SR 461. The landing where Union troops disembarked on the Cumberland River is approximately 2.0 miles due east of the intersection. Turn right, and drive back south to the intersection with US 79. Go left (east) about 0.4 mile, and turn left onto Buckner Road. Proceed east about 500 feet, and pull over at the tablet for Grant's headquarters.

Stop 3: Grant's Headquarters

During the evening of February 12, Johnston made critical decision nine from Bowling Green and ordered Floyd to take command at Fort Donelson. On February 13, Grant made critical decision ten at headquarters and ordered Lew Wallace from Fort Henry to Fort Donelson. On February 15 Grant made critical decision fourteen to leave headquarters and meet Foote at the landing on the Cumberland River.

The Dover Road passed near the Crisp farm, and Grant made his headquarters in the cabin of the Widow Crisp, which was located on the rise beyond Grant's headquarters' tablet. From this location McClernand's division moved toward Lick Creek, while Smith's division moved toward Hickman

Creek. A gap developed between the two divisions, and Grant needed more men. He chose to strip Fort Henry further, making critical decision ten late on February 13 and ordering Lew Wallace and part of his brigade to Fort Donelson.

In response to a message from Foote, Grant made critical decision fourteen at dawn on February 15 and left for the landing. In the crucial moment of the breakout attack, Grant left the army without a commander.

Drive back to US 79, and turn left. Proceed west about 0.6 mile, and turn left onto Fort Donelson Shores Road. Proceed north about 0.4 mile, turn left onto Lakeshore Drive just in front of the sign for the Lake Barclay's Resource and Ft. Donelson National Battlefield. There is no road sign. Travel up the hill about 250 feet, and turn left again. Follow Lakeshore Drive as it curves through the area. This area of houses was occupied by Smith's division from Hickman Creek to US 79. After about 0.4 mile pull over.

Stop 4: Smith's Attack

This stop jumps forward in time to the midafternoon of February 15. It is located about a mile and a quarter from where Grant made critical decision twenty to counterattack and ordered McClernand and Lew Wallace to retake the Wynn's Ferry Road. Grant then rode to Charles Ferguson Smith's location, directing him to attack the rebel fortifications in conjunction with the assault to retake the Wynn's Ferry Road. A drive through the area provides a look at the terrain faced by Smith's men as they assaulted the rebel works. The soldiers formed on the high ground and then advanced down the slope and up the opposite slope to the Confederate earthworks. Somewhere in this vicinity Grant found Smith sitting under a tree awaiting instructions, as he had done the whole day.

Letter from Col. Thomas J. Newsham, Adjutant General, to Gen. William Farrar Smith

About 3 p.m. on Saturday the General and myself were sitting at the base of a large tree on the high ground on our extreme right when General Grant rode up with his staff and said "General Smith all has failed on our right—You must take Fort Donelson." Smith sprung to his feet and brushing his moustache with his right hand said "I will do it."[9]

Report of Brig. Gen. Charles Ferguson Smith, USA, Commanding Second Division

The Second Iowa ... was ordered to lead the assault. The regiment was ordered to rely on the bayonet and not to fire a shot until the enemy's ranks were broken. Right gallantly was the duty performed. The left wing of the regiment, under its colonel [Tuttle] moved steadily over the open space, down the ravine, and up the rough ground, covered with heavy timber, in unbroken line, regardless of the fire poured into it, and paused not until the enemy broke and fled. The movement of this regiment was a very handsome exhibition of soldierly conduct.[10]

Report of Col. James M. Tuttle, USA, Commanding Second Iowa Infantry

We were ordered to storm the fortifications of the enemy in front by advancing the left wing of the regiment, supported a short distance in the rear by the right wing. I took command of the left wing in person and proceeded in line of battle steadily up the hill until we reached the fortifications without firing a gun.[11]

Letter from John M. Duckworth, Second Sergeant, Company G, Second Iowa Infantry, February 18, 1862

The left wing was commanded by Colonel Tuttle.... Up the hill we pushed.... "Steady, boys!" shouted the colonel.... We had scarcely emerged from the woods, when the devils open on us. The first volley sounded like a crash of thunder, and the balls flew round us like hail, but not a waver could be seen in our lines.... We were now on the open ground, right at the breastworks. "Right over, boys!" said the colonel. The "boys" gave a yell, and they did go over.[12]

Drive back to US 79, turn left, and then immediately turn right into the parking lot of the Stewart County Visitor Center. Drive up to the east (left) side of the building, and park.

Stop 5: Lew Wallace's Headquarters

This stop is as close to Lew Wallace's headquarters as possible. Wallace first made critical decision fifteen at his headquarters when he ordered Cruft's brigade to aid McClernand. Then, several hours later, Wallace made critical decision seventeen when he ordered Thayer's brigade to move across the Indian Creek Valley and toward the enemy.

McClernand's column approached this area on February 12 and moved to the right, while Smith came up and moved to the left. Look back to where Fort Donelson Shores Road joins US 79. On February 13 Smith's line of troops extended down off the ridge delineated by Lakeshore Drive and terminated just west beyond Fort Donelson Shores Road and north of US 79. All of McClernand's division had moved east of Indian Creek, leaving a gap in the Union line at this location. Grant created a new division for Wallace to fill the gap. His left ended near this site close to Smith's right. The line went between the Stewart County Visitor Center and the Dover Elementary School, extending southeast to the Indian Creek Valley for approximately 0.5 mile.

The exact spot of Lew Wallace's headquarters is not known, but the approximate center of his line stood about 350 yards from this vicinity to the southeast.

Wallace described the dilemma he faced in the early morning of February 15, 1862, when Grant's orders precluded sending aid to McClernand.

Ulysses S. Grant, *Personal Memoirs*

I directed my adjutant-general to notify each of the division commanders of my absence and instruct them to do nothing to bring on an engagement until they received further orders, but to hold their positions.[13]

Report of Brig. Gen. Lewis Wallace, USA, Commanding Third Division

My orders, received from General Grant, were to hold my position and prevent the enemy from escaping in that direction; in other words, to remain there and repel any sally from the fort. Under the orders I had no authority to take the offensive.[14]

> ### *Lew Wallace: An Autobiography*
> An unusual sound off to the right front of my position attracted me. I listened. The sound broke at a jump into what was easily recognizable as a burst of musketry. . . . I stepped to the tent . . . and said: "Wake, gentlemen, and come out. There's something for you." . . . In a little while guns joined in. "There! That settles it," I said. "Get out your horses. It looks as if we were to have it in boat-loads to-day."[15]

Wallace responded thus to Maj. Brayman's pleas for assistance: "My impulse had been to send help at the first asking; that impulse was now seconded by judgment. . . . If that division were rolled back on me, a panic might ensue. In the absence of the commanding general, the responsibility was mine. A regiment was not enough to meet the demand. . . 'Tell General McClernand that I will send him my first brigade with Colonel Cruft.'"[16]

> ### Report of Col. Charles Cruft, USA, Commanding First Brigade
> At 8:30 o'clock a.m. General Wallace's order was received to put the brigade in rapid motion to the extreme right of our line, for the purpose of re-enforcing General McClernand's division.[17]

Wallace stayed with Thayer's brigade and awaited developments. Capt. John Rawlins arrived, and an increasing stream of rabble passed through the area as the two men talked. Amid a growing chorus of shouts, Wallace determined to advance Thayer's brigade toward the enemy.

> ### Report of Col. John M. Thayer, USA, Commanding Third Brigade
> At about 10:00 o'clock I received orders from General Wallace in person to move forward with my command to the support of General McClernand, who had been engaged with the enemy during the morning. Passing along the central road leading to the breastworks half a mile I met and passed the column of General McClernand retreating. Moving my men at double-quick, we were soon between

the forces of General McClernand and the enemy, who was rapidly approaching.[18]

Return to US 79, go right (east) about 0.2 mile, and turn left to enter Fort Donelson National Battlefield. Proceed through the park to the lower battery, and park.

Stop 6: Water Batteries

This stop is the location where critical decision eleven, Foote's choice to fight at close range, was carried out. The mouth of Hickman Creek is roughly three hundred yards away. One hundred yards beyond that is about how close the gunboats got to the lower battery.

In October 1861 H. L. Bedford reported at Fort Donelson in the position of instructor of artillery. Years later he described the attack.

Paper of H. L. Bedford, CSA, Instructor of Artillery, December 1884

As the boats drew nearer, the firing on both sides became faster, until it appeared as if the battle had dwindled into a contest of speed in firing. When they arrived within three hundred yards of the lower battery they came to a stand, and then it was that the bombardment was truly terrific. The roar of cannons was continuous and deafening, and commands . . . had to be given by signs.[19]

Commander Walke left a vivid account of the carnage endured by the *Carondelet* in the duel with the water batteries at close range.

Statement of Commander Walke on the Gunboat Attack on Fort Donelson

Soon a 128-pounder struck our anchor, smashed it into flying bolts, and bounded over the vessel, taking away part of our smoke-stack. . . . Another shot took away the remaining boat-davits and the boat with them; and still they came, harder and faster, taking flag-staffs and smoke stacks, and tearing off the side armor as lightning tears bark from a tree. . . . The warning words, "Look out!" "Down!" were again soon heard; down went the gunner and his men, as the whizzing shot glanced on the gun, taking off the gunner's cap and the heads of two of the young men who trusted to luck, and in defiance of the order were standing up or passing behind him. This shot killed another man also, who was at the last gun of the starboard side, and disabled the gun. It came in with a hissing sound; three sharp spats and a heavy bang told the sad fate of three brave comrades.[20]

Report of Capt. B. G. Bidwell, CSA, Thirtieth Tennessee Infantry, Commanding Battery

Our men all did well . . . the gallant conduct of John G. Frequa, a private and gunner. At the highest gun in my battery he stood perfectly straight, calm, cool, and collected. I heard him say, "Now, boys, see me take a chimney." The chimney and flag both fell. He threw his cap in the air, shouting to them in defiance. "Come on, you cowardly scoundrels; you are not at Fort Henry," were his words to them. Very soon he sent a ball through a port-hole and the boat fell back.[21]

Flag Officer Foote claimed he had never been under such heavy fire before. He would not venture so close to a fort's guns again. In a letter to his wife he vented his anger.

Letter from Foote to his wife, February 23, 1862

I now am determined to wait till I get the gun and mortar boats ready, and will not obey any orders except the Secretary's and President's. . . . But I tell you the last [Fort Donelson] was a bad fight. I was touching the pilot with my clothes when he was killed, but I won't run into the fire so again, as a burnt child dreads it.[22]

Drive to the park entrance, and turn left on US 79. Proceed east about 0.70 mile, and turn right (south) onto Sandy Road. In about 0.70 mile go straight onto Indian Creek Road, proceed about 0.2 mile, and turn left onto Millers Hill Road. Proceed up Millers Hill Road for about a quarter mile to where Wynn's Ferry Road begins. The original road came in from the right and the trace of the road could be seen prior to the construction of the house and driveway. Proceed east on Wynn's Ferry Road for about 0.2 mile, and pull onto Bomba Lane and park.

Stop 7: Wynn's Ferry Road

In this area Lew Wallace carried out critical decision seventeen, ordering Thayer to deploy his brigade between McClernand's retreating division and the pursuing rebels across the Wynn's Ferry Road. Grant arrived a couple of hours later. After a conversation with Lew Wallace and McClernand, he reached critical decision twenty to order the Wynn's Ferry Road retaken. Grant then rode to Smith's location and directed him to attack the rebel fortifications.

Lew Wallace rode ahead from his headquarters and met William Wallace leading his retreating column.

Report of Brig. Gen. Lewis Wallace, USA, Commanding Third Division

Colonel Wallace, whose coolness under the circumstances was astonishing, informed me that the enemy were following and would shortly attack. The crisis was come. There was no time to await orders. My Third Brigade had to thrust between our retiring forces and the advancing foe.[23]

Lew Wallace asked William Wallace how close the enemy was just as the head of Thayer's column came into view on the Wynn's Ferry Road.

Lew Wallace: An Autobiography

"You will about have time to form a line of battle here." . . . I looked over the ground right and left, and saw the surface open and smooth, then in front, and discovered myself on the brow of a descent, down which the road narrowed as it dipped between walls of brush and low trees of second growth. As a position, the advantages were all mine.[24]

Down the road to the east you can see another ridge that blocks the view from this location. There you can see down into the hollow and visualize the rebels coming up the road and through the trees. This is a good example of the difference between the crest of a ridge and the military crest. Thayer formed his brigade on the lower ridge.

Lew Wallace and his men did not know what they would face.

Statement of Sergeant Henry Otis Dwight of the Twentieth Ohio

My lips began to be very dry. . . . It is the unknown that terrifies and our feeling our way into this battle in the way that we did was to all of us one of the most trying experiences of the whole war.[25]

Wallace sent an aide to hurry Pete Wood's six-gun Chicago battery to the front and later described its arrival.

Lew Wallace: An Autobiography

I heard the rattling of wheels and whips cracking like pistols, and, looking back, beheld Pete Wood coming. I have lived long, and seen many things thrilling, but never anything to approach that battery. It drove forward full speed, the horses running low, the riders standing in their stirrups plying their whips, guns and caissons bouncing over root and rut like playthings, the men clinging to their seats like monkeys. . . . Instead of advancing in line of battle, the enemy marched up the cramped road in files of four, and, meeting us unexpectedly, were trying to deploy. All we had to do was to ply them with fire. I saw their muskets rise and fall steadily as if on a parade-ground.[26]

Confederate George Washington Dillon of the Third Tennessee left this perspective of the engagement: "When I take a retrospective view of that charge I can but shudder at the awful condition we were placed in at that time."[27]

Grant rushed to see the situation on the right, and he stated the fighting had ended and the rebels were back in their trenches when he showed up. The rebel withdrawal gave Grant the opportunity to seize the initiative, and he did.

Ulysses S. Grant, *Personal Memoirs*

I turned to Colonel J. D. Webster, of my staff, who was with me, and said: "Some of our men are pretty badly demoralized, but the enemy must be more so, for he has attempted to force his way out but has fallen back: the one who attacks first now will be victorious and the enemy would have to be in a hurry if he gets ahead of me."[28]

Letter from Lew Wallace to Benson Lossing, August 16, 1863

We were all on horseback. Grant held some dispatches in his hand. He then ordered us to fall back, and commence erecting defensive works on the hills. Or rather he did not order [underlining in original] it in the proper sense of the term, but talked of it as a seeming necessity. He appeared to think the enemy too strong inside his works to be captured by the force he had at command. His face was quite flushed, and his hand, holding a dispatch to which he would every now and then turn his eyes, trembled nervously. It may be that this idea of his had its origin in the dispatch. But the moment it was suggested to him that McClernand's defeat uncovered the road by which the enemy might escape to Clarksville, he closed tightly on the paper. And with the animation of a man who had suddenly come to a firm resolution, ordered McClernand to retake the hill he lost.[29]

Brig. Gen. Lew Wallace on the Meeting with Grant and McClernand

In every great man's career there is a crisis exactly similar to that which now overtook General Grant, and it cannot be better described than as a crucial test of his nature. In his ordinary quiet voice he said, addressing himself to both officers, "Gentlemen, the position on the right must be retaken."[30]

Grant did not know what faced McClernand and Wallace in the effort to retake the road. He rushed back to headquarters (Stop 3) and sent a message to Foote, then rode to Smith's location (Stop 4).

> **Ulysses S. Grant to Andrew Hull Foote, February 15, 1862**
> If all the Gun Boats that can, will immediately make their appearance to the enemy, it may secure us a Victory. Otherwise all may be defeated. A terrible conflict ensued in my absence, which has demoralized a portion of my command. I think the enemy is much more so. If the Gun Boats do not show themselves it will reassure the enemy and still further demoralize our troops. I must order a charge to save appearances. I do not expect the Gun Boats to go into action, but to make their appearance, and throw shells at long range.[31]

Now proceed east on Wynn's Ferry Road for about 0.6 mile, and then turn right into the parking lot of the Fort Donelson Pentecostal Church of God. This is the approximate location of McClernand's headquarters.

Stop 8: McClernand's Headquarters

McArthur's brigade was in position on the left flank of McClernand's line as evening approached on February 14. McClernand made critical decision thirteen at this location when he ordered McArthur's brigade to move approximately one and a half miles to the far-right flank after receiving a request from Oglesby for reinforcements.

Union batteries rimmed the Wynn's Ferry Road in this vicinity. The ground is approximately thirty feet higher here than at Buckner's position in the Confederate earthworks. This area became the focal point of the rebel advance after the Union forces were cleared from in front of Buckner's position. William Wallace ordered the retreat from this area, and the Confederates prepared to pursue.

Return to Wynn's Ferry Road and turn right. Go east about 0.2 mile, turn right onto Leatherwood Road, and proceed south toward Bufford Hollow. There is no road sign for Leatherwood Road. In about 0.4 mile stop where Everett Watson Road and Lick Creek Road attach to Leatherwood Road. Find a place to park, and orient yourself so that you are looking north up Leatherwood Road.

Stop 9: Bufford Hollow

In this location Lew Wallace started the counterattack to retake the Wynn's Ferry Road in response to Grant's critical decision twenty. The Union assault started in Bufford Hollow and drove the rebels back into their earthworks.

Col. Cruft's brigade took position in this vicinity approximately a half mile from the Forge Road. Cruft placed his force to protect a Union hospital to the south, and Drake's Brigade stood opposite his men on the rebel left. Fighting in this area died down while Buckner made his attack against Thayer's brigade.

After Buckner's offensive against Thayer ended, Drake withdrew to a line along a ridge south of the Wynn's Ferry Road. When Lew Wallace rode to determine the position of the enemy, he found only Drake's Brigade and prepared to attack.

Cruft moved to the right and took position at the base of the hill north of Lick Creek Road. Col. Morgan Smith's brigade stretched to the west along the ridge. Farther to the west Wallace placed Col. Ross's brigade.

Report of Col. Morgan Smith, USA, Commanding Fifth Brigade

In obedience to your [Lew Wallace's] order, I stormed the hill on which the enemy were posted with my brigade. The hill was covered at intervals with forest and dense underbrush. . . . After about an hour's hard fighting, the enemy gave way. We pursued them for about a mile, to within 150 yards of their intrenchments.[32]

Report of Col. Charles Cruft, USA, Commanding First Brigade

At about 4 p.m. an order was received from General Wallace to cooperate with Colonel Smith's brigade . . . in carrying the enemy's works on the right, in the front of Dover, by storm. The officers and men, though much fatigued from the action of the morning and worn from loss of rest and lack of food, responded cheerfully to the order and wheeled into column. The enemy was in force on the hill, under cover of the wood on both sides of the only road leading up into the direction of the works. . . . The assault was a complete success.[33]

Report of Brig. Gen. Lewis Wallace, USA, Commanding Third Division

My directions as to the mode of attack were general, merely to form columns of regiments, march up the hill which was the point of assault, and deploy as occasion should require. . . . It is at least 300 steps from the base to the top of the hill. The ascent is much broken by outcropping ledges of rock and for the most part impeded by dense underbrush. Smith's place of attack was clear, but rough and stony. Cruft's was through the trees and brush. The enemy's lines were distinctly visible on the hill-side. Evidently they were ready. . . . Finally the Eighth and Eleventh cleared the hill, driving the rebel regiments at least three-quarters of a mile before them and halting within 150 yards of the intrenchments behind which the enemy took refuge. This was about 5 o'clock and concluded the day's fighting. In my opinion it also brought forth the surrender.[34]

The route to Stop 10 travels through the main killing field. Drive north up Leatherwood Road for about 0.5 mile, and turn right onto modern Forge Road. Travel east about 0.3 mile to the end of the road. The original Forge Road is visible in its descent through the gulch to Lick Creek. To the north the original road ran along the base of the hill. The heaviest fighting occurred along and to the south of the ridge between old Forge Road and modern Natcor Drive. Travel back west about 0.1 mile, and turn right (north) onto Main Street. Old Forge Road is visible where the road bends to the left. After about 0.3 mile, turn left on Natcor Drive. You are now behind the line of entrenchments occupied by Buckner's Division the morning of February 15, 1862. Proceed west on Natcor Drive about 0.2 mile. Go straight through the t-intersection and pull into the small parking area to the left.

Stop 10: Buckner's Salient

During the generals' council the night before, Buckner proposed that he would strike the Union troops in the Wynn's Ferry Road at the same time that Pillow launched his attack on the Union right flank. Buckner made critical decision sixteen when he broke his promise and did not attack as Pillow fought his way up Barn Hollow.

The parking area is located approximately in the center of the line held by Buckner's Division the morning of February 15. Buckner's force occupied the ground to the east (approximately 1,200 feet) to just beyond Main Street (old Forge Road), and to the west the line extended (approximately 1,000 feet) past the position of French's battery overlooking Erin Hollow. Wynn's Ferry Road crossed the entrenchments approximately 550 feet to the east. This location is where the rebel front line was closest to the Union line.

Report of Brig. Gen. Simon B. Buckner, CSA, Commanding Division

In view of the heavy duty which I expected my division to undergo in covering the retreat of the army, I thought it unadvisable to attempt an assault at this time in my front until the enemy's batteries were to some extent crippled and their supports shaken by the fire of my artillery.[35]

McClernand's division occupied the ridge on the higher ground roughly five hundred yards to the south of where you stand. Union artillery occupied the highest ground along the Wynn's Ferry Road approximately seven hundred yards southwest of this location.

Note that the portion of old Wynn's Ferry Road now identified as Natcor Drive is on a ridge that separates two drainage swaths south of Buckner's line. East of the road is the head of Barn Hollow, while on the west is a swale that drains westward to Erin Hollow. Pillow fought his way up Barn Hollow.

Buckner's troops took refuge from Union artillery behind the ridge. Pillow sent a message to Buckner at 9:00 a.m. to launch an attack against the Wynn's Ferry Road to help Pillow's farther advance.

Report of Brig. Gen. Simon B. Buckner, CSA, Commanding Division

About 9 o'clock General Pillow urged an advance to relieve his forces. I accordingly sent forward the Fourteenth Mississippi, Major Doss, deployed as skirmishers. At the request of its commander I assigned the direction of its movements to Maj. Alexander Casseday, of my staff. The line of skirmishers was sustained by the Third and Eighteenth Tennessee.[36]

Walk about five hundred feet to the west, and you will be in the approximate area of French's battery. The Fourteenth Mississippi moved forward from this spot. The Confederates had to pass through their own abatis and cross a drainage swale before ascending another ridge. To the east the Third Tennessee also advanced. There was a gap between the two regiments.

Appendix I

Report of Maj. W. L. Doss, Fourteenth Mississippi Infantry

I received orders to deploy two companies as skirmishers, and soon after the battalion was ordered to dislodge a battery in position, apparently about 400 yards to our front. . . . The regiment suffered severely at this point, and was ordered to retreat by Major Casseday, who had been appointed by General Buckner to assist me. . . . After falling back some 200 yards I endeavored to rally the regiment on the Eighteenth Tennessee, but Major Casseday insisted, and gave the order to the regiment to fall back to the intrenchments, which was done.[37]

Not until three hours into the battle did William Wallace have to contend with an attack by Buckner. Buckner's lack of aggression was evident, because Cruft's brigade found no need to assist Wallace as it marched past Wallace's line to support Oglesby's brigade.

As his forces cleared the road in front of Buckner's line, Pillow wondered where Buckner was. Pillow did not find Buckner, but he ordered Cook to advance the Thirty-Second Tennessee and attack Wallace's new line. Cook and the Tennesseans were to move into Erin Hollow and attack the Federal battery in the rear.

Report of Col. Edward Cook, CSA, Thirty-Second Tennessee Infantry

We remained here until about 10 a.m., [author's note: the time was probably closer to noon] when General Pillow ordered me to move my regiment to the right and to cross the intrenchments and attack a battery of the enemy, which was then firing at us, and seemed to be situated some 800 yards from our intrenchments. Just as we were marching across the intrenchments General Buckner and Colonel Brown came up, and upon learning the order General Pillow had given, General Buckner ordered me to proceed to attack the battery, and ordered Colonel Palmer, with his regiment [Eighteenth Tennessee], to sustain me.[38]

Before Cook's and Palmer's regiments reached the Union battery, Confederate troops in the Wynn's Ferry Road attacked, and the Union forces retreated to the west. A lull fell over the battlefield, but then Buckner ordered Col. Brown to pursue the retreating Federals with his brigade. However, Thayer had his Union brigade across the Wynn's Ferry Road. Brown's attack was repulsed, ending the Confederate breakout attempt.

Return to your car, and proceed north about 0.2 mile to US 79. Turn left, go west about 0.4 mile, and turn left (south) again onto Sandy Road. After about 0.2 mile, pull into the parking area on the right and park. Maney's battery on Heiman's Hill is a walk of approximately 0.3 mile from this spot. Trees prevent a long-range view, so the walk is optional.

Stop 11: Heiman's Hill

Pillow witnessed the repulse of Brown's attack on Thayer's brigade. He then made critical decision eighteen and ordered the rebel forces to return to the entrenchments. Floyd was absent from the area at this time. Upon returning he met Buckner, who told him of Pillow's order. Floyd subsequently went to find Pillow to discuss giving up the Wynn's Ferry Road. After they talked, Floyd made critical decision nineteen and sustained Pillow's order to return the Confederate forces to the entrenchments.

Heiman's Brigade supported Maney's battery atop this prominent hill. Pillow watched Buckner's attack against Thayer from here and could observe Union movements toward Hickman Creek. Floyd probably met Buckner in Erin Hollow and then found Pillow on Heiman's Hill.

Lew Wallace summarized the situation upon the retreat of William Wallace from the Wynn's Ferry Road.

Brig. Gen. Lew Wallace's Statement on the Lost Opportunity

By 11 o'clock Pillow held the road to Charlotte.... The country was once more open to Floyd.... Without pausing to consider whether the Confederate general could now have escaped with his troops, it must be evident that he should have made the effort.... It may be said with strong assurance, consequently, that Floyd could have put his men fairly *en route* for Charlotte before the Federal commander could have interposed an obstruction to the movement.[39]

Buckner contemplated whether to continue the pursuit or position his division to hold the Wynn's Ferry Road.

Report of Brig. Gen. Simon B. Buckner, CSA, Commanding Division

I awaited the arrival of my artillery and reserves, either to continue the pursuit of the enemy or to defend the position I now held.... But General Pillow ... sent me reiterated orders to return to my intrenchments on the extreme right. I was in the act of returning to the lines when I met General Floyd, who seemed surprised at the order.... He directed me to halt my troops and remain in position until he should have conversed with General Pillow.[40]

Pillow revealed inconsistency in his reports when he wrote that Buckner overcame a fresh force but was demoralized by failing to take the Union battery.

Report of Brig. Gen. Gideon J. Pillow, CSA, Commanding Division

I knew, from the great loss my command had sustained during the protracted fight of over seven hours, my command was in no condition to meet a large body of fresh troops, who, I had every reason to believe, were then rapidly approaching the field.... General Buckner's command, so far as labor was concerned, was comparatively fresh, but its demoralization, from being repulsed by the battery, had unfitted it to meet and fight a large body of fresh troops. I therefore called off the pursuit, explained my reasons to General Floyd, who approved the order.[41]

Report of Brig. Gen. John B. Floyd, CSA, Commanding Army

My intention was to hold with Brigadier-General Buckner's command the Wynn's Ferry road, and thus to prevent the enemy during the night from occupying the position on our left which he occupied in the morning. I gave him orders upon the field to that effect. ... Brigadier-General Pillow ordered Brigadier-General Buckner to leave his position on the Wynn's Ferry road and to resume his place in his trenches on the right. This movement was nearly executed before I was aware of it. As the enemy were pressing upon the trenches, I deemed that the execution of this last order was all that was left to be done.⁴²

Pillow compared the success of his division versus that of Buckner's.

Statement of Brig. Gen. Gideon J. Pillow, CSA, Commanding Division

In the battle of Donelson the forces commanded by myself fought with brilliant success and with a gallantry never surpassed. Had General Buckner's command been equally successful we would have destroyed the enemy's army of 30,000 men.⁴³

Return to your car and drive back to US 79, and turn right. Travel east about 0.7 mile, and turn right onto Main Street, which was the Forge Road in 1862. Go south about 0.3 mile, and turn left (east) onto Natcor Drive. Buckner's line ended just beyond this intersection, although the trench continued to the east. In about 0.1 mile turn right (south) onto Fairview Drive. After about 100 yards turn left (east) at Castle Lane. You are in Barn Hollow, where Pillow launched the breakout attack. Travel east about 0.7 mile to Spring Street. Along the way you will pass the area where Pillow was surprised by the presence of McArthur's brigade on Dudley's Hill across the hollow to the south. Pillow's Division formed for the attack on both sides of Spring Street, which was known as the Charlotte Road in 1862. Turn left (west) onto Spring Street, and travel approximately 0.5 mile before turning right onto Petty Street which is just pass the historical marker for the surrender house. There is no street sign. Go north, and in about 100 yards turn left onto Pillow Street. There is no street sign. Pull into the parking lot for the Dover Hotel, and park near the entrance sign, where there is a tablet for the Rice House.

Stop 12: Rice House – Pillow's Headquarters

During the night of February 14 Floyd made critical decision twelve and ordered the breakout attack against the Union right flank to start in the early morning. During the night of February 15 and early morning of February 16, Floyd made critical decision twenty-one to surrender Fort Donelson to Grant.

When Pillow arrived at Dover, Major Rice offered his two-story roomy house to use as headquarters. Floyd and Buckner each made their headquarters in the Dover Hotel. The breakout attack and surrender meetings occurred in the Rice House.

Floyd recognized the continual arrival of Union reinforcements rendered the situation untenable, which led to the breakout attack.

Reports of Brig. Gen. John B. Floyd, CSA, Commanding Army

I then saw clearly that but one course was left by which a rational hope could be entertained of saving the garrison or a part of it—that was to dislodge the enemy from his position on our left, and thus pass our people into the open country lying southward towards Nashville.[44]

The night of February 15 found the three generals first issue orders to evacuate the fort the next morning, but then reports came in that Union forces had reoccupied the ground blocking the escape routes. Floyd and Buckner agreed to surrender the army over Pillow's arguments to fight on. Floyd explained the situation in a report: "The consultation which took place among the officers on the night of the 15th was to ascertain whether a further struggle could be maintained, and it was resolved in the negative unconditionally and emphatically. General Buckner, whose immediate command was the largest in the fort, was positive and unequivocal in his opinion that the fight could not be renewed. I confess I was myself strongly influenced by this opinion of General Buckner."[45]

Pillow wanted to make sure there was no misunderstanding of his position. His aide Lieut. Hunter Nicholson described the scene.

Statement of Lieut. Hunter Nicholson, March 18, 1862

Here General Pillow left the room, but returned in a short time, and, taking a seat between Generals Floyd and Buckner, said, "Gentlemen, in order that we may understand each other, let me state what is my position; I differ with you as to the cost of cutting our way out, but if it were ascertained that it would cost three-fourths of the command, I agree that it would be wrong to sacrifice them for the remaining fourth." Generals Floyd and Buckner replied, "We understand you, general, and you understand us."[46]

This is the last stop. The Dover Hotel is on the other side of the parking lot, and it served as Floyd's and Buckner's headquarters. While many decisions were made in this building, none of them are on the critical decisions list for this book. The initial meeting between Grant and Buckner after the surrender was in the Dover Hotel, known locally as "the Surrender House."

APPENDIX II

UNION ORDER OF BATTLE

FORT HENRY
February 4–6, 1862

ARMY OF THE TENNESSEE
   Brig. Gen. Ulysses S. Grant

FIRST DIVISION
   Brig. Gen. John McClernand

FIRST BRIGADE
   Col. Richard Oglesby
      8th Illinois
      18th Illinois
      29th Illinois
      30th Illinois
      31st Illinois
   Illinois Cavalry Companies
      Carmichael
      Dollins
      O'Harnett
      Stewart

2nd Illinois Cavalry (Battalion)
2nd and 4th US Cavalry (Battalion)
2nd Illinois Light Artillery
    Battery D (Dresser)
    Battery E (Schwartz) (Gumbart)

SECOND BRIGADE
    Col. William Wallace
        11th Illinois
        20th Illinois
        45th Illinois
        48th Illinois
        4th Illinois Cavalry
    1st Illinois Light Artillery
        Battery B (Taylor's Chicago Light Artillery)
        Battery D (McAllister)

SECOND DIVISION
Brig. Gen. Charles Ferguson Smith

FIRST BRIGADE
    Col. John McArthur
        9th Illinois
        12th Illinois
        41st Illinois

SECOND BRIGADE
    Brig. Gen. Lew Wallace
        28th Illinois
        11th Indiana
        23rd Indiana
        8th Missouri
    1st Illinois Light Artillery
        Battery A (Wood's Chicago Light Artillery)

THIRD BRIGADE
    Col. John Cook
        7th Illinois
        50th Illinois
        7th Iowa
        13th Missouri
    1st Missouri Light Artillery
        Battery D (Richardson)

WESTERN FLOTILLA
Flag Officer Andrew Foote
Carondelet
Cincinnati
Essex
St. Louis
Conestoga
Lexington
Tyler

FORT DONELSON
February 12–16, 1862

ARMY OF THE TENNESSEE
Brig. Gen. Ulysses S. Grant

FIRST DIVISION
Brig. Gen. John McClernand

FIRST BRIGADE
Col. Richard Oglesby
8th Illinois
18th Illinois
29th Illinois
30th Illinois
31st Illinois
Illinois Cavalry Companies
Carmichael
Dollins
O'Harnett
Stewart
2nd Illinois Cavalry (Battalion)
2nd and 4th US Cavalry (Battalion)
2nd Illinois Light Artillery
Battery D (Dresser)
Battery E (Schwartz) (Gumbart)
SECOND BRIGADE
Col. William Wallace
11th Illinois
20th Illinois

45th Illinois
48th Illinois
4th Illinois Cavalry
1st Illinois Light Artillery
  Battery B (Taylor's Chicago Light Artillery)
  Battery D (McAllister)
THIRD BRIGADE
  Col. William Morrison
    17th Illinois
    49th Illinois

SECOND DIVISION
  Brig. Gen. Charles Ferguson Smith

FIRST BRIGADE
  Col. John McArthur
    9th Illinois
    12th Illinois
    41st Illinois
THIRD BRIGADE
  Col. John Cook
    7th Illinois
    50th Illinois
    52nd Indiana
    12th Iowa
    13th Missouri
    1st Missouri Light Artillery
      Battery D (Richardson)
      Battery H (Welker)
      Battery K (Stone)
FOURTH BRIGADE
  Col. Jacob Lauman
    25th Indiana
    2nd Iowa
    7th Iowa
    14th Iowa
    14th Missouri (Birge's Sharpshooters)

Fifth Brigade
    Col. Morgan Smith
        11th Indiana
        8th Missouri

THIRD DIVISION
    Brig. Gen. Lew Wallace

First Brigade
    Col. Charles Cruft
        31st Indiana
        44th Indiana
        17th Kentucky
        25th Kentucky
Second Brigade
    Attached to Third Brigade
        46th Illinois
        57th Illinois
        58th Illinois
Third Brigade
    Col. John Thayer
        1st Nebraska
        58th Ohio
        68th Ohio
        76th Ohio
Not Brigaded
    1st Illinois Light Artillery
        Battery A (Wood's Chicago Light Artillery)
    32nd Illinois, Company A

WESTERN FLOTILLA
    Flag Officer Andrew Foote
        Carondelet
        Louisville
        Pittsburg
        St. Louis
        Conestoga
        Tyler

APPENDIX III

CONFEDERATE ORDER OF BATTLE

FORT HENRY
February 4–6, 1862

CONFEDERATE FORCES
    Brig. Gen. Lloyd Tilghman

FIRST BRIGADE
    Col. Adolphus Heiman
        27th Alabama
        10th Tennessee
        48th Tennessee
        Culbertson's Battery
        9th Tennessee Cavalry Battalion

SECOND BRIGADE
    Col. Joseph Drake
        26th Alabama (2 companies)
        15th Arkansas
        4th Mississippi
        51st Tennessee (2 companies)
        Crain's Battery
        Hubbard's and Houston's Alabama Cavalry Battalions

Milner's Cavalry Company
Padgett's Cavalry Company
Milton's Ranger Detachment

FORT HENRY ARTILLERY
Capt. Jesse Taylor
1st Tennessee Artillery, Company B

FORT DONELSON
February 12–16, 1862

CONFEDERATE FORCES
Brig. Gen. John Floyd

PILLOW'S DIVISION
Brig. Gen. Gideon Pillow
Brig. Gen. Bushrod Johnson

HEIMAN'S BRIGADE
Col. Adolphus Heiman
27th Alabama
10th Tennessee
42nd Tennessee
48th Tennessee
53rd Tennessee
Maney's Tennessee Battery

DRAKE'S BRIGADE
Col. Joseph Drake
26th Alabama (2 companies)
15th Arkansas
4th Mississippi
1st Tennessee Battalion

DAVIDSON'S BRIGADE
Col. Thomas Davidson
Col. John Simonton
8th Kentucky
1st Mississippi
23rd Mississippi
7th Texas

BALDWIN'S BRIGADE (Two of five regiments)
    Col. William Baldwin (Served in Pillow's Division)
        20th Mississippi
        26th Mississippi

MCCAUSLAND'S BRIGADE
    Col. John McCausland
        20th Mississippi (Attached to Baldwin's Brigade)
        36th Virginia
        50th Virginia

WHARTON'S BRIGADE
    Col. Gabriel Wharton
        51st Virginia
        56th Virginia

BUCKNER'S DIVISION
    Brig. Gen. Simon Buckner

BROWN'S BRIGADE
    Col. John Brown
        3rd Tennessee
        18th Tennessee
        32nd Tennessee
        Graves's Kentucky Battery
        Jackson's Virginia Battery
        Porter's Tennessee Battery

BALDWIN'S BRIGADE (Three of five regiments)
    Attached to Brown's Brigade
        2nd Kentucky
        14th Mississippi
        41st Tennessee

FORT DONELSON GARRISON
    Col. John Head
        30th Tennessee
        49th Tennessee
        50th Tennessee

FORT DONELSON BATTERIES
    Capt. Joseph Dixon (killed)
    Capt. Jacob Culbertson
        Maury Tennessee Battery (Ross)
        Tennessee Artillery Company (Stankiewicz)
        30th Tennessee, Company A (Bidwell)
        50th Tennessee, Company A (Beaumont)

CAVALRY
    Col. Nathan Bedford Forrest
        3rd Tennessee Cavalry
        9th Tennessee Cavalry Battalion
        1st Kentucky Cavalry Battalion

ARTILLERY (Unattached)
    Adam's Virginia Battery
    French's Virginia Battery
    Guy's Virginia Battery
    Green's Kentucky Battery
    Parker's Battery

NOTES

Introduction

1. James M. McPherson, *Battle Cry of Freedom: The Civil War Era* (New York: Ballantine Books, 1988), 236, 267, 273–74, 278–79.
2. US War Department, *The War of the Rebellion: A Compilation of the Official Records of the Union and Confederate Armies* (Washington, DC: US Government Printing Office, 1880–1901), series 1, vol. 51, part 1, pp. 369–70. (Hereafter cited in the following format: *OR*, ser. 1, vol. 51, pt. 1, pp. 369–70). Unless otherwise noted, all citations are from series 1.); McPherson, *Battle Cry of Freedom*, 282–83, 333–34.
3. George B. McClellan, *McClellan's Own Story* (New York, 1887), 41, 44; *OR*, vol. 51, pt. 1, pp. 338–39.
4. Shelby Foote, *The Civil War, a Narrative: Fort Sumter to Perryville* (New York: Vintage Books, 1986), 112–13; David Herbert Donald, *Lincoln* (New York: Simon and Schuster, 1995), 301; Todd M. Cathey and Ricky W. Robnett, *The River Batteries at Fort Donelson* (Jefferson, NC: McFarland, 2021), 12–14; Robert Erwin Johnson, *Rear Admiral John Rodgers* (Annapolis, MD: United States Naval Institute, 1967), 156.
5. Gary D. Joiner, *Mr. Lincoln's Brown Water Navy: The Mississippi Squadron* (Lanham, MD: Rowman and Littlefield, 2007), 18–19; US War Department, *Official Records of the Union and Confederate Navies in the War of the Rebellion* (Washington, DC: US Government Printing

Office, 1894–1922), series 1, vol. 22, pp. 277–80, 284. (Hereafter cited in the following format: *ORN*, 22:280–81. All citations are from series 1.); *OR*, series 3, vol. 2, pp. 814–15.

6. *ORN*, 22:280–81.

7. Joiner, *Mr. Lincoln's Brown Water Navy*, 21–24; Johnson, *Rear Admiral John Rodgers*, 156–57; *ORN*, 22:283, 299.

8. Joiner, *Mr. Lincoln's Brown Water Navy*, 25–29; Johnson, *Rear Admiral John Rodgers*, 160.

9. *ORN*, 22:297, 491–94; Johnson, *Rear Admiral John Rodgers*, 165–66.

10. Joiner, *Mr. Lincoln's Brown Water Navy*, 25, 29; *ORN*, 22:314, 502–6, 515.

11. E. B. Long, *Civil War Day by Day: An Almanac, 1861–1865*, with Barbara Long (New York: Da Capo, 1971), 83; Timothy B. Smith, *Grant Invades Tennessee: The 1862 Battles for Forts Henry and Donelson* (Lawrence: University Press of Kansas, 2016), 4.

12. Stanley F. Horn, *Army of Tennessee* (1941; repr., Norman: University of Oklahoma Press, 1993), 48; Thomas L. Connelly, *Army of the Heartland: The Army of Tennessee, 1861–1862* (Baton Rouge: Louisiana State University Press, 1967), 25, 37; Edwin C. Bearss, "The Construction of Fort Henry and Fort Donelson," *West Tennessee Historical Society Papers* 21 (1967): 26.

13. Connelly, *Army of the Heartland*, 28–45; Horn, *Army of Tennessee*, 42.

14. Horn, *Army of Tennessee*, 76; Cathey and Robnett, *River Batteries at Fort Donelson*, 8–10.

15. James M. McPherson, *Tried by War: Abraham Lincoln as Commander-in-Chief* (New York: Penguin, 2008), 39–40; McPherson, *Battle Cry of Freedom*, 350–52.

16. McPherson, *Battle Cry of Freedom*, 348–49, 361–62; Bruce Catton, *Terrible Swift Sword* (Garden City, NY: Doubleday, 1963), 93–96, 284–90, 297–301.

17. Catton, *Terrible Swift Sword*, 38–40.

18. *OR*, vol. 4, pp. 185–87.

19. E. Merton Coulter, *The Civil War and Readjustment in Kentucky* (1926; repr., Gloucester, MA: Peter Smith, 1966), 25–26, 96–98, 114; William Preston Johnston, *The Life of General Albert Sidney Johnston* (1879; repr., New York: Da Capo, 1997), 305.

20. Charles P. Roland, *Albert Sidney Johnston: Soldier of Three Republics* (1964; repr., Lexington: University Press of Kentucky, 2001), 260,

272–77; *OR*, vol. 4, p. 405; Johnston, *Life of General Albert Sidney Johnston*, 336–37.

21. Roland, *Albert Sidney Johnston*, 261–63; Smith, *Grant Invades Tennessee*, 13–16; Johnston, *Life of General Albert Sidney Johnston*, 306; Horn, *Army of Tennessee*, 56–57.

22. Connelly, *Army of the Heartland*, 63–65; *OR*, vol. 4, pp. 193–94; Horn, *Army of Tennessee*, 58–59; Roland, *Albert Sidney Johnston*, 274–77; Johnston, *Life of General Albert Sidney Johnston*, 334; Connelly, *Army of the Heartland*, 63–65.

23. Benjamin Franklin Cooling, *Forts Henry and Donelson: The Key to the Confederate Heartland* (Knoxville: University of Tennessee Press, 1987), 12–16; Kenneth A. Hafendorfer, *The Battle of Wildcat Mountain* (Louisville: KH Press, 2003), 15, 23.

24. Patricia L. Faust, ed., *Historical Times Illustrated: Encyclopedia of the Civil War* (New York: Harper and Row, 1986), 435–36.

25. Roland, *Albert Sidney Johnston*, 271.

26. Hafendorfer, *Battle of Wildcat Mountain*, 26, 55–243; *OR*, vol. 4, pp. 424–25.

27. Hafendorfer, *Battle of Wildcat Mountain*, 270–71.

28. *OR*, vol. 4, p. 358; *OR*, vol. 8, p. 369.

29. Stephen D. Engle, *Don Carlos Buell: Most Promising of All* (Chapel Hill: University of North Carolina Press, 1999), 87–89, 110; *OR*, vol. 7. pp. 443–44, 450–52.

30. Stephen E. Ambrose, *Halleck: Lincoln's Chief of Staff* (Baton Rouge: Louisiana State University Press, 1962), 12–22; *OR*, vol. 8, pp. 462–63.

31. *OR*, vol. 8, pp. 462–63; *OR*, vol. 7, pp. 450–52; *OR*, vol. 8, pp. 508–11.

32. George W. Julian, *Political Recollections: 1840 to 1872* (Chicago: Jansen, McClurg, 1884), 201–7.

33. *OR*, vol. 8, pp. 379, 428.

34. Donald, *Lincoln*, 322–23; Foote, *Civil War, a Narrative*, 160.

35. Julian, *Political Recollections: 1840 to 1872*, 201–3.

36. Ethan Rafuse, "Typhoid and Tumult: Lincoln's Response to McClellan's Bout with Typhoid Fever during the Winter of 1861–62," *Journal of the Abraham Lincoln Association* 18 (Summer 1997): 1–16.

37. Donald, *Lincoln*, 330; *OR*, vol. 7, p. 526.

38. *OR*, vol. 7, p. 524.

Chapter 1

1. Ambrose, *Halleck: Lincoln's Chief of Staff*, 3–10.
2. T. Harry Williams, *Lincoln and His Generals* (New York: Grosset and Dunlap, 1952), 46–47.
3. *OR*, vol. 3, pp. 568–69; *OR*, vol. 4, p. 342.
4. *OR*, vol. 8, pp. 382, 389–90; *OR*, vol. 7, pp. 443–44.
5. *OR*, vol. 8, pp. 395, 402–3, 408–10.
6. *OR*, vol. 8, pp. 389–90, 392, 395, 402–3.
7. *OR*, vol. 8, pp. 402–3, 408–10.
8. *OR*, vol. 8, pp. 408–10, 419; *OR*, vol. 7, pp. 487–88.
9. *OR*, vol. 8, pp. 437–39.
10. *OR*, vol. 8, pp. 448–49, 462–63.
11. *OR*, vol. 7, p. 524.
12. *OR*, vol. 7, p. 526.
13. *OR*, vol. 7, p. 527.
14. *OR*, vol. 7, pp. 528–29.
15. Louis S. Gerteis, *The Civil War in Missouri: A Military History* (Columbia: University of Missouri Press, 2012), 119–21.
16. *OR*, vol. 7, pp. 532–34.
17. *OR*, vol. 7, pp. 68–69, 541.
18. *OR*, vol. 7, pp. 69–72.
19. *OR*, vol. 7, pp. 72–73; To Brig. Gen. Charles F. Smith, in *The Papers of Ulysses S. Grant*, ed. John Y. Simon, vol. 4, *January 8, 1862–March 31, 1862* (Carbondale: Southern Illinois University Press, 1972), 11–12; *ORN*, 22:487–88.
20. *OR*, vol. 7, pp. 73–75.
21. *OR*, vol. 7, pp. 73–74; *ORN*, 22:520–21; *OR*, vol. 7, p. 561.
22. Cooling, *Forts Henry and Donelson*, 68; Kendall D. Gott, *Where the South Lost the War* (Mechanicsburg, PA: Stackpole Books, 2003), 61; Smith, *Grant Invades Tennessee*, 58.
23. Gott, *Where the South Lost the War*, 61; A. L. Conger, *Rise of U. S. Grant* (1931; repr., Freeport, NY: Books for Libraries Press, 1970), 145–47, 151.
24. To Maj. Gen. Henry W. Halleck, in *Papers of Ulysses S. Grant*, ed, Simon, 4:90.

25. Johnston, *Life of General Albert Sidney Johnston*, 423–24; Smith, *Grant Invades Tennessee*, 64; Gott, *Where the South Lost the War*, 63.
26. Johnston, *Life of General Albert Sidney Johnston*, 424–26.
27. *OR*, vol. 7, p. 928.
28. *OR*, vol. 7, p. 554; *OR*, vol. 8, pp. 508–11.
29. *OR*, vol. 8, pp. 510, 558–60; Cooling, *Forts Henry and Donelson*, 73.
30. *OR*, vol. 7, pp. 844–45.
31. To Capt. John C. Kelton, in *Papers of Ulysses S. Grant*, ed. Simon, 4:74–75; To Maj. Gen. Henry W. Halleck, in *Papers of Ulysses S. Grant*, ed. Simon, 90–91; To Col. Leonard F. Ross, in *Papers of Ulysses S. Grant*, ed. Simon, 94; *OR*, vol. 7, pp. 561–62; *ORN*, 22:502, 515, 525.
32. Ulysses S. Grant, *Personal Memoirs* (1885; repr., New York: Penguin Books, 1999), 152.
33. To Maj. Gen. Henry W. Halleck, in *Papers of Ulysses S. Grant*, ed. Simon, 4:99–100; To Maj. Gen. Henry W. Halleck, in *Papers of Ulysses S. Grant*, ed. Simon, 103–4.
34. *ORN*, 22:524.
35. *OR*, vol. 5, p. 41; *OR*, vol. 8, p. 510.
36. *OR*, vol. 7, p. 571.
37. *OR*, vol. 7, p. 121.
38. Bruce Catton, *Grant Moves South* (1960; repr., Edison, NJ: Castle Books, 2000), 134; *OR*, vol. 7, p. 572.
39. *OR*, vol. 7, pp. 574, 576.
40. *OR*, vol. 7, pp. 575, 577; *ORN*, 22:534.
41. Cooling, *Forts Henry and Donelson*, 89–90; *OR*, vol. 7, pp. 126, 219.
42. *OR*, vol. 7, pp. 127, 581.
43. *OR*, vol. 7, pp. 124, 128–29.
44. Catton, *Grant Moves South*, 138.

Chapter 2

1. Gott, *Where the South Lost the War*, 93.
2. *OR*, vol. 7, pp. 121–22.
3. Jean Edward Smith, *Grant* (New York: Touchstone, 2001), 27, 52, 71, 73, 76, 86–89, 90–95.
4. Smith, *Grant*, 104–8, 113, 117–18.

5. *OR*, vol. 7, p. 122; Smith, *Grant Invades Tennessee*, 167–68.
6. *OR*, vol. 7, pp. 120–21, 585–86; Grant, *Personal Memoirs*, 154.
7. *OR*, vol. 7, pp. 125, 128.
8. *OR*, vol. 7, pp. 124–25.
9. *OR*, vol. 7, p. 129; Smith, *Grant Invades Tennessee*, 81; Cooling, *Forts Henry and Donelson*, 100; Catton, *Grant Moves South*, 143.
10. Wilbur F. Crummer, *With Grant at Fort Donelson, Shiloh and Vicksburg* (Oak Park, IL: E. C. Crummer, 1915), 19; Robert MacBride, *Civil War Ironclads* (Philadelphia: Chilton Books, 1962), 3; Smith, *Grant Invades Tennessee*, 108.
11. *OR*, vol. 7, pp. 122–23, 142; Rear Admiral Henry Walke, "The Gun-Boats at Belmont and Fort Henry," in *Battles and Leaders of the Civil War*, ed. Robert Underwood Johnson and Clarence Clough Buel (New York: Century, 1884), 1:363; Conrad Hammond Lanza, comp., *Fort Henry and Fort Donelson Campaigns, February 1862: Source Book* (Fort Leavenworth, KS, 1923), 376–77 (hereafter cited as Lanza, *Source Book*).
12. Lew Wallace, *Lew Wallace: An Autobiography* (New York: Harper and Brothers, 1906), 1:368–70; Smith, *Grant Invades Tennessee*, 100–103; Isabel Wallace, *Life and Letters of General W. H. L. Wallace* (1909; repr., Carbondale: Southern Illinois University Press, 2000), 154–55; *OR*, vol. 7, pp. 129–30.
13. *OR*, vol. 7, p. 130.
14. Smith, *Grant Invades Tennessee*, 123–25; *OR*, vol. 7, p. 129.
15. *OR*, vol. 7, pp. 125, 146–47, 151; Grant, *Personal Memoirs*, 156.
16. *ORN*, 22:571–74.
17. *OR*, vol. 7, p. 131.
18. T. Harry Williams, *P. G. T. Beauregard: Napoleon in Gray* (Baton Rouge: Louisiana State University Press, 1954), 118–19.
19. Williams, *P. G. T. Beauregard: Napoleon in Gray*, 118–19; *OR*, vol. 7, pp. 124–25, 861, 864–65.
20. Smith, *Grant Invades Tennessee*, 129–31; Cooling, *Forts Henry and Donelson*, 111.
21. Smith, *Grant Invades Tennessee*, 60–62; Gott, *Where the South Lost the War*, 72–73; Connelly, *Army of the Heartland*, 15–22; *OR*, vol. 7, p. 132.
22. Johnston, *Life of General Albert Sidney Johnston*, 412; *OR*, vol. 4, pp. 496–97.

23. *OR*, vol. 4, p. 560; Cooling, *Forts Henry and Donelson*, 58–59; *OR*, vol. 7, pp. 698–700, 709, 719.
24. Johnston, *Life of General Albert Sidney Johnston*, 423–24; *OR*, vol. 7, pp. 75, 837–38.
25. *OR*, vol. 7, pp. 131–33.
26. *OR*, vol. 7, pp. 133, 137.
27. *OR*, vol. 7, p. 149.
28. *OR*, vol. 7, pp. 137, 149–50.
29. *OR*, vol. 7, pp. 138–40.
30. *OR*, vol. 7, pp. 140, 858–59.
31. *OR*, vol. 7, pp. 139, 145.
32. *OR*, vol. 7, pp. 139–40.
33. *OR*, vol. 7, pp. 143, 145.
34. *OR*, vol. 7, p. 140.
35. Jesse Taylor, "The Defense of Fort Henry," in *Battles and Leaders of the Civil War*, ed. Robert Underwood Johnson and Clarence Clough Buel (New York: Century, 1884), 1:370.
36. *OR*, vol. 7, pp. 132, 141–42; Taylor, "Defense of Fort Henry," 1:370–71.
37. *OR*, vol. 7, pp. 140–41.
38. *OR*, vol. 7, pp. 140, 146–47, 151–52.
39. Taylor, "Defense of Fort Henry," 1:371; *OR*, vol. 7, pp. 142, 147; James Jobe, "Forts Henry and Donelson: Disastrous and Almost without Remedy," *Blue & Gray Magazine* 28, no. 4 (2011): 53.
40. *OR*, vol. 7, p. 141.
41. *OR*, vol. 7, pp. 358, 366.

Chapter 3

1. *OR*, vol. 8, p. 509; *OR*, vol. 7, pp. 574–75, 613; Conger, *Rise of U. S. Grant*, 189.
2. *OR*, vol. 7, pp. 574, 576, 583–84; *OR*, vol. 52, pt. 1, p. 206; Ambrose, *Halleck: Lincoln's Chief of Staff*, 26.
3. Smith, *Grant*, 141–42; *OR*, vol. 7, pp. 583, 594–95; Smith, *Grant Invades Tennessee*, 134.
4. *OR*, vol. 7, pp. 580, 840–41.
5. *OR*, vol. 7, pp. 583–85.

6. *OR*, vol. 7, pp. 583–84.
7. *OR*, vol. 7, pp. 586–89.
8. *OR*, vol. 7, pp. 125, 590.
9. *OR*, vol. 7, p. 125.
10. *OR*, vol. 7, pp. 590–91, 595; Curt Anders, *Henry Halleck's War: A Fresh Look at Lincoln's Controversial General-in-Chief* (Carmel: Guild Press of Indiana, 1999), 344.
11. *OR*, vol. 7, pp. 590–91, 595.
12. *OR*, vol. 7, pp. 590–91, 595.
13. *OR*, vol. 7, pp. 592, 596, 599.
14. *OR*, vol. 7, pp. 576, 584–85.
15. *OR*, vol. 7, pp. 586–87, 593; Cooling, *Forts Henry and Donelson*, 117.
16. *OR*, vol. 7, pp. 591–92, 596–97.
17. *OR*, vol. 7, p. 599.
18. *OR*, vol. 7, pp. 601, 612; To Maj. Gen. Henry W. Halleck, in *Papers of Ulysses S. Grant*, ed. Simon, 4:195-96.
19. Cooling, *Forts Henry and Donelson*, 120–21.
20. *OR*, vol. 7, pp. 524, 527–31.
21. Engle, *Don Carlos Buell*, 21, 38, 40, 41, 48–63, 65, 74–76.
22. *OR*, vol. 7, pp. 509, 545; Engle, *Don Carlos Buell*, 139 (note: author confused Lorenzo Thomas with George Thomas).
23. *OR*, vol. 7, pp. 573–74, 580, 932.
24. *OR*, vol. 7, p. 933.
25. *OR*, vol. 7, pp. 580, 583–84.
26. *OR*, vol. 7, p. 584.
27. *OR*, vol. 7, pp. 580, 583–84, 931–33.
28. *OR*, vol. 7, pp. 576, 587–88, 936–37.
29. *OR*, vol. 7, p. 584.
30. *OR*, vol. 7, p. 584; John H. Rerick MD, *The Forty-Fourth Indiana Volunteer Infantry* (LaGrange, IN, 1880), 31–35; Gail Stephens, *Shadow of Shiloh: Major General Lew Wallace in the Civil War* (Indianapolis: Indiana Historical Society Press, 2010), 48; Simon, *Papers of Ulysses S. Grant*, ed. Simon, 4:196; Gott, *Where the South Lost the War*, 284.
31. *OR*, vol. 7, pp. 473, 586.

32. *OR*, vol. 7, pp. 585, 587–89.

33. General Field Orders No. 14, in *Papers of Ulysses S. Grant*, ed. Simon, 4:205; Wallace, *Lew Wallace: An Autobiography*, 390–92; *OR*, vol. 7, p. 220; Stephens, *Shadow of Shiloh*, 48–49.

34. Charles M. Cummings, *Yankee Quaker Confederate General: The Curious Career of Bushrod Rust Johnson* (Cranbury, NJ: Associated University Presses, 1971), 185; Arndt M. Stickles, *Simon Bolivar Buckner: Borderland Knight* (Chapel Hill: University of North Carolina Press, 1940), 121; Nathaniel Cheairs Hughes Jr. and Roy P. Stonesifer Jr., *Life and Wars of Gideon J. Pillow* (Knoxville: University of Tennessee Press, 2011), 210–11; Charles Pinnegar, *Brand of Infamy: A Biography of John Buchanan Floyd* (Westport, CT: Greenwood, 2002), 125–26; *OR*, vol. 7, pp. 840–41.

35. Roland, *Albert Sidney Johnston*, 6, 15, 18, 31–46, 49–51, 58, 82, 118, 126–27, 130–39, 154, 168, 185, 242, 247, 252, 259–61.

36. Roland, *Albert Sidney Johnston*, 185, 216, 236; Johnston, *Life of General Albert Sidney Johnston*, 247–48.

37. Hughes and Stonesifer, *Life and Wars of Gideon J. Pillow*, 207–11.

38. Roland, *Albert Sidney Johnston*, 261; Stickles, *Simon Bolivar Buckner*, 86–87.

39. Cummings, *Yankee Quaker Confederate General*, 34, 75, 172, 185.

40. *OR*, vol. 7, pp. 358, 863–64.

41. *OR*, vol. 7, pp. 859–60, 864–65; Cooling, *Forts Henry and Donelson*, 128.

42. *OR*, vol. 7, pp. 342, 358.

43. Connelly, *Army of the Heartland*, 111–12; Cooling, *Forts Henry and Donelson*, 128.

44. Cooling, *Forts Henry and Donelson*, 128.

45. Connelly, *Army of the Heartland*, 112; *OR*, vol. 7, p. 865.

46. Gott, *Where the South Lost the War*, 286; Connelly, *Army of the Heartland*, 113; Smith, *Grant Invades Tennessee*, 260; *OR*, vol. 7, pp. 859–60.

47. Smith, *Grant Invades Tennessee*, 154–55.

48. Cummings, *Yankee Quaker Confederate General*, 185; *OR*, vol. 7, p. 858.

49. Cooling, *Forts Henry and Donelson*, 128; Johnston, *Life of General Albert Sidney Johnston*, 308–9; *OR*, vol. 7, pp. 864–65.

50. Hughes and Stonesifer, *Life and Wars of Gideon J. Pillow*, 210–13; Cooling, *Forts Henry and Donelson*, 128; *OR*, vol. 7, p. 358.

51. *OR*, vol. 7, p. 865; Cooling, *Forts Henry and Donelson*, 128–29.

52. *OR*, vol. 7, pp. 278, 865; *OR*, vol. 52, pt. 2, p. 267; Cooling, *Forts Henry and Donelson*, 113.

53. Cummings, *Yankee Quaker Confederate General*, 188–90; Hughes and Stonesifer, *Life and Wars of Gideon J. Pillow*, 213; *OR*, vol. 7, pp. 867–68.

54. *OR*, vol. 7, pp. 261–62, 278–79, 329; Hughes and Stonesifer, *Life and Wars of Gideon J. Pillow*, 213–14.

55. Cooling, *Forts Henry and Donelson*, 121; *OR*, vol. 7, pp. 268, 859–60, 870–71.

56. Gott, *Where the South Lost the War*, 286–88; Lanza, *Source Book*, 1350–51; *OR*, vol. 7, pp. 268, 870–71; *OR*, vol. 52, pt. 2, p. 269.

57. *OR*, vol. 7, p. 869; Roland, *Albert Sidney Johnston*, 290–91; Connelly, *Army of the Heartland*, 85.

58. Cooling, *Forts Henry and Donelson*, 132; *OR*, vol. 7, p. 328.

59. *OR*, vol. 7, pp. 328–29.

60. *OR*, vol. 7, pp. 383–84.

61. Hughes and Stonesifer, *Life and Wars of Gideon J. Pillow*, 216; *ORN*, 22:588; *OR*, vol. 7, p. 338.

62. *OR*, vol. 7, p. 259.

63. Grant, *Personal Memoirs*, 158; Smith, *Grant Invades Tennessee*, 158.

64. To Brig. Gen. John A. McClernand, in *Papers of Ulysses S. Grant*, ed. Simon, 4:165–66.

65. Albert D. Richardson, *Personal History of Ulysses S. Grant* (Hartford, CT, 1868), 217.

66. *OR*, vol. 7, p. 596; Maj. Mason Brayman to Brig. Gen. Ulysses S. Grant, February 7, 1862 [in page note], in *Papers of Ulysses S. Grant*, ed. Simon, 4:166.

67. *OR*, vol. 7, p. 596; Smith, *Grant Invades Tennessee*, 134–35.

68. Smith, *Grant Invades Tennessee*, 134; *OR*, vol. 7, pp. 595–96.

69. To Brig. Gen. Charles F. Smith, in *Papers of Ulysses S. Grant*, ed. Simon, 4:175; Marion Morrison, *History of the Ninth Regiment Illinois Volunteer Infantry, with the Regimental Roster* (1864; repr., Carbondale: Southern Illinois University Press, 1997), 21.

70. To Brig. Gen. John A. McClernand, in *Papers of Ulysses S. Grant,*, ed. Simon, 4:176; To Mary Grant, in *Papers of Ulysses S. Grant*, ed. Simon, 4:179–80.

71. *OR*, vol. 7, p. 600; *ORN*, 22:583.

72. Smith, *Grant*, 151; To Brig. Gen. John A. McClernand, in *Papers of Ulysses S. Grant*, ed. Simon, 4:183.
73. Wallace, *Lew Wallace: An Autobiography*, 376–77; Stephens, *Shadow of Shiloh*, 47.
74. Wallace, *Lew Wallace: An Autobiography*, 377; *OR*, vol. 7, p. 601.
75. *OR*, vol. 7, p. 605.
76. *OR*, vol. 7, pp. 170, 183; Smith, *Grant Invades Tennessee*, 171–73.
77. *OR*, vol. 7, pp. 170–71, 329, 383–84.
78. *OR*, vol. 7, p. 171; Smith, *Grant Invades Tennessee*, 174–76; Jobe, "Forts Henry and Donelson," 15.
79. *ORN*, 22:587–88; Rear Admiral Henry Walke. "The Western Flotilla at Fort Donelson, Island Number Ten, Fort Pillow and Memphis," in *Battles and Leaders of the Civil War*, ed. Robert Underwood Johnson and Clarence Clough Buel (New York: Century), 1:431; *OR*, vol. 52, pt. 2, p. 271.
80. *OR*, vol. 7, p. 184; Smith, *Grant Invades Tennessee*, 175–76; Jobe, "Forts Henry and Donelson," 14.
81. *OR*, vol. 7. p. 329; Connelly, *Army of the Heartland*, 113.
82. Smith, *Grant Invades Tennessee*, 173–74; Hughes and Stonesifer, *Life and Wars of Gideon J. Pillow*, 216–17; *OR*, vol. 7, p. 338.
83. *ORN*, 22:594; Richard L. Kiper, *Major General John Alexander McClernand: Politician in Uniform* (Kent, OH: Kent State University Press, 1999), 75–76; Allen H. Mesch, *Teacher of Civil War Generals: Major General Charles Ferguson Smith, Soldier and West Point Commandant* (Jefferson, NC: McFarland, 2015), 203–4.
84. Smith, *Grant*, 152–53.
85. Cooling, *Forts Henry and Donelson*, 128.
86. Cooling, *Forts Henry and Donelson*, 128; *OR*, vol. 7. pp. 278, 865, 869–71; *OR*, vol. 52, pt. 2, pp. 268–69.
87. *OR*, vol. 7, p. 259.
88. Johnston, *Life of General Albert Sidney Johnston*, 438; *ORN*, 22:609.
89. Johnston, *Life of General Albert Sidney Johnston*, 438.
90. Johnston, *Life of General Albert Sidney Johnston*, 438.
91. *ORN*, 22:609.
92. Johnston, *Life of General Albert Sidney Johnston*, 438.

93. Johnston, *Life of General Albert Sidney Johnston*, 438.
94. *OR*, vol. 7, p. 338; *ORN*, 22:609; Johnston, *Life of General Albert Sidney Johnston*, 438.
95. Gott, *Where the South Lost the War*, 157; Hughes and Stonesifer, *Life and Wars of Gideon J. Pillow*, 217.
96. Johnston, *Life of General Albert Sidney Johnston*, 438; *OR*, vol. 7, p. 271; Roy P. Stonesifer Jr., "The Forts Henry-Heiman and Fort Donelson Campaigns: A Study of Confederate Command" (PhD diss., Pennsylvania State University, 1965), microfilm, 220.
97. *OR*, vol. 52, pt. 2, p. 272; *OR*, vol. 7, p. 159.
98. *OR*, vol. 52, pt. 1, p. 8; *OR*, vol. 7, pp. 172–73, 268; Cooling, *Forts Henry and Donelson*, 145.
99. *OR*, vol. 7, pp. 271, 878–79; *OR*, vol. 52, pt. 2, pp. 272–73.
100. *OR*, vol. 7, p. 260.

Chapter 4

1. Cooling, *Forts Henry and Donelson*, 147–48, 162–65; Lanza, *Source Book*, 560; Rear Admiral Henry Walke, *Naval Scenes and Reminiscences of the Civil War in the United States on the Southern and Western Waters* (New York, 1877), 76; *OR*, vol. 7, pp. 174, 268.
2. *OR*, vol. 7, pp. 261–62; Steven E. Woodworth, *Nothing but Victory: The Army of the Tennessee, 1861–1865* (New York: Alfred A. Knopf, 2005), 82.
3. Grant, *Personal Memoirs*, 88–89; Smith, *Grant Invades Tennessee*, 407–13.
4. *OR*, vol. 7, pp. 601–5.
5. *OR*, vol. 7, pp. 601; Stephens, *Shadow of Shiloh*, 30, 47; Wallace, *Lew Wallace: An Autobiography*, 378.
6. *OR*, vol. 7, p. 613.
7. *OR*, vol. 7, p. 606; Stephens, *Shadow of Shiloh*, 48; Capt. William S. Hillyer to Brig. Gen. Lew Wallace [in page note], in *Papers of Ulysses S. Grant*, ed. Simon, 4:193.
8. To Maj. Gen. Henry W. Halleck [see note no. 2], in *Papers of Ulysses S. Grant*, ed. Simon, 195–96.
9. Wallace, *Lew Wallace: An Autobiography*, 378–80.
10. *OR*, vol. 7, p. 162; Woodworth, *Nothing but Victory*, 85–86; *OR*, vol. 52, pt. 1, p. 7; Smith, *Grant Invades Tennessee*, 174–75; Gott, *Where the South Lost the War*, 147–50; *OR*, vol. 7, pp. 184, 193, 211–12.

11. To Maj. Gen. Henry W. Halleck, near Fort Donaldson Feb. 13/62, to Maj. Gen. Henry W. Halleck, near Fort Donaldson via Cairo, Feb. 14 [13] Feb. 1862, in *Papers of Ulysses S. Grant*, ed. Simon, 4:200.
12. *OR*, vol. 7, pp. 184, 193; Edwin C. Bearss, *Troop Movement Maps—Fort Donelson, Feb. 12–15, 1862*, 11 sheets (Dover, TN: Fort Donelson National Military Park, April–May 1959), 2.
13. *OR*, vol. 52, pt. 1, pp. 7–10; Cooling, *Forts Henry and Donelson*, 140–41.
14. *OR*, vol. 7, p. 220; *OR*, vol. 52, pt. 1, p. 8.
15. *OR*, vol. 7, pp. 172, 190, 212–13, 368, 370.
16. To Brig. Gen. John A. McClernand, in *Papers of Ulysses S. Grant*, ed. Simon, 4:201; To Commander Henry Walke, in *Papers of Ulysses S. Grant*, ed. Simon, 4:203.
17. *OR*, vol. 7, p. 215; Bearss, *Troop Movement Maps*, 2.
18. Stephens, *Shadow of Shiloh*, 48.
19. Wallace, *Lew Wallace: An Autobiography*, 380–83.
20. Wallace, *Lew Wallace: An Autobiography*, 348, 383–85; Stephens, *Shadow of Shiloh*, 48.
21. Wallace, *Lew Wallace: An Autobiography*, 385–87; General Field Orders No. 14 in *Papers of Ulysses S. Grant*, ed. Simon, 4:205–6; Stephens, *Shadow of Shiloh*, 48–49.
22. *OR*, vol. 7, p. 613; Wallace, *Lew Wallace: An Autobiography*, 388–89.
23. Wallace, *Lew Wallace: An Autobiography*, 389–95.
24. *OR*, vol. 7, p. 215; Bearss, *Troop Movement Maps*, 3.
25. Stephens, *Shadow of Shiloh*, 49.
26. Catton, *Grant Moves South*, 150; *ORN*, 22:539; *OR*, vol. 7, p. 261.
27. Spencer C. Tucker, *Andrew Foote: Civil War Admiral on Western Waters* (Annapolis, MD: Naval Institute Press, 2000), 1–6, 10–12, 20–22, 25, 46–52, 71, 81–83, 88–94, 101, 114.
28. *OR*, vol. 7, p. 598.
29. *OR*, vol. 7, pp. 600–601; *ORN*, 22:583–84.
30. *OR*, vol. 7, p. 600.
31. *OR*, vol. 7, pp. 603–4.
32. *ORN*, 22:550; *OR*, vol. 7, p. 604.
33. *OR*, vol. 7, p. 603; Lanza, *Source Book*, 541–42.
34. Edwin C. Bearss, "The Ironclads at Fort Donelson: The Ironclads Sail

for the Cumberland (Part 1)," *Register of the Kentucky Historical Society* 74, no. 1 (1976): 7–8; Lanza, *Source Book*, 542.

35. Edwin C. Bearss, "The Ironclads at Fort Donelson (Part 3): The Ironclads Fail," *Register of the Kentucky Historical Society* 74, no. 3 (1976): 167; Lanza, *Source Book*, 560; *OR*, vol. 7, p. 163.

36. Walke, "Western Flotilla at Fort Donelson," 431.

37. Walke, "Western Flotilla at Fort Donelson," 433; Lanza, *Source Book*, 560–61.

38. Frank R. Donovan and editors of *American Heritage, Ironclads of the Civil War* (New York: American Heritage, 1964), 76.

39. *OR*, vol. 7, pp. 388–89, 394, 410–11; Cooling, *Forts Henry and Donelson*, 87.

40. Cooling, *Forts Henry and Donelson*, 153–55; Lanza, *Source Book*, 562; *OR*, vol. 7, p. 393; Bearss, "Ironclads at Fort Donelson (Part 3)," 170–71; H. L. Bedford, "Fight between the Batteries and Gunboats at Fort Donelson," *Southern Historical Society Papers* 13 (1885): 171.

41. Lanza, *Source Book*, 563; Cooling, *Forts Henry and Donelson*, 155.

42. Lanza, *Source Book*, 563–64, 571; Cooling, *Forts Henry and Donelson*, 157; Bearss, "Ironclads at Fort Donelson (Part 3)," 174.

43. Bearss, "Ironclads at Fort Donelson (Part 3)," 174–75; Lanza, *Source Book*, 571; *ORN*, 22:585.

44. *ORN*, 22:592–93.

45. Walke, "Western Flotilla at Fort Donelson," 433–35; Bearss, "Ironclads at Fort Donelson (Part 3)," 176–77, 182; Walke, *Naval Scenes and Reminiscences*, 78.

46. Lanza, *Source Book*, 571; Tucker, *Andrew Foote*, 89–94; MacBride, *Civil War Ironclads*, 2.

47. Bedford, "Fight between the Batteries and Gunboats," 172; Walke, *Naval Scenes and Reminiscences*, 75; *OR*, vol. 7, p. 396; Walke, "Western Flotilla at Fort Donelson," 431–33.

48. Lanza, *Source Book*, 572.

49. *ORN*, 22:585–86.

50. *ORN*, 22:585–86; James Mason Hoppin, *Life of Andrew Hull Foote, Rear-Admiral United States Navy* (New York, 1874), 228–29.

51. Bedford, "Fight between the Batteries and Gunboats," 172.

52. Johnson, *Rear Admiral John Rodgers*, 156–67.

53. Cooling, *Forts Henry and Donelson*, 159; Johnson, *Rear Admiral John Rodgers*, 168.
54. Grant, *Personal Memoirs*, 162; To Julia Dent Grant, in *Papers of Ulysses S. Grant*, ed. Simon, 4:211; *OR*, vol. 7, pp. 613–14.
55. Smith, *Grant Invades Tennessee*, 206; *OR*, vol. 7, p. 267; Faust, *Historical Times Illustrated*, 51–52, 88, 265, 338, 397, 399, 585.
56. Pinnegar, *Brand of Infamy*, 4–6, 10–13, 17, 45, 51–52, 97, 108–9, 124–25.
57. Robert M. Hughes, "John B. Floyd and His Traducers," *Virginia Magazine of History and Biography* 43, no. 4 (October 1935): 322–23, 325, 328.
58. Hughes, "John B. Floyd and His Traducers," 322; Pinnegar, *Brand of Infamy*, 198n116; Grant, *Personal Memoirs*, 165.
59. *OR*, vol. 7, pp. 172–73, 268, 279, 613, 878–79; *OR*, vol. 52, pt. 1, pp. 7–8; *OR*, vol. 52, pt. 2, p. 273.
60. *OR*, vol. 7, p. 185; Bearss, *Troop Movement Maps*, 2; Cooling, *Forts Henry and Donelson*, 149–51; *OR*, vol. 7, p. 330; Hughes and Stonesifer, *Life and Wars of Gideon J. Pillow*, 221–22.
61. *OR*, vol. 7, pp. 338, 384; Bearss, *Troop Movement Maps*, 3.
62. *OR*, vol. 7, pp. 379, 384.
63. Robert M. Hughes, "Why Fort Donelson Was Surrendered: Gen. John B. Floyd and the Fight at Fort Donelson," *Confederate Veteran*, August 1929, 301–2.
64. Hughes, "Why Fort Donelson Was Surrendered," 302.
65. *OR*, vol. 7, pp. 880–81; Cooling, *Forts Henry and Donelson*, 149.
66. Gott, *Where the South Lost the War*, 184; *OR*, vol. 7, p. 185.
67. *OR*, vol. 52, pt. 2, p. 273; *OR*, vol. 7, pp. 263, 285–86.
68. *OR*, vol. 7, p. 271; Cooling, *Forts Henry and Donelson*, 202.
69. *OR*, vol. 7, p. 286.
70. *OR*, vol. 7, pp. 268, 286.
71. *OR*, vol. 7, p. 263.
72. *OR*, vol. 7, pp. 314–15, 330–31, 338–39, 347.
73. *OR*, vol. 7, pp. 281–82; Cooling, *Forts Henry and Donelson*, 163–64; Bearss, *Troop Movement Maps*, 3.
74. Smith, *Grant Invades Tennessee*, 258–59; Gott, *Where the South Lost the War*, 286–88; Bearss, *Troop Movement Maps*, 4; *OR*, vol. 7, pp. 282, 330–31.

75. *OR*, vol. 7, p. 286.
76. Bearss, *Troop Movement Maps*, 3; *OR*, vol. 7, pp. 286, 330–31, 369, 377.
77. Smith, *Grant Invades Tennessee*, 217; *OR*, vol. 7, pp. 338–39.
78. *OR*, vol. 7, pp. 329, 331, 347; Bearss, *Troop Movement Maps*, 4.
79. *OR*, vol. 7, pp. 369, 377; Randal W. McGavock, journal entry for Feb. 14, [1862], in *Pen and Sword: The Life and Journals of Randal W. McGavock*, ed. Hershel Gower and Jack Allen (Nashville: Tennessee Historical Commission, 1959), 591.
80. Cooling, *Forts Henry and Donelson*, 164–65; *OR*, vol. 7, pp. 268, 360, 365.
81. *OR*, vol. 7, pp. 263, 276–77, 330–31, 347, 360, 369, 384.
82. *OR*, vol. 7, pp. 268, 330–31, 317–18.
83. Stonesifer, "Forts Henry-Heiman and Fort Donelson Campaigns," 265–66; *OR*, vol. 7, pp. 268, 880.
84. *OR*, vol. 4, p. 197; *OR*, vol. 3, pp. 471, 528.
85. *OR*, vol. 7, pp. 219, 575, 578.
86. Smith, *Grant Invades Tennessee*, 76–79; Grant, *Personal Memoirs*, 154.
87. Wallace, *Lew Wallace: An Autobiography*, 370–73; Stonesifer, "Forts Henry-Heiman and Fort Donelson Campaigns," 155, 165.
88. Kiper, *Major General John Alexander McClernand*, 1–6, 11, 15, 23–25, 28–29.
89. *OR*, vol. 7, pp. 170–71, 183–84, 192–93, 211, 215, 220; *OR*, vol. 52, pt. 1, p. 7; Smith, *Grant Invades Tennessee*, 174–76.
90. Smith, *Grant Invades Tennessee*, 174–76; *OR*, vol. 7, pp. 171–72, 184, 193, 211–12, 215, 220; *OR*, vol. 52, pt. 1, p. 7.
91. *OR*, vol. 52, pt. 1, pp. 9–10; *OR*, vol. 7, pp. 172, 184–85, 193, 215, 220.
92. *OR*, vol. 7, p. 215.
93. Grant, *Personal Memoirs*, 161–62; *OR*, vol. 7, p. 174.
94. *OR*, vol. 7, pp. 174, 185.
95. *OR*, vol. 7, pp. 215, 218.
96. *OR*, vol. 7, pp. 174, 217–18; Gott, *Where the South Lost the War*, 194; Stonesifer, "Forts Henry-Heiman and Fort Donelson Campaigns," 271–72; Bearss, *Troop Movement Maps*, 4.
97. *OR*, vol. 7, pp. 175, 286, 338–39; Bearss, *Troop Movement Maps*, 4.
98. *OR*, vol. 7, pp. 218, 339.
99. *OR*, vol. 7, pp. 282, 339; Bearss, *Troop Movement Maps*, 5.

100. *OR*, vol. 7, pp. 185, 218, 339; Smith, *Grant Invades Tennessee*, 269–70.
101. *OR*, vol. 7, pp. 218, 282, 339, 380.
102. *OR*, vol. 7, pp. 185–86, 188, 190, 276–77, 282, 373; Smith, *Grant Invades Tennessee*, 274–76.
103. *OR*, vol. 7, pp. 185–86, 218.
104. *OR*, vol. 7, pp. 216–17, 385.
105. *OR*, vol. 7, pp. 186, 277–78, 339; Bearss, *Troop Movement Maps*, 5.
106. *OR*, vol. 7, pp. 216–19; Bearss, *Troop Movement Maps*, 5.
107. Morrison, *History of the Ninth Regiment*, 22–23; *OR*, vol. 7, pp. 188–90; Bearss, *Troop Movement Maps*, 5.
108. *OR*, vol. 7, pp. 186, 190, 216, 219.
109. *OR*, vol. 7, pp. 185–87, 216.
110. *OR*, vol. 7, pp. 269, 276, 282, 340, 385.

Chapter 5

1. Cooling, *Forts Henry and Donelson*, 155–59; *ORN*, 22:584–85, 593; Walke, "Western Flotilla at Fort Donelson," 433–34.
2. Walke, "Western Flotilla at Fort Donelson," 429; Bearss, "Ironclads at Fort Donelson (Part 3)," 182.
3. *ORN*, 22:585–86.
4. *ORN*, 22:588–89, 593.
5. Hoppin, *Life of Andrew Hull Foote*, 227–28, 312; Tucker, *Andrew Foote*, 195–96; Adam Badeau, *Military History of General U. S. Grant, from April, 1861 to April, 1865* (New York, 1885), 1:42–43.
6. Grant, *Personal Memoirs*, 163.
7. Grant, *Personal Memoirs*, 162–63.
8. Badeau, *Military History of General U. S. Grant*, 42–43; Grant, *Personal Memoirs*, 163.
9. Charles Whittlesey, *War Memoranda* (Cleveland: William W. Williams, 1884), 29–31; Joseph A. Rose, *Grant under Fire.* (New York: Alderhanna, 2015), 78.
10. Grant, *Personal Memoirs*, 163.
11. Grant, *Personal Memoirs*, 163; *OR*, vol. 7, p. 600.
12. *ORN*, 22:586.
13. Wallace, *Lew Wallace: An Autobiography*, 390; Rose, *Grant under Fire*, 78.

14. Thomas B. Buell, *The Warrior Generals: Combat Leadership in the Civil War* (New York: Crown, 1997), 164.
15. Jobe, "Forts Henry and Donelson," 14, 16; Wallace, *Lew Wallace: An Autobiography*, 389, 393–95.
16. Stephens, *Shadow of Shiloh*, 1–8, 14, 17–19, 23–45; Wallace, *Lew Wallace: An Autobiography*, 8.
17. Wallace, *Lew Wallace: An Autobiography*, 397–98.
18. Wallace, *Lew Wallace: An Autobiography*, 399–400; *OR*, vol. 7, pp. 176–77.
19. *OR*, vol. 7, p. 176.
20. *OR*, vol. 7, pp. 176–77; Wallace, *Lew Wallace: An Autobiography*, 399–400; Smith, *Grant Invades Tennessee*, 284.
21. *OR*, vol. 7, p. 177; Wallace, *Lew Wallace: An Autobiography*, 399.
22. *OR*, vol. 7, p. 177; Wallace, *Lew Wallace: An Autobiography*, 400.
23. *OR*, vol. 7, p. 237; Wallace, *Lew Wallace: An Autobiography*, 400.
24. Buell, *Warrior Generals*, 164.
25. Wallace, *Lew Wallace: An Autobiography*, 399–400.
26. Wallace, *Lew Wallace: An Autobiography*, 399–400; *OR*, vol. 7, p. 243.
27. Bearss, *Troop Movement Maps*, 6–7; Stonesifer, "Forts Henry-Heiman and Fort Donelson Campaigns," 283–84.
28. *OR*, vol. 7, pp. 182, 186, 219; Bearss, *Troop Movement Maps*, 5.
29. *OR*, vol. 7, pp. 175, 243, 251.
30. *OR*, vol. 7, pp. 186, 188–89.
31. *OR*, vol. 7, pp. 186, 190, 216; Smith, *Grant Invades Tennessee*, 287–89; Bearss, *Troop Movement Maps*, 6.
32. Bearss, *Troop Movement Maps*, 6; Smith, *Grant Invades Tennessee*, 290–91; *OR*, vol. 7, pp. 186, 189, 251.
33. *OR*, vol. 7, p. 216; Gott, *Where the South Lost the War*, 283.
34. *OR*, vol. 7, p. 246.
35. Smith, *Grant Invades Tennessee*, 293–94; *OR*, vol. 7, p. 244; Bearss, *Troop Movement Maps*, 7.
36. Gott, *Where the South Lost the War*, 282–84.
37. *OR*, vol. 7, 282; Bearss, *Troop Movement Maps*, 2.
38. *OR*, vol. 7, pp. 263, 268, 327–28, 331; Bearss, *Troop Movement Maps*, 4.

39. Stickles, *Simon Bolivar Buckner*, 4–10, 13, 16–17, 32, 41–42, 46, 67–69, 78–79, 86–89, 93.
40. Gott, *Where the South Lost the War*, 286–88; Cooling, *Forts Henry and Donelson*, 164; Bearss, *Troop Movement Maps*, 4.
41. *OR*, vol. 7, pp. 344, 350, 352, 356, 377.
42. *OR*, vol. 7, p. 347.
43. *OR*, vol. 7, pp. 331, 343; Bearss, *Troop Movement Maps*, 3.
44. Bearss, *Troop Movement Maps*, 5.
45. Bearss, *Troop Movement Maps*, 5.
46. Bearss, *Troop Movement Maps*, 5.
47. *OR*, vol. 7, pp. 186, 188–90, 282, 286, 331.
48. *OR*, vol. 7, p. 6.
49. *OR*, vol. 7, pp. 186, 189, 251, 286.
50. *OR*, vol. 7, pp. 331, 344–45, 347–48, 350.
51. *OR*, vol. 7, pp. 345, 352.
52. *OR*, vol. 7, pp. 195–96, 352.
53. *OR*, vol. 7, p. 343.
54. *OR*, vol. 7, p. 343; Bearss, *Troop Movement Maps*, 6.
55. *OR*, vol. 7, p. 343.
56. *OR*, vol. 7, pp. 195–96; Jim Huffstodt, *Hard Dying Men* (Bowie, MD: Heritage Books, 1991), 69; Lanza, *Source Book*, 840.
57. Huffstodt, *Hard Dying Men*, 69–70; Jobe, "Forts Henry and Donelson," 27, 56.
58. *OR*, vol. 7, pp. 263–64, 282.
59. *OR*, vol. 7, pp. 282, 356; Hughes and Stonesifer, *Life and Wars of Gideon J. Pillow*, 227–28.
60. *OR*, vol. 7, pp. 263–64, 356.
61. *OR*, vol. 7, pp. 331; Gott, *Where the South Lost the War*, 215.
62. Cooling, *Forts Henry and Donelson*, 174; Hughes, "Why Fort Donelson Was Surrendered," 303.
63. Cooling, *Forts Henry and Donelson*, 174.
64. *OR*, vol. 7, pp. 331, 344–45, 350, 352.
65. Gott, *Where the South Lost the War*, 282–87.
66. Bearss, *Troop Movement Maps*, 6.

67. OR, vol. 7, pp. 282, 331–32, 348; Hughes and Stonesifer, *Life and Wars of Gideon J. Pillow*, 228.
68. Bearss, *Troop Movement Maps*, 8.
69. OR, vol. 7, p. 237; Wallace, *Lew Wallace: An Autobiography*, 401.
70. Wallace, *Lew Wallace: An Autobiography*, 403.
71. Wallace, *Lew Wallace: An Autobiography*, 402; Bearss, *Troop Movement Maps*, 7; Benjamin Franklin Cooling, "The First Nebraska Infantry Regiment and the Battle of Fort Donelson," *Nebraska History* 45, no. 2 (June 1964): 140; Gott, *Where the South Lost the War*, 284.
72. Wallace, *Lew Wallace: An Autobiography*, 402–3.
73. Wallace, *Lew Wallace: An Autobiography*, 404–5.
74. Wallace, *Lew Wallace: An Autobiography*, 405–6; OR, vol. 7, pp. 210, 237–38, 252; Bearss, *Troop Movement Maps*, 8.
75. Wallace, *Lew Wallace: An Autobiography*, 385.
76. OR, vol. 7, pp. 348, 356, 385; Bearss, *Troop Movement Maps*, 8.
77. OR, vol. 7, p. 269.
78. OR, vol. 7, pp. 269, 315.
79. OR, vol. 7, pp. 332, 369.
80. OR, vol. 7, pp. 348, 356.
81. OR, vol. 7, pp. 348, 353; Cooling, *Forts Henry and Donelson*, 180.
82. Cooling, *Forts Henry and Donelson*, 179; OR, vol. 7, p. 238; Wallace, *Lew Wallace: An Autobiography*, 406–8.
83. Wallace, *Lew Wallace: An Autobiography*, 407–8; OR, vol. 7, pp. 348, 350, 353, 356.
84. Wallace, *Lew Wallace: An Autobiography*, 332.
85. Wallace, *Lew Wallace: An Autobiography*, 408.
86. Bearss, *Troop Movement Maps*, 8.
87. OR, vol. 7, p. 332; Cooling, *Forts Henry and Donelson*, 174–75.
88. Cooling, *Forts Henry and Donelson*, 176; OR, vol. 7, pp. 245, 290.
89. OR, vol. 7, p. 361.
90. OR, vol. 7, pp. 282–83; Bearss, *Troop Movement Maps*, 8.
91. OR, vol. 7, pp. 253, 283, 348, 350, 353, 356.
92. OR, vol. 7, pp. 264, 332.
93. OR, vol. 7, pp. 282–83, 290.

94. *OR*, vol. 7, p. 332; Smith, *Grant Invades Tennessee*, 324.
95. Bearss, *Troop Movement Maps*, 8; *OR*, vol. 7, pp. 276, 278, 340, 374.
96. *OR*, vol. 7, pp. 244–45, 361.
97. Gott, *Where the South Lost the War*, 286–87; *OR*, vol. 7, pp. 338–39.
98. *OR*, vol. 7, pp. 319, 348, 350.
99. *OR*, vol. 7, p. 332.
100. *OR*, vol. 7, pp. 332–33; Stickles, *Simon Bolivar Buckner*, 151.
101. *OR*, vol. 7, pp. 269, 333; Cooling, *Forts Henry and Donelson*, 181.
102. *OR*, vol. 7, p. 269.
103. *OR*, vol. 7, pp. 263–64, 290.
104. *OR*, vol. 7, pp. 269, 314–15.
105. *OR*, vol. 7, pp. 315, 333.
106. *OR*, vol. 7, pp. 276, 278, 340, 374.
107. *OR*, vol. 7, p. 361.
108. *OR*, vol. 7, p. 361.
109. *OR*, vol. 7, p. 269; Lew Wallace, "The Capture of Fort Donelson," in *Battles and Leaders of the Civil War*, ed. Robert Underwood Johnson and Clarence Clough Buel (New York: Century, 1884), 1:421.
110. *OR*, vol. 7, pp. 369, 377.
111. *OR*, vol. 7, pp. 400–401.
112. *OR*, vol. 7, pp. 315, 385.
113. *OR*, vol. 7, p. 163; Grant, *Personal Memoirs*, 163.
114. Grant, *Personal Memoirs*, 163.
115. Badeau, *Military History of General U. S. Grant*, 44; Rose, *Grant under Fire*, 79–80; Richardson, *Personal History of Ulysses S. Grant*, 215.
116. Grant, *Personal Memoirs*, 163; *OR*, vol. 52, pt. 1, p. 8.
117. *OR*, vol. 52, pt. 1, p. 8; *OR*, vol. 7, p. 237; David W. Reed, *Campaigns and Battles of the Twelfth Regiment Iowa Veteran Volunteer Infantry* (Evanston, IL, 1903), 19.
118. Woodworth, *Nothing but Victory*, 107.
119. Wallace, "Capture of Fort Donelson," 421; Wallace, *Lew Wallace: An Autobiography*, 410–11; Catton, *Grant Moves South*, 166.
120. Wallace, "Capture of Fort Donelson," 422: Wallace, *Lew Wallace: An Autobiography*, 411; Grant, *Personal Memoirs*, 164.

121. Wallace, *Lew Wallace: An Autobiography*, 412.
122. Grant, *Personal Memoirs*, 164–65; *OR*, vol. 7, p. 238.
123. *OR*, vol. 7, pp. 210–11, 245; Wallace, *Lew Wallace: An Autobiography*, 412–14; Bearss, *Troop Movement Maps*, 9.
124. Wallace, *Lew Wallace: An Autobiography*, 413–15; Jobe, "Forts Henry and Donelson," 60; *OR*, vol. 7, p. 245.
125. Wallace, *Lew Wallace: An Autobiography*, 414–17; *OR*, vol. 7, p. 233.
126. Gott, *Where the South Lost the War*, 283; Wallace, *Lew Wallace: An Autobiography*, 416–19; Wallace, "Capture of Fort Donelson," 424; *OR*, vol. 7, pp. 211, 239.
127. Wallace, *Lew Wallace: An Autobiography*, 420; *OR*, vol. 7, pp. 361–62.
128. *OR*, vol. 7, p. 618; *ORN*, 22:588.
129. *OR*, vol. 52, pt. 1, p. 8; Lanza, *Source Book*, 935; *OR*, vol. 7, p. 229; John T. Bell, *Tramps and Triumphs of the Second Iowa Infantry* (Omaha, 1886), 5.
130. *OR*, vol. 52, pt. 1, p. 10; *OR*, vol. 7, p. 221; V. P. Twombly, *Second Iowa Infantry at Fort Donelson, February 15, 1862* (Des Moines, IA: Plain Talk, 1901), 15–16; Bell, *Tramps and Triumphs*, 5–6; Mesch, *Teacher of Civil War Generals*, 217–18.
131. Twombly, *Second Iowa Infantry at Fort Donelson*, 7, 16; *OR*, vol. 52, pt. 1, p. 8; Mesch, *Teacher of Civil War Generals*, 217, 310n42.
132. *OR*, vol. 52, pt. 1, p. 10; *OR*, vol. 7, pp. 221, 229, 333, 344, 378.
133. *OR*, vol. 7, pp. 221, 228–29, 333, 344; *OR*, vol. 52, pt. 1, p. 9; Jobe, "Forts Henry and Donelson," 61.
134. *OR*, vol. 52, pt. 1, p. 8; *OR*, vol. 7, p. 635; Mesch, *Teacher of Civil War Generals*, 229.
135. *OR*, vol. 52, pt. 1, p. 11; Grant, *Personal Memoirs*, 164; Jobe, "Forts Henry and Donelson," 61.
136. *OR*, vol. 7, pp. 361–62, 381; Wallace, *Lew Wallace: An Autobiography*, 420–23; Jobe, "Forts Henry and Donelson," 61.
137. Wallace, *Lew Wallace: An Autobiography*, 423; Stephens, *Shadow of Shiloh*, 60.
138. *OR*, vol. 7, p. 239; Grant, *Personal Memoirs*, 163.
139. Gott, *Where the South Lost the War*, 284.
140. Wallace, *Lew Wallace: An Autobiography*, 422; *OR*, vol. 7, pp. 233, 245–46.

141. Wallace, *Lew Wallace: An Autobiography*, 419; Wallace, "Capture of Fort Donelson," 424–25.

Chapter 6

1. *OR*, vol. 7, pp. 269, 287.
2. Jobe, "Forts Henry and Donelson," 61; *OR*, vol. 7, p. 216.
3. *OR*, vol. 7, p. 385; Cooling, *Forts Henry and Donelson*, 200.
4. McGavock, journal entry for Feb 15th, [1862], in *Pen and Sword*, 591-92; Smith, *Grant Invades Tennessee*, 164; *OR*, vol. 7, pp. 255–56.
5. Edwin C. Bearss, *Unconditional Surrender: The Fall of Fort Donelson* (1962; repr., Fort Washington, PA: Eastern National, 2004), 3.
6. *OR*, vol. 7, pp. 269, 287, 293.
7. *OR*, vol. 7, pp. 287, 293, 333.
8. *OR*, vol. 7, p. 287.
9. *OR*, vol. 7, pp. 246, 287, 293.
10. John Allan Wyeth, *Life of General Nathan Bedford Forrest* (New York, 1899), 64.
11. *OR*, vol. 7, pp. 293, 295, 299; Wyeth, *Life of General Nathan Bedford Forrest*, 64.
12. *OR*, vol. 7, pp. 295, 297–98, 385–86; Thomas Jordan and J. P. Pryor, *The Campaigns of Lieut.-Gen. N. B. Forrest and of Forrest's Cavalry, with Portraits, Maps, and Illustrations* (New Orleans, 1868), 88.
13. Adam R. Johnson, *The Partisan Rangers of the Confederate States Army* (Louisville, KY: G. G. Fetter, 1904), 67–68.
14. *OR*, vol. 7, pp. 295, 386; Jordan and Pryor, *Campaigns of Lieut.-Gen. N. B. Forrest*, 88–89.
15. *OR*, vol. 7, pp. 269, 273, 287, 295–96, 300, 333, 386.
16. *OR*, vol. 7, pp. 269; McGavock, journal entry for Feb 16th, [1862], in *Pen and Sword*, 592-93.
17. *OR*, vol. 7, pp. 287–88, 365–66, 369–70, 378.
18. *OR*, vol. 7, pp. 295, 334.
19. *OR*, vol. 7, pp. 287, 295.
20. *OR*, vol. 7, pp. 334, 349.
21. *OR*, vol. 7, p. 288.
22. *OR*, vol. 7, pp. 288, 294–95, 298, 300; Jordan and Pryor, *Campaigns of Lieut.-Gen. N. B. Forrest*, 90–91.

23. *OR*, vol. 7, pp. 273, 294, 297, 302.
24. *OR*, vol. 7, pp. 349, 362–63, 369–70, 378.
25. *OR*, vol. 7, p. 269.
26. Johnson, *Partisan Rangers*, 67–69; Jordan and Pryor, *Campaigns of Lieut.-Gen. N. B. Forrest*, 92–93; Andrew Nelson Lytle, *Bedford Forrest and His Critter Company* (Seminole, FL: Green Key, 1984), 77–78.
27. *OR*, vol. 7, pp. 295, 386; Jordan and Pryor, *Campaigns of Lieut.-Gen. N. B. Forrest*, 92–93.
28. Jobe, "Forts Henry and Donelson," 62–63.
29. Wyeth, *Life of General Nathan Bedford Forrest*, 60–62; *OR*, vol. 7, pp. 415–16.
30. Wyeth, *Life of General Nathan Bedford Forrest*, 60, 64–65; M. L. Vesey, "Why Fort Donelson Was Surrendered," *Confederate Veteran*, October 1929, 370.
31. *OR*, vol. 7, pp. 273–75, 302, 381–82; Hughes and Stonesifer, *Life and Wars of Gideon J. Pillow*, 238; W. N. Brown to Jefferson Davis, in *Jefferson Davis; Constitutionalist; His Letters, Papers and Speeches*, ed. Dunbar Rowland (Jackson MS, 1923), 8:485–88.
32. *OR*, vol. 7, pp. 362–63; Wallace, *Lew Wallace: An Autobiography*, 426–29; Stickles, *Simon Bolivar Buckner*, 33–34.
33. Hughes and Stonesifer, *Life and Wars of Gideon J. Pillow*, 236–38; John H. Brinton, *Personal Memoirs* (New York: Neale, 1914), 129; *OR*, vol. 7, pp. 161, 335.
34. *OR*, vol. 7, pp. 625–26; Cooling, *Forts Henry and Donelson*, 212.
35. *OR*, ser. 2, vol. 3, pp. 271–72, 276–78; George Levy, *To Die in Chicago: Confederate Prisoners at Camp Douglas, 1862–1865* (Gretna, LA: Pelican, 1999), 47; *OR*, ser. 2, vol. 3, pp. 275, 287, 333; Camilla A. Corlas Quinn, "Forgotten Soldiers: The Confederate Prisoners at Camp Butler 1862-1863," *Illinois Historical Journal* 81 (Spring 1988): 36; Hattie Lou Winslow and Joseph R. H. Moore, "Camp Morton, 1861–1865: Indianapolis Prison Camp," *Indiana Historical Society Publications* 13, no. 3 (1940): 258.
36. Lonnie R. Speer, *Portals to Hell: Military Prisons of the Civil War* (Mechanicsburg, PA: Stackpole Books, 1997), 101–2; *OR*, ser. 2, vol. 3, pp. 812–13; *OR*, ser. 2, vol. 4, pp. 266–67.
37. Bearss, *Unconditional Surrender*, 42–43; *OR*, ser. 2, vol. 3, pp. 276, 279–80, 283, 320; *OR*, vol. 7, p. 328.

38. Gott, *Where the South Lost the War*, 288; Johnston, *Life of General Albert Sidney Johnston*, 493.

39. Levy, *To Die in Chicago*, 101; *OR*, vol. 7, p. 274; David J. Bodenhamer and Robert G. Barrows, eds. *The Encyclopedia of Indianapolis* (Indianapolis: Indiana University Press, 1994), 441–42; Speer, *Portals to Hell*, 74. Retired Lieutenant Colonel James Vaughan researched military records and other sources to compile a list of Confederate prisoners of war from Fort Donelson who died in the various Union prisons. His list currently contains 1526 names.

40. Cooling, *Forts Henry and Donelson*, 232–34; Stickles, *Simon Bolivar Buckner*, 169.

41. Johnston, *Life of General Albert Sidney Johnston*, 495; Horn, *Army of Tennessee*, 102.

42. Hughes and Stonesifer, *Life and Wars of Gideon J. Pillow*, 238–39; Johnston, *Life of General Albert Sidney Johnston*, 504; *OR*, vol. 7, pp. 428–29.

43. Johnston, *Life of General Albert Sidney Johnston*, 503, 515–18; Smith, *Grant Invades Tennessee*, 388.

44. *OR*, vol. 7, pp. 254, 256–57, 269, 283–84.

45. Hughes and Stonesifer, *Life and Wars of Gideon J. Pillow*, 242; *OR*, vol. 7, pp. 288, 293, 295–96, 298, 300.

46. *OR*, vol. 7, pp. 405–6.

47. *OR*, vol. 7, pp. 270–73.

48. *OR*, vol. 7, pp. 257–60.

49. *OR*, vol. 7, p. 260.

50. *OR*, vol. 7, pp. 305–6.

51. *OR*, vol. 7, pp. 306–13.

52. Bearss, *Unconditional Surrender*, 43; Stickles, *Simon Bolivar Buckner*, 192; McGavock, journal entry for March 10th, [1862], in *Pen and Sword*, 602–3; McGavock, journal entry for March 12th, [1862], in *Pen and Sword*, 603; McGavock, journal entry for Apr 4, [1862], in *Pen and Sword*, 611; McGavock, journal entry for July 31, [1862], in *Pen and Sword*, 657; McGavock, journal entry for Aug 6, [1862], in *Pen and Sword*, 660.

53. McGavock, journal entry for March 12th, [1862], in *Pen and Sword*, 603; *OR*, vol. 7, pp. 332–34, 348–51, 353–54, 356–57.

54. *OR*, vol. 7, pp. 252, 287–88, 332–32, 348, 350, 353, 356.

55. *OR*, vol. 7, pp. 313.
56. *OR*, vol. 7, pp. 314–16.
57. *OR*, vol. 7, pp. 316–20.
58. *OR*, vol. 7, pp. 320–21.
59. *OR*, vol. 7, pp. 321–25.

Chapter 7

1. *OR*, vol. 7, pp. 861–64; Johnston, *Life of General Albert Sidney Johnston*, 328.
2. *OR*, vol. 7, pp. 524, 528–29, 533–34.
3. William Swinton, *The Twelve Decisive Battles of the War* (New York, 1867), 80–82; Smith, *Grant Invades Tennessee*, 150–53.
4. Gott, *Where the South Lost the War*, 87; Johnston, *Life of General Albert Sidney Johnston*, 484–86; Roland, *Albert Sidney Johnston*, 295.
5. Roland, *Albert Sidney Johnston*, 290–91; *OR*, vol. 7, pp. 864–65; Johnston, *Life of General Albert Sidney Johnston*, 485–86.
6. Johnston, *Life of General Albert Sidney Johnston*, 510–13; Swinton, *Twelve Decisive Battles of the War*, 83; James D. Richardson, *Compilation of the Messages and Papers of the Confederacy, including the Diplomatic Correspondence, 1861-1865* (Nashville: United States Publishing, 1906), 2:193–206.
7. Cooling, *Forts Henry and Donelson*, 128; J. F. C. Fuller, *The Generalship of Ulysses S. Grant* (1929; repr., New York: Da Capo, 1991), 6.
8. *OR*, vol. 7, pp. 870–71; Johnston, *Life of General Albert Sidney Johnston*, 438–39.
9. Johnston, *Life of General Albert Sidney Johnston*, 437; *OR*, vol. 7, pp. 259, 334, 426–27.
10. Stonesifer, "Forts Henry-Heiman and Fort Donelson Campaigns," 364; *OR*, vol. 7, pp. 862–63.
11. *OR*, vol. 7, pp. 271–72, 880; Pinnegar, *Brand of Infamy*, 144.
12. McGavock, journal entry for Feb. 15th, [1862], in *Pen and Sword*, 591–92; *OR*, vol. 7, pp. 316–17; Hughes and Stonesifer, *Life and Wars of Gideon J. Pillow*, 234–36.
13. Hughes and Stonesifer, *Life and Wars of Gideon J. Pillow*, 237; *OR*, vol. 7, p. 300.
14. Stickles, *Simon Bolivar Buckner*, 159.

15. Pinnegar, *Brand of Infamy*, 144–47.
16. Stickles, *Simon Bolivar Buckner*, 192, 194, 256, 272, 346.
17. Stickles, *Simon Bolivar Buckner*, 159–60, 423.
18. OR, vol. 7, p. 325; Hughes and Stonesifer, *Life and Wars of Gideon J. Pillow*, 266–67; Wyeth, *Life of General Nathan Bedford Forrest*, 278–79.
19. OR, vol. 7. p. 325.
20. Hughes and Stonesifer, *Life and Wars of Gideon J. Pillow*, 312.
21. Hughes and Stonesifer, *Life and Wars of Gideon J. Pillow*, 301–2, 310, 315, 321.
22. OR, vol. 7, p. 395; McGavock, journal entry for Feb. 16th, [1862], in *Pen and Sword*, 592–94; Cooling, *Forts Henry and Donelson*, 213.
23. OR, vol. 7, pp. 595, 624–25, 630.
24. OR, vol. 7, pp. 625, 628–29, 632–33.
25. Samuel Richey Kamm, "Civil War Career of Thomas A. Scott" (PhD diss., University of Pennsylvania, 1940), 108–10; OR, vol. 7, pp. 643, 645, 648, 652, 660.
26. OR, vol. 7, pp. 422–23, 638; ORN, 22:584.
27. OR, vol. 7, pp. 625, 633, 640–41, 655; To Brig. Gen. William T. Sherman, in *Papers of Ulysses S. Grant*, ed. Simon, 4:259–60.
28. To Brig. Gen. George W. Cullum in *Papers of Ulysses S. Grant*, ed. Simon, 4:278–79; OR, vol. 7, pp. 425, 662–63; Engle, *Don Carlos Buell*, 176.
29. OR, vol. 7, p. 425; Engle, *Don Carlos Buell*, 177–78.
30. OR, vol. 7, pp. 661, 668.
31. OR, vol. 7, pp. 666–68; To Julia Dent Grant in *Papers of Ulysses S. Grant*, ed. Simon, 4:292; Grant, *Personal Memoirs*, 172.
32. OR, vol. 7, pp. 670–71; Grant, *Personal Memoirs*, 172–73.
33. OR, vol. 7, p. 674.
34. OR, vol. 7, p. 677; To Brig. Gen. George W. Cullum, in *Papers of Ulysses S. Grant*, ed. Simon, 4:296–98.
35. OR, vol. 7, pp. 676, 679–80.
36. OR, vol. 10, pt. 2, p. 3.
37. OR, vol. 10, pt. 2, pp. 4–5, 15.
38. Smith, *Grant*, 176.
39. OR, vol. 10, pt. 2, pp. 13–14.

40. *OR*, vol. 10, pt. 2, p. 21.
41. *OR*, vol. 10, pt. 2, pp. 22, 36.
42. *OR*, vol. 7, p. 683.
43. *OR*, vol. 10, pt. 2, pp. 20–21, 27; *OR*, vol. 8, p. 602.
44. *OR*, vol. 10, pt. 2, pp. 9–10, 17, 29–30; Smith, *Grant Invades Tennessee*, 13.
45. *OR*, vol. 10, pt. 2, pp. 28–29.
46. *OR*, vol. 10, pt. 2, pp. 32, 36.
47. *OR*, vol. 7, pp. 683–84; *OR*, vol. 10, pt. 2, p. 43.
48. Roland, *Albert Sidney Johnston*, 305; *OR*, vol. 7, pp. 426–27, 438, 878, 889–92; *OR*, vol. 6, pp. 825, 828, 836; Horn, *Army of Tennessee*, 111, 114; Alfred Roman, *The Military Operations of General Beauregard in the War between the States, 1861–1865* (New York, 1884): 1:510–11.
49. Roland, *Albert Sidney Johnston*, 307–9; Johnston, *Life of General Albert Sidney Johnston*, 505, 522.
50. *OR*, vol. 7, p. 674; *OR*, vol. 8, p. 602; *OR*, vol. 10, pt. 2, p. 35; *OR*, vol. 10, pt. 1, pp. 8–11, 22–24.
51. *OR*, vol. 10, pt. 2, pp. 28–29, 48, 55; *OR*, vol. 8, p. 611.
52. Grant, *Personal Memoirs*, 170; *OR*, vol. 10, pt. 2, pp. 42–43, 387; Ambrose, *Halleck: Lincoln's Chief of Staff*, 44.
53. Niccolo Machiavelli, "A Battle That You Win Cancels All Your Mistakes," AZQuotes.com, Wind and Fly LTD, 2021, https://www.azquotes.com/quote/1206786.
54. McPherson, *Battle Cry of Freedom*, 402, 415.
55. Larry J. Daniel, *Shiloh: The Battle That Changed the Civil War* (New York: Touchstone, 1998), 305–6; M. F. Force, *Campaigns of the Civil War: From Fort Henry to Corinth* (1881; repr., Edison, NJ: Castle Books, 2002), 183–84.
56. Woodworth, *Nothing but Victory*, 206–8; Stephen D. Engle, *Struggle for the Heartland: The Campaigns from Fort Henry to Corinth* (Lincoln: University of Nebraska Press, 2001), 182–85.
57. Benjamin Franklin Cooling, *Fort Donelson's Legacy: War and Society in Kentucky and Tennessee, 1862–1863* (Knoxville: University of Tennessee Press, 1997), 66–67, 70.
58. *OR*, vol. 16, pt. 2, pp. 15, 62–63; Long, *Civil War Day by Day*, 222–23; Cooling, *Fort Donelson's Legacy*, 24, 62; Engle, *Don Carlos Buell*, 267.

59. Long, *Civil War Day by Day*, 227–28; McPherson, *Battle Cry of Freedom*, 515.
60. *OR*, vol. 17, pt. 2, p. 90; Catton, *Grant Moves South*, 287.
61. Engle, *Don Carlos Buell*, 177.
62. McPherson, *Battle Cry of Freedom*, 517–20; Horn, *Army of Tennessee*, 162–72, 186–89; Long, *Civil War Day by Day*, 260.
63. Horn, *Army of Tennessee*, 172–75.
64. Horn, *Army of Tennessee*, 172–75.
65. Catton, *Grant Moves South*, 328–44.
66. McPherson, *Battle Cry of Freedom*, 520–22, 579–83; Long, *Civil War Day by Day*, 281; Horn, *Army of Tennessee*, 210.
67. McPherson, *Battle Cry of Freedom*, 586–88, 629–36; Catton, *Grant Moves South*, 425–27.
68. McPherson, *Battle Cry of Freedom*, 668–70; Horn, *Army of Tennessee*, 236–37.
69. McPherson, *Battle Cry of Freedom*, 670; Stickles, *Simon Bolivar Buckner*, 159.
70. McPherson, *Battle Cry of Freedom*, 670, 672–76; Horn, *Army of Tennessee*, 279–81.
71. McPherson, *Battle Cry of Freedom*, 676; Bruce Catton, *Grant Takes Command* (Boston: Little, Brown, 1969), 63–65, 70–72, 79–85; Long, *Civil War Day by Day*, 440.
72. Lanza, *Source Book*, v.
73. Smith, *Grant*, 286.

Appendix I

1. Wallace, *Lew Wallace: An Autobiography*, 367.
2. Philip Smith, entry for February 5, 1862, in Diary of Philip Smith, Peoria Historical Society, Peoria, IL, 85.
3. McGavock, journal entry for Feb. 4, 1862, in *Pen and Sword*, 582–83.
4. *OR*, vol. 7, p. 149.
5. *OR*, vol. 7, p. 140.
6. *OR*, vol. 7, p. 145.
7. Wallace, *Lew Wallace: An Autobiography*, 376–77.
8. *OR*, vol. 7, p. 601.

9. William Farrar Smith, "Operations before Fort Donelson," *Magazine of American History* 15 (January–June 1886): 40–41.
10. *OR*, vol. 52, pt. 1, p. 8.
11. *OR*, vol. 7, p. 229.
12. Twombly, *Second Iowa Infantry at Fort Donelson*, 15–16.
13. Grant, *Personal Memoirs*, 162–63.
14. *OR*, vol. 7, p. 236.
15. Wallace, *Lew Wallace: An Autobiography*, 397–98.
16. Wallace, *Lew Wallace: An Autobiography*, 400.
17. *OR*, vol. 7, p. 243.
18. *OR*, vol. 7, p. 252.
19. Bedford, "Fight between the Batteries and Gunboats," 171.
20. Walke, "Western Flotilla at Fort Donelson," 433–35.
21. *OR*, vol. 7, p. 395.
22. *ORN*, 22:626.
23. *OR*, vol. 7, p. 237.
24. Wallace, *Lew Wallace: An Autobiography*, 404–5.
25. Henry Otis Dwight, *Henry Otis Dwight Papers*, 13-14, Ohio History Connection, Columbus.
26. Wallace, *Lew Wallace: An Autobiography*, 405–6.
27. Cooling, *Forts Henry and Donelson*, 180.
28. Grant, *Personal Memoirs*, 164.
29. Stephens, *Shadow of Shiloh*, 54–55.
30. Wallace, "Capture of Fort Donelson," 422.
31. *OR*, vol. 7, p. 618.
32. *OR*, vol. 7, p. 233.
33. *OR*, vol. 7, p. 245.
34. *OR*, vol. 7, pp. 238–39.
35. *OR*, vol. 7, p. 331.
36. *OR*, vol. 7, p. 331.
37. *OR*, vol. 7, pp. 344–45.
38. *OR*, vol. 7, p. 356.
39. Wallace, "Capture of Fort Donelson," 418–19.

40. *OR*, vol. 7, pp. 332–33.
41. *OR*, vol. 7, p. 290.
42. *OR*, vol. 7, p. 269.
43. *OR*, vol. 7, pp. 316–17.
44. *OR*, vol. 7, p. 268.
45. *OR*, vol. 7, p. 273.
46. *OR*, vol. 7, p. 300.

BIBLIOGRAPHY

Ambrose, D. Leib. *History of the Seventh Regiment Illinois Volunteer Infantry.* Springfield, IL: Illinois Journal, 1868.

Ambrose, Stephen E. *Halleck: Lincoln's Chief of Staff.* Baton Rouge: Louisiana State University Press, 1962.

Anders, Curt. *Henry Halleck's War: A Fresh Look at Lincoln's Controversial General-in-Chief.* Carmel: Guild Press of Indiana, 1999.

Avery, P. O. "Donelson and Henry." *National Tribune*, September 8, 1887, 2.

———. *History of the Fourth Illinois Cavalry Regiment.* Humboldt, NE: Enterprise, 1903.

Badeau, Adam. *Military History of General U. S. Grant, from April, 1861 to April, 1865.* Vol. 1. New York: D. Appleton, 1885.

Ballard, Michael B. *U. S. Grant: The Making of a General, 1861–1863.* Lanham, MD: Rowman and Littlefield, 2005.

Barber, Flavel C. *Holding the Line: The Third Tennessee Infantry, 1861–1864.* Edited by Robert H. Ferrell. Kent, OH: Kent State University Press, 1994.

Barnwell, Robert W. "Gen. John B. Floyd." *Confederate Veteran*, April 1931, 141–43.

Bearss, Edwin C. "The Construction of Fort Henry and Fort Donelson." *West Tennessee Historical Society Papers* 21 (1967): 24–47.

———. *The Fall of Fort Henry: Dover, Tennessee.* 1963. Reprint. Fort Washington, PA: Eastern National, 1999.

———. "General C. F. Smith's Attack on Rebel Right." Fort Donelson National Military Park Service, Research Project #10, December 1959.

———. "The Ironclads at Fort Donelson: The Confederates Prepare for the Ironclads (Part 2)." *Register of the Kentucky Historical Society* 74, no. 2 (1976): 73–84.

———. "The Ironclads at Fort Donelson: The Ironclads Sail for the Cumberland (Part 1)." *Register of the Kentucky Historical Society* 74, no. 1 (1976): 1–9.

———. "The Ironclads at Fort Donelson (Part 3): The Ironclads Fail." *Register of the Kentucky Historical Society* 74, no. 3 (1976): 167–91.

———. *Troop Movement Maps—Fort Donelson, Feb. 12–15, 1862.* 11 sheets. Dover, TN: Fort Donelson National Military Park, April–May 1959.

———. *Unconditional Surrender: The Fall of Fort Donelson.* 1962. Reprint. Fort Washington, PA: Eastern National, 2004.

Bedford, H. L. "Fight between the Batteries and Gunboats at Fort Donelson." *Southern Historical Society Papers* 13 (1885): 165–73.

Bell, John T. *Tramps and Triumphs of the Second Iowa Infantry.* Omaha: Gibson, Miller and Richardson, 1886.

Black, J. S. "Mr. Black to Mr. Wilson." *Galaxy* 11 (February 1871): 257–276.

Bodenhamer, David J., and Robert G. Barrows, eds. *The Encyclopedia of Indianapolis.* Indianapolis: Indiana University Press, 1994.

Boynton, Charles B. *The History of the Navy during the Rebellion.* Vol. 1. New York: D. Appleton, 1867.

Brinton, John H. *Personal Memoirs.* New York: Neale, 1914.

Buell, Thomas B. *The Warrior Generals: Combat Leadership in the Civil War.* New York: Crown, 1997.

Casseday, Morton M. "The Surrender of Fort Donelson." *Southern Bivouac,* April 1887, 694–97.

Cathey, Todd M., and Ricky W. Robnett. *The River Batteries at Fort Donelson.* Jefferson, NC: McFarland, 2021.

Catton, Bruce. *Grant Moves South.* 1960. Reprint. Edison, NJ: Castle Books, 2000.

———. *Grant Takes Command.* Boston: Little, Brown, 1969.

———. *Terrible Swift Sword.* Garden City, NY: Doubleday, 1963.

Chetlain, Augustus L. *Recollections of Seventy Years.* Galena, IL: Gazette, 1899.

Conger, A. L. *The Rise of U. S. Grant.* 1931. Reprint. Freeport, NY: Books for Libraries Press, 1970.

Connelly, Thomas L. *Army of the Heartland: The Army of Tennessee, 1861–1862.* Baton Rouge: Louisiana State University Press, 1967.

Cooling, Benjamin Franklin. *The Campaign for Fort Donelson.* National Park Civil War Series. Fort Washington, PA: Eastern National, 1999.

———. "The First Nebraska Infantry Regiment and the Battle of Fort Donelson." *Nebraska History* 45, no. 2 (June 1964): 131–45.

———. *Fort Donelson's Legacy: War and Society in Kentucky and Tennessee, 1862–1863.* Knoxville: University of Tennessee Press, 1997.

———. *Forts Henry and Donelson: The Key to the Confederate Heartland.* Knoxville: University of Tennessee Press, 1987.

Coulter, E. Merton. *The Civil War and Readjustment in Kentucky.* 1926. Reprint. Gloucester, MA: Peter Smith, 1966.

Crummer, Wilbur F. *With Grant at Fort Donelson, Shiloh and Vicksburg.* Oak Park, IL: E. C. Crummer, 1915.

Cummings, Charles M. "Forgotten Man at Fort Donelson: Bushrod Rust Johnson." *Tennessee Historical Quarterly* 27, no. 4 (1968): 380–97.

———. *Yankee Quaker Confederate General: The Curious Career of Bushrod Rust Johnson.* Cranbury, NJ: Associated University Presses, 1971.

Daniel, Larry J. *Shiloh: The Battle That Changed the Civil War.* New York: Touchstone, 1998.

Donald, David Herbert. *Lincoln.* New York: Simon and Schuster, 1995.

Donovan, Frank R., and editors of *American Heritage. Ironclads of the Civil War.* New York: American Heritage, 1964.

Dyer, Frederick H. *A Compendium of the War of the Rebellion.* Des Moines, IA: Dyer, 1908.

Eicher, John H., and David J. Eicher. *Civil War High Commands.* Stanford, CA: Stanford University Press, 2001.

Emerson, Col. John W. "Grant's Life in the West." *Midland Monthly Illustrated* 9 (January–June 1898): 47–54, 109-19, 219-38, 318-25, 409-23, 500-26.

Engle, Stephen D. *Don Carlos Buell: Most Promising of All.* Chapel Hill: University of North Carolina Press, 1999.

———. *Struggle for the Heartland: The Campaigns from Fort Henry to Corinth.* Lincoln: University of Nebraska Press, 2001.

Faust, Patricia L., ed. *Historical Times Illustrated: Encyclopedia of the Civil War.* New York: Harper and Row, 1986.

Foote, Shelby. *The Civil War, a Narrative: Fort Sumter to Perryville.* New York: Vintage Books, 1986.

Force, M. F. *Campaigns of the Civil War: From Fort Henry to Corinth.* 1881. Reprint, Edison, NJ: Castle Books, 2002.

Foster, Wilbur F. "Building of Forts Henry and Donelson." In *Battles and Sketches of the Army of Tennessee,* by Bromfield L. Ridley, 64–66. Mexico, MO: Missouri Printing and Publishing, 1906.

Fuller, J. F. C. *The Generalship of Ulysses S. Grant.* 1929. Reprint. New York: Da Capo, 1991.

"Gen. Grant at Donelson." *Chicago Tribune,* September 23, 1865, 3.

Gerteis, Louis S. *The Civil War in Missouri: A Military History.* Columbia: University of Missouri Press, 2012.

Gott, Kendall D. *Where the South Lost the War.* Mechanicsburg, PA: Stackpole Books, 2003.

Grant, Ulysses S. *Personal Memoirs.* 1885. Reprint. New York: Penguin Books, 1999.

Greenawalt, John G. "The Capture of Fort Henry and Fort Donelson, February 1862." - Military Order of the Loyal Legion of the United States, District of Columbia Commandery, War Papers 87, Washington, DC, 1912.

———. "A Charge at Fort Donelson, February 15, 1862." Military Order of the Loyal Legion of the United States, District of Columbia Commandery, War Papers 41, Washington, DC, 1902.

Hafendorfer, Kenneth A. *The Battle of Wildcat Mountain.* Louisville: KH Press, 2003.

———. *Mill Springs: Campaign and Battle of Mill Springs, Kentucky.* Louisville: KH Press, 2001.

Hamilton, James J. *The Battle of Fort Donelson.* Cranbury, NJ: Thomas Yoseloff, 1968.

Harlan, Edgar Rubey. *A Narrative History of the People of Iowa.* Chicago: American Historical Society, 1931.

Henry, Robert Selph. *"First with the Most" Forrest.* 2nd printing. Wilmington, NC: Broadfoot, 1992.

Hicken, Victor. *Illinois in the Civil War.* 1966. Reprint. Urbana: University of Illinois Press, 1991.

Hoppin, James Mason. *Life of Andrew Hull Foote, Rear-Admiral United States Navy.* New York: Harper and Brothers, 1874.

Horn, Stanley F. *Army of Tennessee.* 1941. Reprint. Norman: University of Oklahoma Press, 1993.

Howison, Robert R. "History of the War." *Literary Messenger* 38, no. 6 (June 1864): 321-33.

Huffstodt, Jim. *Hard Dying Men.* Bowie, MD: Heritage Books, 1991.

Hughes, Nathaniel Cheairs, Jr., and Roy P. Stonesifer Jr. Life and Wars of Gideon J. Pillow. Knoxville: University of Tennessee Press, 2011.

Hughes, Robert M. "Facts Not to Be Controverted." *Confederate Veteran*, March 1931, 90-91.

———. "John B. Floyd and His Traducers." *Virginia Magazine of History and Biography* 43, no. 4 (October 1935): 316-29.

———. "Sacrificing Truth." *Confederate Veteran*, November 1930, 417–19.

———. "The Situation at Fort Donelson." *Confederate Veteran*, December 1929, 449–50.

———. "A Vindication of John B. Floyd." *William and Mary Quarterly* 5, no. 4 (October 1925): 279-84.

———. "Why Fort Donelson Was Surrendered: Gen. John B. Floyd and the Fight at Fort Donelson." *Confederate Veteran*, August 1929, 300–303, 317.

Jobe, James. "Forts Henry and Donelson: Disastrous and Almost without Remedy." *Blue & Gray Magazine* 28, no. 4 (2011): 6-27, 43-65.

Johnson, Adam R. *The Partisan Rangers of the Confederate States Army.* Louisville, KY: Geo. G. Fetter, 1904.

Johnson, Robert Erwin. *Rear Admiral John Rodgers.* Annapolis, MD: United States Naval Institute, 1967.

Johnston, William Preston. *The Life of General Albert Sidney Johnston.* 1879. Reprint. New York: Da Capo, 1997.

Joiner, Gary D. *Mr. Lincoln's Brown Water Navy: The Mississippi Squadron.* Lanham, MD: Rowman and Littlefield, 2007.

Jordan, Thomas, and J. P. Pryor. *The Campaigns of Lieut.-Gen. N. B. Forrest and of Forrest's Cavalry, with Portraits, Maps, and Illustrations.* New Orleans: Blelock, 1868.

Julian, George W. *Political Recollections: 1840 to 1872*. Chicago: Jansen, McClurg, 1884.

Kamm, Samuel Richey. "The Civil War Career of Thomas A. Scott." PhD diss., University of Pennsylvania, 1940.

Kelley, D. C. "Forrest's (Old) Regiment, Cavalry." In *The Military Annals of Tennessee—Confederate, First Series*, edited by John Berrien Lindsley, 761–69. Nashville, 1886.

Kiner, F. F. *One Year's Soldiering*. 1863. Reprint. Prior Lake, MN: Morgan Avenue, 2000.

Kiper, Richard L. *Major General John Alexander McClernand: Politician in Uniform*. Kent, OH: Kent State University Press, 1999.

Knight, James R. *The Battle of Fort Donelson*. Charleston, SC: History Press, 2011.

Lanza, Conrad Hammond, comp. *Fort Henry and Fort Donelson Campaigns, February 1862: Source Book*. Fort Leavenworth, KS: General Service Schools, 1923.

"Last Surviving Lieutenant General—Simon Bolivar Buckner." *Confederate Veteran*, February 1909, 61–64, 83–85.

Levy, George. *To Die in Chicago: Confederate Prisoners at Camp Douglas, 1862–1865*. Gretna, LA: Pelican, 1999.

Long, E. B. *The Civil War Day by Day: An Almanac, 1861–1865*. With Barbara Long. New York: Da Capo, 1971.

Lytle, Andrew Nelson. *Bedford Forrest and His Critter Company*. Seminole, FL: Green Key, 1931.

MacBride, Robert. *Civil War Ironclads*. Philadelphia: Chilton Books, 1962.

Marszalek, John F. *Commander of All Lincoln's Armies: A Life of General Henry W. Halleck*. Cambridge, MA: Harvard University Press, 2004.

McClellan, George B. *McClellan's Own Story*. New York: Charles L. Webster, 1887.

McGavock, Randal W. *Pen and Sword: The Life and Journals of Randal W. McGavock*. Edited by Hershel Gower and Jack Allen. Nashville: Tennessee Historical Commission, 1959.

McPherson, James M. *Battle Cry of Freedom: The Civil War Era*. New York: Ballantine Books, 1988.

———. *Tried by War: Abraham Lincoln as Commander-in-Chief*. New York: Penguin, 2008.

Mesch, Allen H. *Teacher of Civil War Generals: Major General Charles Ferguson Smith, Soldier and West Point Commandant.* Jefferson, NC: McFarland, 2015.

Miller, Edward A., Jr. *Lincoln's Abolitionist General: The Biography of David Hunter.* Columbia: University of South Carolina Press, 1997.

"Monthly Record of Current Events." *Harper's New Monthly Magazine* 24 (December 1861–May 1862): 696–98.

Moore, Frank, ed. *The Rebellion Record: A Diary of American Events.* Vol. 4. New York: G. P. Putnam, 1862.

Morrison, Marion. *A History of the Ninth Regiment Illinois Volunteer Infantry, with the Regimental Roster.* 1864. Reprint. Carbondale: Southern Illinois University Press, 1997.

Pinnegar, Charles. *Brand of Infamy: A Biography of John Buchanan Floyd.* Westport, CT: Greenwood, 2002.

Poppin, James Mason. *Life of Andrew Hull Foote, Rear-Admiral United States Navy.* New York: Harper and Brothers, 1874.

Quinn, Camilla A. Corlas. "Forgotten Soldiers: The Confederate Prisoners at Camp Butler, 1862–1863." *Illinois Historical Journal* 81 (Spring 1988): 35–44.

Quisenberry, A. C. "Kentucky's 'Neutrality' in 1861." *Register of Kentucky State Historical Society* 15, no. 43 (1917): 7–21.

Rafuse, Ethan. "Typhoid and Tumult: Lincoln's Response to McClellan's Bout with Typhoid Fever during the Winter of 1861–62." *Journal of the Abraham Lincoln Association* 18 (Summer 1997): 1–16.

Reece, Brig. Gen. J. N., reviser. *Report of the Adjutant General of the State of Illinois.* Vol. 1. Springfield, IL: Phillips Brothers, 1900.

———, reviser. *Report of the Adjutant General of the State of Illinois.* Vol. 3. Springfield, IL: Phillips Brothers, 1900.

Reed, David W. *Campaigns and Battles of the Twelfth Regiment Iowa Veteran Volunteer Infantry.* Evanston, IL: n.p, 1903.

Rerick, John H., MD. *The Forty-Fourth Indiana Volunteer Infantry.* LaGrange, IN: n.p., 1880.

Richardson, Albert D. *Personal History of Ulysses S. Grant.* Hartford, CT: D. L. Guernsey, 1868.

Richardson, James D. *Compilation of the Messages and Papers of the Confederacy.* Vol. 2. Nashville: United States Publishing, 1906.

Ridley, Bromfield L. *Battles and Sketches of the Army of Tennessee.* Mexico, MO: Missouri Printing and Publishing, 1906.

"River Batteries at Fort Donelson." *Confederate Veteran*, November 1896, 392–98.

Roland, Charles P. "Albert Sidney Johnston and the Loss of Forts Henry and Donelson." *Journal of Southern History* 23, no. 1 (February 1957): 45–69.

———. *Albert Sidney Johnston: Soldier of Three Republics.* 1964. Reprint. Lexington: University Press of Kentucky, 2001.

Roman, Alfred. *The Military Operations of General Beauregard in the War between the States, 1861–1865.* Vol. 1. New York: Harper and Brothers, 1884.

Rose, Joseph A. *Grant under Fire.* New York: Alderhanna, 2015.

Rowland, Dunbar, ed. *Jefferson Davis, Constitutionalist: His Letters, Papers and Speeches.* Vol. 8. Jackson, MS: Mississippi Department of Archives and History, 1923.

Simon, John Y., ed. *The Papers of Ulysses S. Grant.* Vol. 3, October 1, 1861–January 7, 1862. Carbondale: Southern Illinois University Press, 1970.

———, ed. *The Papers of Ulysses S. Grant.* Vol. 4, January 8, 1862–March 31, 1862. Carbondale: Southern Illinois University Press, 1972.

Smith, H. I. *History of the Seventh Iowa, Veteran Volunteer Infantry during the Civil War.* Mason City, IA: E. Hitchcock, 1903.

Smith, Jean Edward. *Grant.* New York: Touchstone, 2001.

Smith, John Thomas. *A History of the Thirty-First Regiment of Indiana Volunteer Infantry in the War of the Rebellion.* Cincinnati: Western Methodist Book Concern, 1900.

Smith, Timothy B. *Grant Invades Tennessee: The 1862 Battles for Forts Henry and Donelson.* Lawrence: University Press of Kansas, 2016.

Smith, William Farrar. "Operations before Fort Donelson." *Magazine of American History* 15 (January–June 1886): 20–43.

Speer, Lonnie R. *Portals to Hell: Military Prisons of the Civil War.* Mechanicsburg, PA: Stackpole Books, 1997.

Stephens, Gail. *Shadow of Shiloh: Major General Lew Wallace in the Civil War.* Indianapolis: Indiana Historical Society Press, 2010.

Stickles, Arndt M. *Simon Bolivar Buckner: Borderland Knight.* Chapel Hill: University of North Carolina Press, 1940.

Stonesifer, Roy P., Jr. "The Forts Henry-Heiman and Fort Donelson Campaigns: A Study of Confederate Command." PhD diss., Pennsylvania State University, 1965. Microfilm.

Swinton, William. *The Twelve Decisive Battles of the War*. New York: Dick and Fitzgerald, 1867.

Taylor, Jesse. "The Defense of Fort Henry." In *Battles and Leaders of the Civil War*, edited by Robert Underwood Johnson and Clarence Clough Buel, 1:368–72. New York: Century, 1884.

Thompson, Ed Porter. *History of the Orphan Brigade*. Louisville, KY: L. N. Thompson, 1898.

Treichel, James A. "Lew Wallace at Fort Donelson." *Indiana Magazine of History* 59, no. 1 (March 1963): 3–18.

Tucker, Spencer C. *Andrew Foote: Civil War Admiral on Western Waters*. Annapolis, MD: Naval Institute Press, 2000.

———. *Unconditional Surrender: The Capture of Forts Henry and Donelson*. Abilene, TX: McWhiney Foundation Press, 2001.

Twombly, Capt. V. P. *The Second Iowa Infantry at Fort Donelson, February 15, 1862*. Des Moines, IA: Plain Talk, 1901.

US War Department. *Official Records of the Union and Confederate Navies in the War of the Rebellion*. 29 vols. Washington, DC: US Government Printing Office, 1894–1922.

———. *The War of the Rebellion: A Compilation of the Official Records of the Union and Confederate Armies*. 70 vols. Washington, DC: US Government Printing Office, 1880–1901.

Vaughan, James. *Staff Ride Handbook for the Battle of Fort Donelson, February 13-16, 1862*. n.p. 2009.

Vesey, M. L. "Why Fort Donelson Was Surrendered." *Confederate Veteran*, October 1929, 369–70.

Walke, Rear Admiral Henry. "The Gun-Boats at Belmont and Fort Henry." In *Battles and Leaders of the Civil War*, edited by Robert Underwood Johnson and Clarence Clough Buel, 1:358–67. New York: Century, 1884.

———. *Naval Scenes and Reminiscences of the Civil War in the United States on the Southern and Western Waters*. New York: F. R. Reed, 1877.

———. "The Western Flotilla at Fort Donelson, Island Number Ten, Fort Pillow and Memphis." In *Battles and Leaders of the Civil War*, edited by Robert Underwood Johnson and Clarence Clough Buel, 1:430–52. New York: Century, 1884.

Walker, Peter Franklin. "Command Failure: The Fall of Forts Henry and Donelson." *Tennessee Historical Quarterly* 16, no. 4 (1957): 335–60.

Wallace, Isabel. *Life and Letters of General W. H. L. Wallace.* 1909. Reprint. Carbondale: Southern Illinois University Press, 2000.

Wallace, Lew. "The Capture of Fort Donelson." In *Battles and Leaders of the Civil War,* edited by Robert Underwood Johnson and Clarence Clough Buel, 1:398–428. New York: Century, 1884.

———. *Lew Wallace: An Autobiography.* Vol. 1. New York: Harper and Brothers, 1906.

Whittlesey, Charles. *War Memoranda.* Cleveland: William W. Williams, 1884.

Williams, T. Harry. *Lincoln and His Generals.* New York: Grosset and Dunlap, 1952.

———. *P. G. T. Beauregard: Napoleon in Gray.* Baton Rouge: Louisiana State University Press, 1954.

Winslow, Hattie Lou, and Joseph R. H. Moore. "Camp Morton, 1861–1865: Indianapolis Prison Camp." *Indiana Historical Society Publications* 13, no. 3 (1940).

Woodbury, Henry H. *Complete History of the Forty-Sixth Illinois Veteran Volunteer Infantry.* Freeport, IL: Bailey and Ankeny, 1866.

Woodworth, Steven E., ed. *Grant's Lieutenants: From Cairo to Vicksburg.* Lawrence: University Press of Kansas, 2001.

———. *Nothing but Victory: The Army of the Tennessee, 1861–1865.* New York: Alfred A. Knopf, 2005.

Wyeth, John Allan. *Life of General Nathan Bedford Forrest.* New York: Harper and Brothers, 1899.

INDEX

Page numbers in **boldface** refer to illustrations.

Abingdon, VA, 167
Alabama, 1, 5, 173; battlefield guide, 185
Alabama troops
—infantry: *27th*, 154
Alps, 77
Anaconda Plan, 1
Anderson, Adna, 3
Anderson, Gen. Robert, 6, 84
Appalachian Mountains, 5
Appomattox Court House, VA, 179
Arkansas, 1, 5
Army of East Tennessee (South), 178
Army of the Mississippi (North), 175
Army of the Ohio (North), 175
Army of the Potomac (North), 4, 7
Army of the Tennessee (North), 175, 179
Army of the West (South), 175
Atlanta, GA, 176, 179

Badeau, Adam, 133
Bailey's Landing, 19, 23, 30

Baker, Lieut. Col. James, 139
Baldwin, Col. William, 85–86, 89, **96–97**, 99, 116, 128, 131; brigade of, 85, 89, 98, 112
Baldwyn, MS, 175
Ball's Bluff, Battle of, 7
Barn Hollow, battlefield guide, 198–99, 203
Bates, Attorney General Edward, 2
Bear Creek Bridge, 171
Beauregard, Gen. Pierre Gustave Toutant, 1, 17–18, 20, 28, 36, 38, 84, 163, 173–76
Bedford, Lieut. H. L., 82; battlefield guide, 191; narrative of, 191
Belmont, Battle of, 12
Benton, USS, 3, 105
Bidwell, Capt. B. G., 169; battlefield guide, 192; narrative of, 192
Big Black, Battle of, 178
Blandville, KY, 13
Boston Harbor, 156

Index

Bowling Green, KY, 5, 7–9, 11–14, 16, 20, 23, 28, 34, 36, 39–42, 45–49, 52, 61, 64, 84, 86–87, 156, 163, 165–66, 169; battlefield guide, 184, 186
Boyd's place, battlefield guide, 181, 183
Bragg, Gen. Braxton, 176–78
Brayman, Maj. Mason, 107, 109; battlefield guide, 190
Bridgeport, AL, 176
Britain, 7
Brown, Col. John, 89–90, 112, 117–18, 122–23, 126, 128, 151, 153, 159; battlefield guide, 201; brigade of, 89, 117, 122–23, 125–26, 130, 153, 159
Brown, Maj. William, 85–86, 154
Bruinsburg, MS, 178
Buchanan, President John, 45, 84
Buckner, Brig. Gen. Simon Bolivar, 5, 44–50, **51**–52, 57–62, 64–66, 84, 86–91, 93, 99, 101, 111–13, **114**–19, 122–23, 125–32, 141–42, 144–45, 147–51, 153–60, 164–69, 178–79; battlefield guide, 197–205; command of, 48; critical decision, 111–19; division of, 28–29, 47–48, 50–**51**, 64–65, 85, 88–89, 112, 116, 131; narratives of, 199, 202; personal background, 112
Buell, Brig. Gen. Don Carlos, 6–13, 16, 18–19, 28, 35–**40**, 41–43, 47, 49, 121, 163–66, 169–77; battlefield guide, 184; critical decision, 39–43; personal background, 39–40
Buena Vista, Battle of, 154
Bufford, G. W., 154
Bufford Hollow, 99, 110–11, 116, 118, 122, 125, 127–28, 137; battlefield guide, 196
Bull Run, First Battle of, 4
Burnside, Maj. Gen. Ambrose, 178
Burnsville, MS, 174
Byrd Bay, battlefield guide, 183

Cairo IL, 2–4, 8–9, 11–13, 16–17, 19–20, 22, 34, 36, 38, 40, 53, 70, 72, 75, 83, 92, 103–5, 139, 156, 169, 171; battlefield guide, 184
Cairo, USS, 3
Calhoun, KY, 42
California, 44–45
Calloway, KY, 14
Cameron, Secretary of War Simon, 2
Camp Butler, 156
Camp Chase, 156
Camp Dick Robinson, 6
Camp Douglas, 156
Camp Floyd, 45
Camp Halleck, battlefield guide, 183
Camp Morton, 156
Camp Wildcat, Battle of, 6
Canton, KY, 77
Canton (now Guangzhou), China, 81
Carondelet, MO, 2
Carondelet, USS, 2, 19, 51, 54, **58**, 65, 77–82, 103, 169; battlefield guide, 191
Carter, Lieut, 106
Casseday, Maj. Alexander, 115, 118
Champion Hill, Battle of, 178
Chandler, James, 154
Charleston Harbor, SC, 84
Charlotte Road, 112, 137, 147–49, 158, 161; battlefield guide, 203
Charlotte, TN, 88, 147–48
Chattanooga, TN, 157, 173–74, 176, 178–79
Cheairs, Maj. Nathaniel, 115, 126–27
Chicago, IL, 156
Chickamauga, Battle of, 178
Chickasaw Bayou, 177
Chickasaw, MS, 174
Cincinnati, OH, 2–3, 178
Cincinnati, USS, 3, 19
Clark, Brig. Gen. Charles, 47; brigade of, 47–50
Clarksville, TN, 29, 44, 46–50, 52–53, 60, 62–63, 76, 134, 145, 165, 169–71

Index

Collantes, Calderon, Spanish secretary of foreign affairs, 165
Columbia, TN, 154, 157, 168, 174
Columbus, KY, 4–5, 7–9, 11–14, 23, 28–29, 31, 38, 163, 165, 175
Columbus, OH, 156
Conestoga, USS, 2, 14, 19, 79
Confederate States of America, 3; War Department, 17, 157–58, 160–61
Cook, Col. Edward, 117, 126; battlefield guide, 200; narrative of, 200
Cook, Col. John, 19, 43, 70–71, 74, 91–93, 139, 141
Corinth, MS, 171, 173–75, 177
Crimean War, 26
critical decisions: criterion, x; hierarchy of, x; list of, xi; summary of, 163–64; types, x
Crittenden, Maj. Gen. George, 173
Cruft, Col. Charles, 42–43, 70, 74, 105, **108**–11, 116, 118–20, 125, 128, 131, 135, 137, 143; battlefield guide, 189–90, 197, 200; narratives of, 190, 197
Cullum, Brig. Gen. George W., 53, 76, 171
Cumberland City, TN, 51–52, 57–59, 61–62, 64, 66, 90, 166
Cumberland Gap, 5, 178
Cumberland River, 2–4, 7–13, 16, 35–38, 40–41, 45–47, 49–51, 54, 60–65, 71–72, 76, 87, 91, 153, 165, 169–70; battlefield guide, 186
Curtis, Brig. Gen. Samuel R., 16

Danville, TN (site flooded by Kentucky Lake) area, 30; railroad bridge, 28
Davidson, Col. Thomas, 47, 89, 96
Davis, President Jefferson, 5, 52, 61, 154, 157–58, 160, 167–68, 174
Decatur, AL, 157, 173, 175
Department No. 2 (CSA), 5

Department of Kansas, 7
Department of the Mississippi, 167, 173
Department of the Missouri, 6, 10
Department of the Ohio, 1–2, 6, 10, 39–40
Department of the West, 167, 169, 176
Dickey, Col. T. Lyle, 137
Dillon, George Washington, Third Tennessee, battlefield guide, 194
Dix-Hill Cartel, 156
Doss, Maj. W. L., 115, battlefield guide, 200; narrative of, 200
Dove, Commander Benjamin M., 139
Dover Hotel, 87, **155**; battlefield guide, 203–5
Dover Road, battlefield guide, 186
Dover, TN, 13, 19, 22–23, 50, 52, 57, 67, 69–70, 77, 83, 87, 90, 97, 127, 132–33, 137, 148–49, 151, 153; battlefield guide, 181, 204
Drake, Col. Joseph, 89, 131, 137, 142; battlefield guide, 197; brigade of, 98, 128, 131, 137
Dresser, Capt. Jaspar, 116
Duck River, 174, 177
Duckworth, John M., Second Iowa, battlefield guide, 188; narrative of, 188
Dudley's Hill, 96–99, 109, 113–14, 145, 153–54; battlefield guide, 203
Dwight, Sergeant Henry Otis, Twentieth Ohio, battlefield guide, 194; narrative of, 194

Eads, James Buchanan, 2–3
Edgar, Capt. G. P., 107
Edgefield, TN, 170
Erin Hollow, 118, 122; battlefield guide, 198–201
Essex, USS, 3, 19, 26, **27**, 32

First Mississippi Rifles, 154
Florence, AL, 28

Index

Florida, 1, 173
Floyd, Brig. Gen. John, 34, 44–51, 58–**62**, 63–67, 84–91, 99, 101, 111, 117–18, 122–23, 125–32, 144–145, 147–51, 153–61, 164–69; battlefield guide, 186, 201, 203–5; brigade of, 28, 47, 50; critical decisions, 84–91, 129–33, 145–61; narratives of, 202, 204; personal background, 84
Foote, Flag Officer Andrew Hull, 3, 8, 17–20, 23–25, **26**, 27–29, 32, 34, 36, 38, 53–54, 67, 72, 74–83, 85–87, 93, 101, 103–5, 133, 135, 137, 139, 164, 169–70; battlefield guide 186–87, 191–92; critical decision, 75–83; narrative of, 192; personal background, 75–76
Forge Road, 66, 85–86, 88–89, 93, 97–99, 109, 111, 113–19, 122–23, 126, 128, 130–32, 137, **143**, 145, 148, 154, 158, 161; battlefield guide, 197–98
Forrest, Col. Nathan Bedford, 51, 57–59, 66, 70, 85–86, 88, 90, **98**–99, 112, 116, 118, 122, 128–29, 132, 137, 148–51, 153–54, 156–58, 161, 168, 175, 177
Forrest, Lieut. Jeffrey, 153
Fort Clark, 4
Fort Donelson, 3–4, 14, 16, 23, 26–32, 34–39, 42–43, 46–55, 57–66, 69–78, **79, 80, 81**, 82–84, 87–88, 90, 92, 101, 103, 105, 127, 133, 135, 141, 145, 151, 156–60, 163–72, 174, 179; battlefield guide, 184–87, 191, 203
Fort Hatteras, 4
Fort Heiman, 14, 19, 23–24, 26, 30–31, 38, 69–70, 74–75, 91–92; battlefield guide, 184
Fort Henry, 4, 9, 14, 16–21, 23, **24**, 25–32, 34–43, 46–48, 51, 53–55, 57, 59–60, 67, 69–73, 75, 77–79, 82, 91–92, 102–3, 106, 122, 163–65, 169–72; battlefield guide, 183–87
Fort Jefferson, KY, 13

Fort Leavenworth, KS, 179
Fort Moultrie, 84
Fort Sumter, 1, 84
Fort Warren, 156, 159
Forts Henry and Donelson, 3, 5, 8–10, 12, 14, 19, 29, 34, 39, 103, 164, 166, 171–72, 179; campaign and battles for, ix-x, xii, **xiii**, xiv
Fourteenth Mississippi, battlefield guide, 199
Frémont, Maj. Gen. John C., 3, 10, 22
French's battery, battlefield guide, 198–99

Galena, IL, 22
General Service Schools, 179
General War Order No. 1, 17–18
Georgia, 1, 178
Gilmer, Maj. Jeremy, 29–30, 50, 52, 75, 87–88, 90, 111, 116, 153
Gordon, Lieut. Col. Thomas M. 123
Grant, Brig. Gen. Ulysses S., 4, 8, 12–14, 16–**22**, 23–29, 32, 34–39, 42–43, 46–47, 49–55, 57–63, 65–67, 69–78, 82–83, 85–88, 90–94, 101, 103–8, 119, 122, 125–29, 133–35, 137, 139, 142–44, 150–51, 155, 157, 160–61, 163–65, 167, 169–79; battlefield guide, 183–87, 189, 193–96, 203, 205; critical decisions, 21–29, 52–60, 67–75, 101–5, 133–44; narratives of, 189, 195–96; personal background, 21–22

Halleck, Maj. Gen. Henry Wager, 6, **10**, 12–14, 16–23, 28, 35–42, 52–54, 69–70, 74, 76–77, 82–83, 105, 141, 156, 163–64, 169–76; battlefield guide, 183–84; critical decisions, 9–20, 35–39; personal background, 9–10
Hanson, Col. Roger, 116, 141
Hardee, Maj. Gen. William, 5, 28, 47, 84, 86, 163
Harris, Governor Isham, 3, 5, 50, 62, 64

262

Harrodsburg, KY, 176
Hay Ford, 154
Haynes, Lieut. Col. Milton, 31, 78; battlefield guide, 185; narrative of, 185
Head, Col. John, 89–90, 111–12, 132, 141, 149, 153; brigade of, 153
Heiman, Col. Adolphus, 30, 34, 89–90, 112, 123, 132; battlefield guide, 185, 201; brigade of, 90, 115, 125, 129, 131, 153; narrative of, 185
Heiman's Hill, battlefield guide, 201
Henry, Gustavus, Confederate senator, 45
Henry, Maj. Gus, 149
Hickman Creek, 58, 92–93; battlefield guide, 186–87, 191, 201
Hillyer, Capt. William, 69, 133, 142
Holly Springs, MS, 177
Hooker, Maj. Gen. Joe, 178
Hopkinsville, KY, 47
Hughes Bay, battlefield guide, 183
Humboldt, TN, 171
Huntsville, AL, 176

Illinois, 1–2, 10, 22, 38, 40, 121
Illinois troops
—artillery: A, *1st Illinois Light*, 121–23, 125; B, *1st Illinois Light*, 116, 122; D, *1st Illinois Light*, 116; D, *2nd Illinois Light*, 116 — cavalry: *4th*, 137 — infantry: *8th*, 99, 109–10, 143; *9th*, 91, 96, 98–99; *11th*, 115–16, 143; *12th*, 91, 96, 98–99; *18th*, 96, 99, 109–10; *20th*, 143; *21st*, 22; *29th*, 110; *30th*, 110; *31st*, 99, 110, 115; *41st*, 96–98; *46th*, 74; *57th*, 70, 74; *58th*, ix, 74, 137
Indiana, 2, 38, 42–43, 74, 156
Indiana troops
—infantry: *11th*, 74, 137; *31st*, 110; *52nd*, 43
Indian Creek, 71–72, 74, 89, 93, 119–21, 129–32, 151; battlefield guide, 189

Indian Creek Valley, 57–59, 65, 70–71, 75, 93–94, 105, 109, 119–20, 128; battlefield guide, 189
Indian Territory, 5, 7
Iowa troops
—infantry: *2nd*, 139, 141–42; *7th*, 91; *12th*, 133
Island No. 10, 175
Itra Landing, 19
Iuka, MS, 174, 177

Jackson, MS, 178; Battle of 178
Jackson, TN, 171
Jeffersonville, IN, 3
Johnson, Adam Rankin, 148–49
Johnson, Andrew, 176
Johnson, Brig. Gen. Bushrod, 3–4, 34, 43, **45**–50, 64, 84, 90, 125–26, 128, 131, 137, 149, 153, 155
Johnson's Island, 156
Johnston, Gen. Albert Sidney, 5–8, 10, 12, 14, 16–17, 20, 23, 27–31, 35–37, 43–52, 55, 58–66, 84–87, 91, 112, 125, 127, 147, 149, 151, 156–59, 163–66, 169–70, 173–74; battlefield guide 184, 186; critical decisions, 43–52, 60–66; personal background, **44**
Joint Committee on the Conduct of the War, 7
Jones, Lieut., 106

Kansas, 7
Kentucky, 3–6, 8, 10, 13–14, 16, 18, 28, 156, 166–67, 173, 176, 179
Kentucky (CSA) troops
—infantry: *2nd*, 46, 89, 113, 116–17, 141
Kentucky Lake, 27; battlefield guide, 183
Kentucky (USA) troops
—infantry: *25th*, 109–10
Knoxville, TN, 3, 5, 157–58, 173, 176, 178–79

Index

Lafayette, IN, 156
Lagow, Capt. Clark, 104
Lauman, Col. Jacob, 70–71, 74, 92–93, 139, 141
Lee, Gen. Robert E., 179
Lenthall, John, chief of the Navy Bureau of Construction, Equipment, and Repair, 2
Lexington, KY, 6, 176
Lexington, MO, siege of, 6
Lexington, USS, 2, 14, 19
Lick Creek, 59, 67, 72, 86–87, 93–94, 96, 105, 112, 129, 148, 153–54, 161; battlefield guide, 186, 198
Lick Creek Ford, 147–49, 154
Lincoln administration, 4, 7, 11, 156
Lincoln, President Abraham, 1–2, 6–9, 11–13, 16–18, 39, 163, 169, 172–73, 176–79
Logan, Col. John A. "Black Jack," 99
Longstreet, Lieut. Gen. James, 179
Lossing, Benson, American historian, battlefield guide, 195
Louisiana, 1, 5, 173
Louisville, KY, 10
Louisville, USS, 2, 77, 79–80, 82, 103

Machiavelli, 165, 175
Madrid, Spain, secretary of foreign affairs, 165
Magoffin, Governor Beriah, 4–5
Maney, Capt. Frank, 89, 125, 128
Maney's battery, battlefield guide, 201
Martin, Bob, 148–49
Maryland, 4
Mayfield, KY, 13
McAllister, Capt. Edward, 116–18, 125
McArthur, Col. John, 70, 72, 75, 91–**94**, 96–100, 106, 109–11, 113–14, 118–19, 145; battlefield guide, 196, 203
McCausland, Col. John, 90, 97, 116, 127, 131

McClellan, Maj. Gen. George B., 1–2, 4, 7–8, 10–12, 16–18, 22, 36–42, 82, 169–73
McClernand, Brig. Gen. John, 13, 19, 23–26, 30, 32, 34, 43, 52–55, 57–59, 65, 67, 69–75, 77, 85–88, 91–**92**, 93–94, 96–97, 99, 101, 104–11, 113, 115, 118–20, 125, 128, 132–35, 160, 164, 177; battlefield guide, 181, 186–87, 189–90, 193, 195–96, 199; critical decision, 91–100; personal background, 92
McCook, Brig. Gen. Alexander, 170
McGavock, Col. Randall, 90, 147, 159, 169; battlefield guide, 184; narrative of, 184
Meigs, Quartermaster Montgomery C., 7
Memphis, TN, 3, 174–75, 177
Memphis and Charleston Railroad, 176
Mexican War, 45, 67, 154–55, 167–68
Milburn, KY, 13
Military Division of the Mississippi, 178
Milliken's Bend, 177
Mill Springs, KY, 6, 8, 16–17
Missionary Ridge, 178
Mississippi, 1, 5, 173–77
Mississippi Central Railroad, 177
Mississippi River, 1–4, 7, 13, 16, 177
Mississippi troops
—infantry: *14th*, 113, 115, 117, 154; *20th*, 85–86, 97, 128, 154–55; *26th*, 85
Missouri, 4–7, 9–12, 16–18, 22–23, 38–39, 43, 172
Missouri State Guard, 4, 6
Missouri troops
—infantry: *8th*, 74, 137
Mitchel, Brig. Gen. Ormsby, 170, 176
Mobile, AL, 176
Morgan, John Hunt, 175
Mormon expedition, 45, 84
Morrison, Col. William, 58, 70–71, 92–93

Mound City, IL, 2–3
Mound City, USS, 3
Munford, Col. Edward, 163
Murfreesboro, TN, 157, 173, 176–78

Nashville, TN, 1–2, 5, 7, 11, 13–14, 16, 28–29, 34, 38–39, 43, 45–47, 50–52, 59, 64, 86–91, 101, 119, 122, 125, 127, 131–32, 142, 145, 147, 149, 151, 156–57, 161, 163, 165–66, 169–73, 176
Nashville Banner, 167
Nebraska, 43
Nebraska troops
—infantry: *1st*, 43, 70, 121, 123, 125
Nelson, Brig. Gen. William "Bull," 170
New Orleans, LA, 1, 5
Newsham, Col. Thomas, Adjutant General to Gen. William Farrar Smith, battlefield guide, 187; narrative of, 187
New York, NY, 155
New York Herald reporter, 77, 82
New York Times, 164
New York Tribune, 53
Nicholson, Lieut. Hunter, 149; battlefield guide, 204; narrative of, 204–5
North Carolina, 1, 4

Oglesby, Col. Richard, 58, 70–72, 92–93, 96–100, 106, 109–11, 114–16, 119, 145; battlefield guide, 196, 200
Ohio, 1–2, 36, 38, 41–43, 121
Ohio River, 2–3
Ohio troops
—infantry: *20th*, 43, 104; *58th*, 43; *68th*, 43; *76th*, 43
Ord, Maj. Gen. Edward, 177
Otey, Maj. Peter, 86

Paducah, KY, 4, 6, 9, 11–14, 16, 19, 30, 38, 40, 72, 77, 91–92, 106, 171–72
Palmer, Col. Joseph, 123, 126; battlefield guide, 200

Panther Creek, 19, 23
Paris, TN, 36
Pemberton, Lieut. Gen. John C., 178
Perryville, Battle of, 176–77
Phelps, Lieut. Seth, 14, 28
Pillow, Brig. Gen. Gideon, 3–4, 34, 44–49, 50–52, 54, 57–66, 84–91, 96–99, 101, 105, 109, 111–19, 122, 125–32, 145, 147–51, 153–54, 157–61, 164–69; battlefield guide, 184, 198–204; critical decision, 125–29; division of, 89, 112, 115–16, 118, 125, 127, 129, 132; narrative of, 202–3
Pittsburg, USS, 2, 79–80, 103
Pittsburg Landing, 175
Polk, Maj. Gen. Leonidas, 4–5, 13, 29, 31, 45
Pook, Samuel M., naval constructor, 2, 82–83
Pope, Maj. Gen. John, 175
Port Gibson, MS, Battle of, 178
Price, Maj. Gen. Sterling, 6, 11, 16, 176–77
Provisional Army of Tennessee, 3
Pugh, Col. Isaac, 96–98

Randolph, George, Confederate secretary of war, 158–61, 167
Randolph Forge, 123
Rawlins, Capt. John, 74, 119–20; battlefield guide, 190
Raymond, MS, Battle of 178
Rhoads, Lieut. Col. Frank, 109–10
Rice, Maj. J. E., 147–48, 151; battlefield guide, 204
Rice House, 147; battlefield guide, 203–4
Richardson, Albert, *New York Tribune* reporter, 53, 133
Richmond, KY, 176
Richmond, VA, 1, 3, 5, 28, 45, 157, 159–60, 163
Ridge Road, 23, 27, 34, 55, 92

Rodgers, Commander John, 2–3, 82–83
Rosecrans, Maj. Gen. William, 175–78
Ross, Col. Leonard F., 135, 137
Ross, Lieut. James, 70
Russell, Col. Daniel R., 154
Russellville, KY, 14, 36, 44, 46, 48, 60

San Jacinto, USS, 7
Savannah, TN, 173–74
Scott, Lieut. Gen. Winfield, 1–2, 67, 168
Scott, Thomas, assistant secretary of war, 36, 169
Shackelford, Col. James, 109–10
Sherman, Brig. Gen. William, 6, 10, 171, 177–78
Shiloh, 159, 174–75
Shirk, Lieut. James, 14
Simonton, Col. John, 96–97, 127, 131
Slidell, John, Confederacy Commissioner, 165
Smith, Brig. Gen. Charles Ferguson, 13–14, 17, 19, 23–24, 26, 30, 52–55, 57–59, 65, 69–75, 77, 85, 91–93, 105, 107, 119–20, 128, 133, **134**–35, 137, 139, 141–42, 145, 170–71, 173–74; battlefield guide, 186–87, 189, 195; narrative of, 188
Smith, Col. Morgan, 70, 74–75, 134–35, 137; battlefield guide, 197; narrative of, 197
Smith, Dr. James W, 148–49, 153–54
Smith, Gen. William Farrar, battlefield guide, 187
Smith, Maj. Gen. Edmund Kirby, 176
Smith, Philip, Eighth Missouri Infantry, battlefield guide, 183; narrative of, 183–84
Smithland, KY, 6, 16, 91
South Carolina, 1
Springfield, IL, 156, 179
Standing Rock Creek, 34
Stanton, Attorney General Edwin, 84, 169

Stevenson, AL, 163, 176
Stewart, Capt. Warren, 53
St. Louis, IL, 2–3, 10, 14, 17, 169, 171–72; battlefield guide, 183–84
St. Louis, USS, 2, 19, 77, 79–80, 103–4
Stones River, 177
Swinton, William, *New York Times* correspondent, 164

Taylor, Capt. Erza, 116, 122
Taylor, Capt. Jesse, 32
Taylor, Zachary, 67
Telegraph Road, 23–24, 26, 55, 92; battlefield guide, 181, 183
Tennessee, 1, 3, 5–6, 8, 10, 16–17, 27–28, 50, 64, 151, 154, 166, 171, 176, 179; East, 3, 7, 39, 41–42, 176, 178–79; Middle, 176; West, 175, 177
Tennessee Corps of Artillery, 78
Tennessee River, 2–4, 7–14, 16, 18–19, 27–30, 35, 37–38, 40–41, 53, 65, 75, 91, 165–66, 169–74, 176; battlefield guide, 185
Tennessee troops
—artillery: *Maney's Battery*, 89, 125, 128 —infantry: *3rd*, 113, 115, 117, 123, 127; *18th*, 115, 117, 123; *26th*, 85; *30th*, 89–90; *32nd*, 113, 117; *41st*, 113; *49th*, 141; *50th*, 141
Texas, 1, 5, 7, 45
Terre Haute, IN, 156
Terry's Texas Rangers, 5
Thayer, Col. John, 43, 70, 74, 105, 108, 119–20, **121**–23, 125–128, 130, 135, 159–60; battlefield guide, 189–90, 193–94, 197, 201; narrative of, 190–91
Third Tennessee, battlefield guide, 199
Thirty-Second Tennessee, battlefield guide, 200
Thomas, Adjutant General Lorenzo, 40, 172–73
Thomas, Maj. Gen. George, 175, 178

Tilghman, Brig. Gen. Lloyd, 14, 21, 27, **29**–32, 34, 43, 46, 156, 164; battlefield guide, 184–85; critical decision, 29–34; narrative of, 185; personal background, 29–30
Tod, Governor David, 42
Trent, HMS, 7
Tullahoma, TN, 177–78
Tullahoma Campaign, 178
Tupelo, MS, 176
Tuscumbia, MS, 174
Tuttle, Col. James Madison, **139**, 141–42; battlefield guide, 188; narrative of, 188
Twombly, Volare, 141
Tyler, USS, 2, 19, **28**, 79

United States Army, 2, 10; War Department, 2
Utah, 45

Van Dorn, Maj. Gen. Earl, 175–77
Vesey, M. L., 154
Vicksburg, MS, 174, 176–78; campaign, 177
Virginia, 1, 3–4, 44, 66, 154–55, 159, 167, 179; west, 42, 167
Virginia troops
—infantry: *51st*, 99

Walke, Commander Henry, 54, **57**–59, 72, 80–81; battlefield guide, 191; narrative of, 191–92
Wallace, Brig. Gen. Lew, 42–43, 54, 69–72, **73**–75, 77, 86–87, 91, 93, 101, 105–9, 118–23, 125–26, 129, 132–35, 137, 142–43, 145, 147, 155, 159, 164; battlefield guide, 183, 186–87, 189–90, 193–97, 201; critical decisions, 105–11, 119–25; narratives of, 183, 186, 189–90, 193–95, 197–98, 201; personal background, 106

Wallace, Col. William Hervey Lamme, 58, 70–71, 92–93, 109–11, 114–16, 118–19, 121, 125, 130, 164; battlefield guide, 193, 196, 200–1
Ware, Lieut. Addison, 107
Washburne, Elihu, 172
Washington, DC, 2, 4, 16, 172, 175–77
Webster, Col. Joseph D., 134–35, 143
Welles, Secretary of the Navy Gideon, 2, 77, 82, 103, 105
Western Department of United States, 6
Western Flotilla, 2
West Point, 45, 78, 155
Wharton, Col. Gabriel, 89–90, 98–99, 128, 131
White House, 179
Widow Crisp, 57, **71**, 74; battlefield guide, 186
Wilderness Road, 6
Wilson's Creek, MO, 4
Wood, Lieut. Peter, 121–23; battlefield guide, 194
Woodard, James, 154
Wynn's Ferry Road, 57, 70, 75, 88–89, 93–94, 99, 101, 109–18, **122**–23, 125–28, 130–32, 135, 137, 142–43, 145, 149, 159–60, 166; battlefield guide, 187, 193, 196–201

Yates, Governor Richard, 22

Zollicoffer, Brig. Gen. Felix, 5–6

www.ingramcontent.com/pod-product-compliance
Lightning Source LLC
Chambersburg PA
CBHW030513080526
44586CB00011B/175